Underwater Reflections

Gary Gentile

Bellerophon Bookworks

Copyright 2011 by Gary Gentile

All rights reserved. Except for the use of brief quotations embodied in critical articles and reviews, this book may not be reproduced in part or in whole, in any manner (including mechanical, electronic, photographic, and photocopy means), transmitted in any form, or recorded by any data storage and/or retrieval device, without express written permission from the author. Address all queries to:

Bellerophon Bookworks
3 Lehigh Gorge Drive
Jim Thorpe, PA 18229

Additional copies of this book may be purchased from the same address by sending a check or money order in the amount of $20 U.S. for each copy (plus $4 postage per order, not per book, in the U.S. Inquire for shipping cost to foreign countries). Alternatively, copies may be ordered from the author's website and paid by credit card:

http://www.ggentile.com

Picture Credits
The front cover art is titled "Cave of the Storm Nymphs." It was painted by Edward Poynter in 1903. All uncredited photographs were taken by the author.

International Standard Book Numbers (ISBN)
1-883056-42-X
978-1-883056-42-1

First Edition

Printed in U.S.A.

Contents

Introduction: a Life of Adventure	4
The Bell Boys	5
Lost on the Wide, Wide Sea	14
Shipwreck Potpourri	31
A Whopper of a Bell	48
Robinson Crusoes of St. Paul Island	76
Rescue and Redemption	91
Yucatan Caves and Mayan Cenotes	123
The Rise of the Fourth Reich	173
Homage to Occam's Razor	179
Photographic Memories	205

Introduction
a Life of Adventure

Human life is many things to many people.

Each person chooses the kind of life that he wishes to lead; or, by omission of choice, allows his life to wander aimlessly or to proceed at the will of others.

I chose a life of adventure. At first my adventures were local: within walking distance of my house. Later I expanded my sphere of adventure to driving distance; then to flying distance. Not content with confining my adventures to the surface of the planet, I started exploring underground; then under water. Finally I explored both underground *and* under water: in submerged caves.

My many and varied explorations and adventures eventually led to my chosen occupation: that of a photojournalist. In this guise I not only sought new adventures, but I shared those adventures afterward with my readers.

As the title suggests, in the present book I reflect upon some of the adventures that I have experienced under water: mostly as a participant but sometimes as an observer who happened to be on the spot.

If these adventures appeal to you in any way other than vicarious, keep in mind that you can pursue adventures of similar kind. The choice is yours.

The Bell Boys

In the wreck-diving community, the Italian passenger liner *Andrea Doria* is generally perceived as the ultimate wreck-dive and pinnacle of achievement. The potential challenges are paramount: great depth, strong current, limited visibility, long decompression, and – for those who venture inside the hallowed hull – the possibility of entanglement and disorientation.

The Grand Dame of the Sea is justly renowned for the number of artifacts that divers have recovered throughout the years. Many of these artifacts were rescued from the wreck's capacious interior before they were destroyed by the ongoing and accelerating process of collapse.

Artifacts are still being recovered. The breakdown of the hull has enabled divers to reach interior compartments that were never accessible before. Windows, portholes, and floor tiles are now being recovered with increasing regularity from the constantly growing debris field that has resulted from the collapse of the upper decks. The dedicated diver never knows what he might find. Case in point . . .

On June 25, 2010, the dive boat *Explorer* departed from Rhode Island's Stone Cove Marina into uncertain seas. She was *Doria* bound. On board were nine eager divers: owner and operator Dave Sutton; trip organizer Joel Silverstein; crewmembers Ernest Rookey, Rick Simon, and this author; and passengers Carl Bayer, Chris Gini, Kathy Mallon, and Laila Richard. Five of these divers were looking forward with enthusiasm to their very first dive on the historic wreck: Ernie, Carl, Chris, Kathy, and Laila.

Both Ernie and Carl were last minute replacements for a crewmember and a passenger who canceled participation. Ironically, they had dived together before and had known each other for about eight years.

Before the boat left the dock, I had a serious and down-to-earth talk with Rick Simon. He was slated to be my tie-in buddy. I entertained no doubts about his deep-diving experience and technical ability. I had been on one previous *Doria* trip with him, and he had been on several other *Doria* trips besides that one. Yet I was afraid that because I was older and more experienced, he might feel that it was his place to be subordinate to me.

A buddy team works best when it is based on mutual respect: not with a leader and a follower, but with a pair of equals each of whom is willing to defer to a decision that the other makes for both of them if a situation calls for it. A buddy team is much like a marriage or a relationship between lovers: it fails when one member tries to dominate the other. The consequences can be dire, both under water as well as in a shared household.

I told Rick about my very first *Doria* trip, in 1974. I was the youngest diver among a group of twelve. I was paired with John Starace because he was the oldest diver. The rationale was that his wisdom borne of age would temper my youthful derring-do, and that my strength and stamina would compensate for his waning physical prowess. They called us the Ford and the Ferrari: he was the Ford and I was the Ferrari.

Now the tables were turned. I wanted Rick to appreciate that I was passing the torch to him; that now I was the Ford and he was the Ferrari. Under water, we would equally share the responsibility of making decisions. We reached a clear understanding.

Rough seas portended an auspicious beginning. The heavily-laden boat rolled and bounced with sickening motion as darkness overtook the sky. After only a few hours underway, the weather moderated and the waves laid down and stretched to long and gentle swells. Stars adorned the heavens like silvery sequins on a coal-black dress. By morning, the ocean was calm and the sun shone brightly above a cloudless horizon. The sea assumed the appearance of a sheet of glass. Anticipation ran high.

The first day's diving promised to be exciting for all, especially for the first-timers. Ambient light visibility exceeded thirty feet on the surface. Current was negligible to nonexistent.

Rick and I were the first to splash into the water. We were full of enthusiasm. Our job was to descend a sturdy down-line to the bottom, detach the line from its sacrificial weight, and secure the line to the wreck. Subsurface currents existed at various depths with varying strengths, but did not unduly hinder us from making our descent. We hit the sandy bottom in limited visibility. The wreck was nowhere in sight.

My depth gauge registered 249 feet. My breathing gas was trimix-19/50, which kept me clear-headed. I peered into the gloom. Obviously, the drop weight had dragged off the wreck. The standard practice under such a circumstance was to swim into the current. Rick maintained a grip on the line and pointed his light as a beacon. I took a short jaunt ahead – out of sight of Rick but not out of sight of his light. After going twenty feet without spotting wreckage, I turned around and returned to the down-line. I shook my head.

I explored to the right of the down-line while Rick explored to the left. After going about fifteen feet, I noticed that the ambient light was growing darker – as if a cloud were passing in front of the sun. I looked up and – what to my surprise – spotted the bulbous tip of the stem about twenty feet above my head. I had swum into a washout under the hull!

I quickly retreated and waved my light. I pointed with my finger. Rick understood. I started to detach the weight from the down-line so we could swim the line to the wreck. Rick shook his head vehemently. He did not want me to detach the 60-pound weight just yet. I understood his concern. Although we had not had any difficulty in descending the down-line, the subsurface currents were exerting considerable pull against the 300 feet of nylon rope and the marker buoy on the surface.

We took up station on opposite sides of the downline. We started humping the heavy weight along the bottom. I let go of my light and let it dangle from its lanyard. I grabbed the sand with the fingers of my right hand, kicked hard with my fins, then pulled my arms together. Rick worked equally as hard on his side of the line. Yet we were able to move the weight only a few inches per "hump."

We advanced incrementally in this manner for a couple of minutes. Then we were able to advance the weight no farther. I was breathing harder than I should have been at that depth. I looked up and saw that we had reached a point underneath the sharp stem of the bow. I jabbed a finger upward. Rick now saw – and understood – where we were located with respect to the hull.

I shrugged. Rick shrugged.

There was no way we would be able to lift the weight to the height of the stem. It was too heavy to lift, especially with the current tugging against all that line. I figured that the only chance we had of accomplishing our goal was to release the weight and hope that we could ascend to the hull, grab onto the steel, and haul the line some fifty feet aft to the forward scupper.

I indicated the weight. Rick shrugged.

I detached the weight. Immediately the current started to drag us upward and away from the hull. We both kicked for all we were worth. By the time we ascended twenty feet to the height of the stem, we were out of arm's reach and being pulled away from the wreck. Our combined kicking was not enough to overcome the force of the current.

We shrugged at each other and stopped fighting the implacable force. During the ascent I got my breathing rate under control.

Being trammeled by the *Doria* was a first-time experience for Rick, but it was nothing new to me. On more than one occasion I had been overwhelmed by the current on tie-in dives that had to be aborted. Mother Nature had won another round.

Rick and I had accumulated too much residual nitrogen to attempt another tie-in dive without waiting for a couple of hours. Instead, Dave Sutton dropped a grapnel near the middle of the wreck. Joel Silverstein and Ernie Rookey went down to do the tie-in. The hook was in part of the debris field that had once been the Promenade Deck. They had a relatively easy task of securing the chain to a prominent piece of wreckage. They made tying-in look easy.

The down-line now terminated at a hull plate that lay at a depth of 220 feet, and which was located some thirty feet abaft the barely recognizable wreckage of the wheelhouse. There was no end of awe at the immensity of the wreck. The customers made their first descent. The midday sun made the bottom a great deal brighter than it had been on the early morning dive that Rick and I had made. Ambient light visibility exceeded thirty feet. Everyone had now lost his or her *Doria* virginity.

Rick and I made another dive late in the afternoon.

That evening, the full moon shed its reflected light with brilliant luminosity. Camaraderie filled the cabin during dinner and dessert. Newfound friendships were forged. The night remained calm.

The morning was fraught with a strong current that kept divers gasping for breath as they pulled themselves down the line. The three California passengers (Chris, Kathy, and Laila) dived as a threesome. After their return, Carl and Ernie descended together; their goal was to relocate the cache of bathroom tiles that Carl had found the day before.

On the bottom, Ernie tied a guideline to the chain. He and Carl proceeded to explore the debris field that extended perpendicular to the standing hull. Carl led the way as Ernie laid line. They swam over the remains of the upper decks until they reached the seabed that lay beyond. They dropped to the sand at 241 feet.

Carl spotted a curved green patina of bronze protruding from the sand in the distance. He decided to check it out. Ernie was right on his heels – or, more accurately, on his fin tips. Ernie reached the object a bare four seconds after Bayer.

It took only a cursory examination to ascertain that the bronze object was a bell!

Their initial dive plan called for a maximum bottom time of 25 minutes. After experiencing the strength of the current on the surface, they reduced their planned bottom time to 20 minutes. They found the bell at 15 minutes into the dive. This meant that they had only 5 minutes remaining before they had to turn back, retrieve the line-reel line, reach the tie-in spot, and commence their ascent.

The bell was three-quarters buried in the sandy bottom. They started digging furiously: Carl scooped sand out of the inside of the bell while Ernie used both hands to dig trenches along the outer sides of the bell. In seconds they were surrounded by a cloud of silt that reduced visibility to inches.

They continued to dig out the object. After several minutes of excavation – with only two minutes remaining of their planned bottom time – Carl planted both fins firmly on the seabed, grabbed the bell by its lip, and started tugging. Ernie then commenced to pull on the top of the bell. Facing each other, they resembled a pair of construction workers who were lifting a block of concrete out of mud.

Their combined effort finally broke the suction and freed the bell from the sediment. Now they had to send it to the surface.

Ernie deployed his 50-pound liftbag and secured it to the bolt hole (the hole in the knob on top of the bell, used to swing the bell from its hanger by means of a bolt or drift pin). He inflated the bag to full capacity. The bell continued to sit on the bottom.

Carl then deployed a 125-pound liftbag, which he secured to the bolt hole. Now an important difference between a rebreather and open-circuit scuba became apparent. Carl could not inflate a liftbag from his rebreather. Ernie, who was wearing two 108-cubic-foot tanks, pressed the purge button on his regulator to inflate this second liftbag.

The bell rose off the bottom. Ernie and Carl skedaddled for the anchor line, with Ernie pushing the bell ahead of him, and Carl reeling in Ernie's line-reel line. The tie-in point was higher than the seabed. When they reached the anchor chain, the slight reduction in pressure caused the gas in the liftbag to expand. The bell was pulled out of Ernie's hand before Carl arrived. The bell sped for the surface without the line-reel attached as a security measure.

Their total bottom time was 26 minutes. Now that their team recovery effort was concluded, they faced an hour and a half of decompression without knowing whether those of us on the boat had managed to retrieve their valuable prize.

The rest of the recovery operation was anticlimactic by contrast. The liftbags hit the surface forward of the *Explorer*, and drifted to within three feet of the gunwale. Captain Sutton used a boat hook to grab the liftbag line. He pulled the bell onto the swim platform, then placed it on the deck.

Rick Simon and I were next down the anchor line. We grinned and gave the thumbs-up sign to Ernie and Carl as we passed them at their decompression stop. They nodded and beamed at confirmation of the successful rescue of the bell.

Dave Sutton.

Carl and Ernie were ecstatic when they completed their decompression, boarded the boat, and were able to read the lettering that was cast in bronze: ANDREA DORIA; and underneath the name was the date of manufacture, 1952.

Congratulations to the "bell boys" Carl Bayer and Ernie Rookey for a great find and a job well done!

The bell is about half the size of the one that was

recovered from the stern, a quarter century earlier. (For details of that recovery operation, see *Andrea Doria: Dive to an Era*.)

Initially there was some speculation about the origin of the smaller bell. It could have been mounted on the outside of the bulkhead that was the front wall of the wheelhouse, or it might have been mounted on the mast above or inside the crow's nest.

The way Ernie and Carl described the bell's location to me – in the sand some twenty feet from the edge of the debris field – I leaned toward a crow's nest bell; but it is not known if a bell was ever mounted there. John Moyer obtained a photograph of the *Andrea Doria* under construction. This picture shows a bell mounted above the center wheelhouse window. In deference to this picture, a wheelhouse bell seems more likely than a crow's nest bell.

A great deal of fanfare resulted from the recovery of this second *Andrea Doria* bell. Carl and Ernie were interviewed by newspaper and television reporters. They each told how they had worked together to effect the momentous recovery, and how they shared equally in ownership of the bell as a result of their underwater teamwork. They vowed to put the bell on public display for everyone to see.

Ordinarily, a story such as this would end at this point. There was little more to do other than conserve the bell for posterity. Carl took the bell home and placed it in a weak bath of muriatic acid. After the acid dissolved the encrustation, he soaked the bell in continually changing baths of fresh water; this process leeched the acids and chlorides from interstices in the bronze.

Unfortunately, however, this story has an unsavory and unsatisfactory conclusion.

Carl decided that he did not want Ernie to have an ownership interest in the prize that Ernie had helped to recover. Carl wanted full ownership for himself.

They say that possession is nine tenths of the law. This overused aphorism is not true. The law does not recognize possession as a merit of legal ownership. A court order can dispossess a person of any so-called possession that a judge determines has alternate or multiple ownership. The problem that arises in America's litigious society is that lawsuits cost money. It may be possible to prove a point in court, but it can cost tens of thousands of dollars to do so.

Carl retained a lawyer to establish his claim; or rather, to disestablish any claim that Ernie might presume to make. Mediation failed after nearly a year of out-of-court wrangling. Carl's position on the matter was unswerving: he did not want Ernie to share ownership of the bell; he did not want Ernie to ever possess the bell; he did not even want Ernie to have visiting rights.

Bayer offered to buy out Ernie's half share for $1,500 – this for a bell that was appraised at $50,000. And there the matter stands. For now.

Ernie is now a bellless boy.

Shame on Carl for adopting such a reprehensible attitude; for exhibiting the basest side of human nature. They say that greed often rears its ugly head. This aphorism is unfortunately true.

Carl Bayer. Ernie Rookey.

Lost on the Wide, Wide Sea

Being lost at sea is a concept that few recreational divers ever contemplate. Training courses seldom even mention the possibility. Instructors do their best to impress students with the fun, beauty, and safety of diving – generally without mentioning many of the hazards that may be encountered. Thus novices receive their certification cards in blissful ignorance that sometimes unanticipated events can occur that might leave them alone and stranded on the broad reaches of the sea.

This form of training with awareness prevention is a disservice to naïve people who place trust in their instructors. Imagine a driver education course in which the instructor avoided any reference to the possibility of car crashes and traffic accidents, except to wear seatbelts because it is law.

Divers may be forced to learn harsh realities the hard way – often with painful or disastrous results. There are numerous cases on record of recreational divers being left adrift after the departure of their dive boat. Sometimes the skipper or dive master neglected to take a head count before leaving the dive site. Sometimes divers surfaced far from the boat, couldn't swim against the current, and were dragged out of sight – leaving those onboard to wonder whether the diver failed to surface at all, or whether he disappeared over the horizon (and in which direction). Sometimes mechanical problems made it impossible for the boat to collect its divers. Whatever the cause, recreational divers are seldom prepared to deal with such a catastrophe.

Fatalities have occurred. Some bodies have never been found.

The problem of being lost at sea has been compounded with the advent of technical diving, in which diving deep and staying down long require extended decompression. This is due largely to the fact that the majority of technical dives are made on shipwrecks that lie far from shore.

A recent incident is a case in point.

Topside Perspective

On July 2, 2010, a group of nine wreck-divers departed from Captree State Park for a trip to the *Andrea Doria*. The dive boat was the *Garloo*, Captain Hank Garvin. Also on board were Marcie Bilinski, Jeff Downing, Wes Carmen, Joe King, Mark Shannon, Marty Schutsbank, Bill Vogel, and this author.

The seas were calm; the winds were light and variable. After an overnight passage of fifteen hours, the *Garloo* reached the site and, after some difficulty, hooked into the deteriorating hull. Some divers made their very first descent to the Grand Dame of the Sea.

Day two dawned with building seas that were manifested by swells rather than by breaking waves: five to six feet in height but with a long period between crests. The boat rolled but not uncomfortably so.

Some divers hit the water early; others waited until the sun was higher and shed more light on the bottom.

A strong current was running. Perhaps it could be called "super strong." Sometimes the current runs so strongly across the *Doria* that diving is impossible. This current was diveable, but just barely. Along with the high swells, decompression on the anchor line was an excruciating experience that was extremely bad on the shoulder joints.

Jeff Downing went in around 11 o'clock. He was alone and was diving on a rebreather.

All the early birds returned in due course. There was no sign of Jeff more than two hours after his descent. There was concern on the boat. People started looking for bubbles and scanning the horizon. Looking for bubbles was largely fruitless, because the only time a rebreather is supposed to emit bubbles is during ascent, when the counterlung becomes overinflated and dumps excess gas. A rebreather diver who is stabilized at a decompression stop is not likely to reveal his presence by means of exhaust bubbles.

A marker buoy was spotted off the starboard side of the boat, at a distance of more than one hundred feet. Was Jeff underneath it, or had he used it as a liftbag to raise the sink that he had found the previous day?

The *Garloo* was equipped for rescue and retrieval. An inflatable chase boat was already in the water; the motor was mounted and had been test-started. Mark pulled in the painter, jumped into the inflatable, started the motor, and took off at flank speed. By this time the current had dragged the surface marker buoy for a distance of several hundred yards.

The wind had picked up speed and was now blowing better than twenty knots.

From the *Garloo*, we could not see what was happening on the inflatable. We saw Mark sit for a moment on one pontoon, then stand straight and tall. He remained standing. He made no effort to return to the *Garloo*. Had the motor conked out?

To those of us on the *Garloo*, it appeared that Mark was standing in order to increase his profile, and to make himself more visible as he continued to drift away from the dive boat. Already he was more than a quarter

of a mile away. We couldn't go after him because the *Garloo* was tied to the wreck, and granny lines streamed from the anchor line to port and starboard cleats near the stern. We didn't *want* to move the boat because Jeff might be decompressing on the anchor line or on one of the granny lines.

Hank peered through binoculars at the inflatable. He did not see a diver floating next to it. Nor was Mark looking in our direction.

Before Hank could go after the inflatable, he had to ascertain if Jeff was decompressing under the dive boat. Bill Vogel donned drysuit and dive gear. He entered the water on the port side, swam along the granny line to the anchor line, descended to fifty feet, and returned along the starboard granny line. There was no sign of Jeff.

Anyone who was not assisting in handling lines or in the operation of the boat, took station on the walk-around wheelhouse deck. Each person scanned a different quadrant. There was still no sign of Jeff, and the inflatable was now nearly half a mile in the distance: hardly more than an orange speck that was visible only when it rose onto the crest of a swell. When it sank into the trough it was all but invisible.

Equipment lines and granny lines were pulled into the boat. A mooring ball was secured to the anchor line, then the anchor line and mooring ball were thrown free. Hank steered the *Garloo* toward the inflatable.

After our arrival, Mark quickly explained the situation. When he pulled alongside the surface marker buoy, he reached out to secure it to the inflatable. He felt tension on the line for only a moment. Then the tension relaxed. Now a limp line hung beneath the SMB. He didn't know what happened, but he wasn't about to pull up the line in case Jeff was clinging to it.

We all surmised that a diver must have been doing a drift decompression, and for some reason had let go of or lost his grip on the line reel. By this reasoning we all hoped – or prayed – that Jeff was adrift and decompressing at depth under water.

Mark had initially spotted bubbles rising to the surface, but then lost sight of them. He stood in order to have a better view of the water around the inflatable. He let the inflatable drift with the current in the hope that Jeff would surface not far away. He did not see anything more to indicate the presence of a diver, but he didn't stop looking. He was confident that the *Garloo* would eventually come for him.

By this time, Jeff had been absent for two and a half hours. Under normal circumstances, we would have presumed that he had long since run out of gas. But because he was using a rebreather, there was a strong possibility that he was alive – either still decompressing, or on the surface but not visible because of the state of the sea.

The *Garloo* circled the inflatable. We kept searching visually.

Meanwhile, Joe King, still wet from his early morning dive, took an entirely different tack. Afterward, he described his actions and thought processes to me.

When he first learned that Jeff was missing, he climbed to the wheelhouse deck and, using Hank's binoculars (which had a built-in compass), took an azimuth reading on the raft. The rough seas caused the bearing to vary between 270° and 310°. The average bearing was 290°.

At that time the inflatable was between one-half and three-quarters of a mile from the mooring on the *Doria*. After the *Garloo* reached the inflatable, and conducted a search in the vicinity, Joe asked Hank to stop the boat and let it drift. Using his handheld GPS receiver, Joe stored a waypoint at that location, and set his timer. After precisely five minutes he stored a second waypoint.

The difference between these two waypoints provided a heading and a distance. The direction of the surface current approximated 353°. The travel distance approximated one-tenth of a mile. To obtain the speed of the current, he multiplied the travel distance by 12 (60 minutes divided by 5 minutes), which yielded a product of 1.2 miles per hour.

Based on the approximate passage of time, Joe estimated that Jeff must have drifted for about thirty minutes after Mark picked up the SMB. Half of 1.2 miles was .6 mile, which he rounded down to half a mile. He then suggested to Hank that he search in an arc at a distance of half a mile downcurrent of the inflatable. After sweeping in one direction along the arc, the boat could then move farther out and sweep back along the second arc. The reason for the arc was to compensate for any inaccuracies that resulted from variations in wind speed or current speed and direction.

The *Garloo* was proceeding along the first arc when Joe shouted, "There he is! Diver ahead! He's alive!" (Or words to that effect.) He pointed so Hank could see where to steer the boat.

Joe deserves kudos not only for being a mathematical genius – he made all the calculations in his head – but for incredible eyesight. Although Jeff was waving, he was extremely difficult to spot because his black-clad body spent more time in the troughs and on the slopes than it did on the crests.

It is informative to note that Jeff was found in a straight line that extended from the mooring on the *Doria* through the position of the inflatable when Mark first arrived at the surface marker buoy. After Mark arrived at the SMB, the drift of the inflatable diverged more than 30° from Jeff's line of drift. This implies that the wind was blowing the raft in a direction that was different from the direction of the current. The direction of Jeff's drift possessed no wind component.

In retrospect, the above story comes across as somewhat mundane and too much "by the book." I related only the facts in chronological sequence. The plot boils down to three major scenes: a diver was missing, we searched for him, we found him.

Until you have been in a similar situation, you cannot appreciate the intense anxiety that we all felt when it first appeared that Jeff might have drowned under water and sank to the bottom, never to be seen again – especially in light of the alarming number of recent rebreather fatalities.

I suffered a hollow feeling in the pit of my stomach that resulted from a general sense of helplessness. A stark sense of gloom and doom pervaded the boat. *But,* no one yielded to fatalistic impotence. Despite deep emotional turmoil, everyone acted with strength and determination, and did everything possible to effect Jeff's rescue, working on the premise that he could still be alive.

A positive attitude and affirmative action are quintessentially important in such dire situations.

Underwater Perspective

Now for Jeff Downing's side of the story.

This was his first trip to the *Doria*. On his second dive (the previous day) he made a deep penetration. He found a porcelain sink in the interior, hauled it out of the wreck, and prepared it for recovery by rigging it with a liftbag and line reel. On his third dive – the one on which he went missing – he planned to float the sink to the surface.

It is not possible to fill a liftbag from a rebreather, especially at such a depth as the *Doria*. In addition to two 80-cubic-foot bailout tanks, Jeff carried a 30-cubic-foot sling bottle that was filled with air and that was designated for inflating the liftbag. He also carried a scooter.

The anchor line was secured to the middle scupper on the port bow, at a depth of 200 feet. The sink lay on the high side of the hull forward of the anchor line.

Because of the strong current, Jeff scootered to the anchor line and then made his descent unassisted. He reached the tie-in point without difficulty. He clipped a marker strobe to the anchor line. Now he saw that his line-reel line was no longer secured to the anchor line; his line was draped over the anchor line.

He followed his line down to the seabed, on the hull side of the wreck (as opposed to the top or superstructure side). There he discovered that he had left the locking screw open. The line had unspooled and the reel had slid down the hull to 250 feet. He commenced to reel himself up to the anchor line.

The hull is smooth and without protuberances. The current kept pushing him aft as he reeled in line. He was unable to reel in the line quickly enough to maintain tension on the line. When he reached the high side of the wreck at the tie-in point, the line reel jammed.

He spent some time trying to free the line, but eventually came to the conclusion that the line could not be freed under water. He cut the line and stowed the reel.

By now he had seven or eight minutes remaining of his planned 35-minute bottom time. He decided to send up the sink without a safety line. He unclipped the air-filled sling bottle only to find that the first stage of the attached regulator had come off the valve.

Both he and Marty had personally checked the tank and regulator before the dive, and he had charged the regulator before entering the water. His only explanation for the loosened first stage was that because Marty had slung the tank by clipping the nose to the hip D-ring, the second stage purge button must have pressed against the adjacent sling bottle, discharged the air, and the tank had then rolled against the other sling bottle in such a way that it gradually unscrewed the first stage from the valve.

He tried to reseat the valve but was unable to do so. By then he had reached the limit of his planned bottom time. He restowed the sling bottle, retrieved his marker strobe, and commenced his ascent. By now the topside conditions were worsening: the current was stronger and wave heights were increasing.

On the way up the line, somewhere deeper than 100 feet, the jolting anchor line hit him in the face and dislodged his mask. He normally sealed the mask on the smooth side of his cold-water hood, or skullcap, which he wore underneath his regular hood. He was unable to readjust the mask in order to get a good seal. The mask kept flooding (not just leaking). Because he was venting gas through his nose in order to constantly clear the mask, instead of exhaling through his mouth and keeping the gas in the breathing loop, he was losing great quantities of diluent. (During ascent, a rebreather no longer uses diluent; oxygen is injected when necessary in order to maintain its partial pressure.)

Finally he had to pull his hood completely back off his head, remove the mask, don the mask anew, and re-seal it against the cold-water hood – all this while not losing his grip on the bouncing anchor line.

After he resolved the mask situation, he resumed his ascent and made his deep decompression stops at the end of a jonline. When he reached the depth of the granny lines, he worked his way aft along the starboard line. Granny lines tend not to bounce the way an anchor line does; this makes for a more comfortable decompression. On the *Garloo*, the aft end of each granny line was secured to a weighted down-line.

At this point Jeff still had about an hour of decompression to complete. As he settled into his 20-foot stop, he decided to relieve himself of some of his encumbrances. He let go of the granny line and swam to an equipment line that was weighted with a stainless steel hammer.

As soon as he grabbed the equipment line, the current pushed him like the counterweight of a pendulum, lifting him above his decompression stop. He immediately let go of the line and kicked downward as hard as he could in order to regain his proper depth. After he stabilized his depth, he looked for the equipment line but it was nowhere in sight – the current had swept him out of visual range of the boat and all its lines.

He then attempted to scooter into the current toward the boat. After about a minute of this, he realized that he had no way to gauge his forward progress, if any, and no way to ascertain if he was going in the right direction. He could see neither lines nor the shadow of the boat. He switched off the scooter.

He deployed a surface marker buoy – securing it not to the reel that had jammed, but to a backup finger spool. He burped some gas out of the side of his mouth into the open bottom of the SMB. The SMB rose lazily to the surface, but it was inflated with such a small amount of gas that it sank when he put only the slightest amount of tension on the line.

He retrieved the SMB. He used the purge valve of a regulator on one of his bailout bottles to blast a large quantity of gas into the SMB. This time it stayed on the surface.

He still had about 45 minutes of decompression remaining at his fifteen-foot stop.

A few minutes later, he heard the motor of the inflatable roar into life. Now he knew that his SMB had been spotted, and that someone was coming after him. Shortly afterward, he saw the shadow of the inflatable approaching, then he saw the inflatable above him.

Mark stopped the motor and drifted to the SMB. When he grabbed the SMB, the wind pushed the inflatable and dragged Jeff's emergency line sideways, once again swinging him like the counterweight of a pendulum above his decompression stop. This gave Jeff the feeling that someone was pulling the line to the surface.

Jeff let go of the line. He kicked downward hard in order to regain his decompression depth. After he was stabilized, he could no longer see either his line or the inflatable. He burped gas from one of his sling bottle regulators to indicate his location to whoever was in the inflatable. As noted in the previous section, Mark spotted bubbles rising to the surface, but then lost sight of them.

Jeff still had 36 minutes of decompression remaining. Now he had to complete his decompression without the ease of hanging heavily on a line beneath a surface marker buoy.

A drift decompression on open circuit can be difficult, exhausting, and wasteful of breathing gas. This is because the lungs inflate with every inhale, and deflate with every exhale, causing the diver to rise and fall with every breath as a result of constant changes in buoyancy. Each minute change in depth also affects the inflation gas in the drysuit and buoyancy compensator.

Not only is this yo-yo affect not a safe way to decompress, but the diver finds himself rising above his prescribed decompression stop and venting inflation gas to compensate, or sinking too deep and adding inflation gas. The trick is to breathe shallowly, stay slightly heavy, and kick the fins in order to maintain depth.

Buoyancy control is exacerbated by heavy seas, when deep troughs are followed by high crests.

A drift decompression is somewhat easier on a rebreather. The exhaled gas passes through the breathing loop into the counterlung, which inflates at the same time that the lungs deflate; then inhaled gas passes through the breathing loop from the counterlung, which deflates at the same time that the lungs inflate. A near perfect balance is achieved because of this closed loop.

The only time that balance is lost is when the solenoid injects oxygen into the loop. Whenever Jeff heard the solenoid actuating, he compensated for the slight inflation by burping a little gas out of the side of his mouth.

Finally he completed his decompression obligation, and surfaced. To achieve and maintain positive buoyancy, he fully inflated the bladder of his buoyancy compensator; then he locked down the exhaust valve of his drysuit and added inflation gas. He also closed the overpressure relief valve of his counterlung.

The problem he then encountered was insufficient oxygen to maintain a suitable partial pressure. His onboard diluent was trimix-10/60. Ten percent oxygen is not a high enough partial pressure to sustain life on the surface, at one atmosphere. Because the solenoid kept injecting oxygen in order to increase the partial pressure, his oxygen supply was quickly being depleted.

Now he started to scan the horizon for the *Garloo*. Only on occasion, when both he and the *Garloo* were on the crest of a wave, was he able to spot the boat. He estimated that this occurred about once every five minutes or so. He could tell that the *Garloo* was searching for him because one time he would see the port side of the boat, and the next time he would see the starboard side. This indicated to him that the *Garloo* was sweeping back and forth in a regular search pattern.

Joe King provided a valuable perspective to the wave crest situation: "The only time we could see Jeff was when both [he and the boat] were sitting on the apex of the wave. I estimate that with Jeff a half mile away (approximately 41 boat lengths) and accounting for eyeballs being 15 feet above the water (on the boat), we could only see Jeff for less than 20 degrees of the 360 degrees in the wave sinusoid – or about 5% of the wave length. This same 5% applies to the time component of the wave period (the time between crests). Assuming 10 seconds between crests means that we had about 1/2 second to see Jeff (5% times 10 seconds). To put this in a bit more perspective, a human blink is .3-.4 seconds. Quite literally, it only took a blink of an eye to miss Jeff!"

Jeff was dressed like a stealth diver: black drysuit, black hood, black mask, black gloves, and black rebreather cover. The only thing on his person that had any noticeable color was the sling bottle filled with air for liftbag inflation – it was painted fluorescent yellow. He unclipped the yellow tank and placed it on his head, then swung his body back and forth as a way to attract attention.

The weight of the tank overhead pushed his face beneath the surface.

By this time the rebreather's oxygen cylinder was empty. Jeff had to switch off the rebreather because the solenoid kept activating, trying to inject oxygen into the loop when there was no oxygen in the tank. His rebreather was fitted with an offboard gas kit. This kit enabled him to plug in a hose from his bailout bottle and pipe nitrox-50 into the diluent regulator, so he could continue to use the unit in semi-closed-rebreather mode.

At this point Jeff suffered a malfunction of a different kind. His P-valve had operated flawlessly on his first urination. When he urinated a second time, something went wrong with the mechanism. Now his drysuit was less than dry.

When the yellow tank failed to attracted attention from the boat, Jeff resorted to his scooter. He restowed the tank and unclipped the scooter. Scootering was challenging because of the big waves. It was difficult to track the boat because it was moving, and with his face in the water he couldn't determine his direction of travel. So he scootered for a minute or so, surfaced and realigned himself with the boat, then repeated the process.

Eventually, Jeff and the *Garloo* got close enough for Joe King to spot him on the crest of a wave. By this time Jeff had been in the water for four hours: three hours under water and one hour on the surface. He was greatly relieved to see the bow of the *Garloo* charging toward him.

Jeff's greatest relief, however, was the fact that he did not feel any symptoms of decompression injury.

Afterward, Jeff described his experience as a Murphy's Law kind of dive: one in which just about everything that could go wrong, did go wrong. The saving grace was that the wrongs were not simultaneous or cumulative, but were isolated and sequential.

In the relief that came after the rescue operation ended happily, Jeff was dubbed Lost Boy, and Joe was dubbed Eagle Eye.

Parsing Perspectives

There are lessons to be learned by parsing this incident, and there is much food for thought to be consumed by chewing over the circumstances. In this section I intend to raise questions, but I must state up front that I don't have all the answers. My purpose is to increase awareness of the potential hazards of remote technical diving expeditions – first, so that others may understand the risks involved; second, so that they can better prepare themselves for similar eventualities; and third, so that they might offer suggestions for dealing with relevant safety issues.

The most important aspect of technical diving – indeed, of any activity that might be life-threatening – is decision making. Each individual must make his own decisions, and is solely responsible for accepting the results of those decisions, without assigning blame else-

Stealth diver returning safely.

where.

Jeff Downing's dive involved two crucial decisions. The first – and the one that is likely to receive the most vigorous objection from non-technical divers – was whether to dive at all in conditions that were less than ideal. There are two parts to this answer.

First, if one were to wait for ideal conditions before making a dive on the *Doria*, one might never get in the water. I have seen ideal conditions on the *Doria*, but only on rare occasions. For the most part, you take what you get and make do with it.

Second, conditions that one person might find too difficult, another person might find acceptable (although uncomfortable). In this regard, the biggest mistake that people make is in using their own abilities and levels of experience to judge the actions of others who possess different abilities and levels of experience. Despite Thomas Jefferson's oft-quoted phrase in the Declaration of Independence, all people are *not* created equal.

Jeff's second crucial decision was to complete his decompression after he drifted away from the boat, instead of surfacing immediately and calling for help while it was still nearby. These two choices – to decompress or to surface – beg the question: which was the better choice? Or rather, since neither choice led to immediate safety, which choice constituted the best possibility of survival?

There is no right answer to this question. There is no way to know – either beforehand, during, or afterward – which choice is, was, or will be the better of the two. Est quod est, as the Romans used to say. It is what it is.

When Jeff chose to complete his decompression, he accepted certain possibilities: that he might never be found, or that he might be overwhelmed by another equipment failure, or that he might run out of gas and drown on the surface, or that he might be attacked by a shark, or . . .

Had he chosen to surface, he would have faced different possibilities: that he might die shortly afterward from massive decompression injury; that he could breathe oxygen on the boat and ameliorate or never manifest symptoms; that he could be airlifted to a recompression chamber for treatment whose prognosis was dubious; that he could be paralyzed for life, or . . .

He also could have surfaced temporarily next to the dive boat or the inflatable, called attention to himself, and resubmerged in order to complete his decompression.

The possibilities are as endless as they are uncertain. Either choice could have been right – or could just as well have been wrong. Second guessing is impossible to do.

Perhaps he would have chosen differently if he had less decompression to complete, or if he had less faith in the captain and crew, or if the seas were more violent, or if he was on an open-circuit rig that was nearly out of gas, or if Great White sharks had been spotted in the vicinity, or . . .

I repeat: the possibilities are endless.

The real question is: what *did* we learn from the experience? Or, what questions were raised, whether or not any solutions were found.

The number one gripe on the boat was the lack of

bubbles. The tried and true method of locating a diver under water doesn't work when the diver is using a rebreather, because there is no continuous telltale volume of bubbles breaking the surface. The idea of a rebreather that was equipped with a bubble maker was kicked around, but without any serious attempt to determine how such a mechanism would operate with the limited gas supply that is available from the small tanks with which a rebreather is equipped. No solution was forthcoming.

Jeff could have made himself more visible on the surface by adding color to his equipment: an orange drysuit instead of a black one, a brightly colored rebreather cover, retro-reflective tape on his hood, and so on. A signal mirror would have been helpful. A submersible strobe would have been invaluable. A plastic whistle or air horn (attached to a bailout bottle) could have been useful. Water dye, flares, or rockets should not be discounted; they can be carried in watertight containers. I've even known people to carry an EPIRB in a waterproof housing. (EPIRB is the acronym for Emergency Position Indicating Radio Beacon, a device that is not just standard but is mandated by the Coast Guard for all licensed passenger vessels.)

At least one company sells a personal locator beacon that is based on GPS technology; it comes installed in a pressure-proof housing that can be taken to nearly 500 feet. Recently, another company started marketing a device that incorporates a two-way VHF radio, and a GPS transmitter and display unit, both of which are housed together in a waterproof case that is pressure tested to more than 400 feet. The retail price is only a few hundred dollars. In an emergency, it might be worth several million.

Don't laugh at any of these putative extravagances until you've been adrift at sea more than fifty miles from shore. The modern day version of "My kingdom for a horse" could be "My kingdom for a signaling device."

In fact, Jeff did have a submersible strobe with him, as well as three dive lights. He was saving their battery power for use after sunset. Considering the wave height, the strobe or light would have worked better for signaling an aircraft overhead than a boat on the same plane.

There was one last recourse. Had we not found Jeff shortly after we did, Hank would have called for Coast Guard assistance. The Coast Guard would have dispatched a helicopter to scour the area for the missing diver. It has been done before, and it will be done again. But a helicopter search and rescue mission is a major undertaking: a privilege that is not to be abused. Responsible skippers know and respect the protocol of not calling for airborne support until all avenues of self-help have been exhausted.

Objectors might note that Jeff's drift decompression could have been avoided if he had stayed on the granny line instead of moving to the equipment line. While this fact may be obvious in retrospect, Jeff did not think at the time that the conditions were bad enough to create any problems. Because he was able to swim with the current in order to reach the equipment line that was secured to the aftermost cleat, he failed to consider that there might not be enough weight on the line to keep him at his prescribed decompression depth.

There is no way to foresee every difficulty that might arise from every action. But the diver who is trained and mentally prepared for unanticipated events has a better chance of surviving than one who is not.

I have seen people who lacked the resolve or the will to live – who did not possess what I call the survival instinct: they gave up and died when there was much they could have done to effect their rescue and survival.

A true technical diver must be fully aware of the risks that are involved in the activity. He must be familiar with his equipment. He must be self-assured and self-reliant. He must be willing to keep working toward his survival no matter what the odds are against it.

Most important of all, a technical diver must exercise good judgment and be able to make firm decisions – and to accept responsibility for the results of those decisions.

Andrea Doria Breakthroughs

In 2005, I published *Deep, Dark, and Dangerous: Adventures and Reflections on the Andrea Doria*. The book included a Collapse Chronology in which I detailed the changes that occurred from year to year, ending with my observations of 2004: the year in which the bow broke away from the rest of the wreck, to create a feature that became known as the "break."

I continued my Collapse Chronology to 2008 in *Shipwreck Sagas*.

To recapitulate: Because the forward end of the hull curves inward (toward the centerline) and comes together at the stem, one hundred fifty feet of the bow has been unsupported ever since the wreck sank on its starboard side. The weight of the bow and the lack of support placed tremendous stress on transverse bulkheads and crossthwart trusses. In effect the bow was a massive cantilever.

The weakest point of the hull – or the location of greatest instability – was the trunk of number two hatch. This broad void in the beam occurred precisely where the curvature began. The port hull cracked in 2000, then broke completely away between the 2003 and 2004 diving seasons. This "break" permitted access to the lower decks, both forward and aft.

C Deck (the bottommost deck) was not accessible at first because the opening to it was too small to squeeze through. Over succeeding years, the bow continued to roll slowly onto its keel. This process widened the crack and opened the way to C Deck in 2005, although it was still a squeeze. The "squeeze" enlarged until today it has the appearance of a garage door.

The crack in the port hull above the break is shaped

like a V. The open end of the V measures some twenty feet across. The closed end of the V touches the bottom of the hull. Because the wreck lies on its side, the bottom of the hull is vertical. In 2011, I noticed a six-inch crack that ran down about fifteen feet from the high side. This crack was not in evidence in 2010.

As soon as it appeared, the so-called break made it easy to enter areas that were never accessible before. These decks were crammed with small cabins whose partitions have long since disintegrated, leaving bunk beds and bathroom fixtures exposed, and fields of debris that have yielded a trove of artifacts.

By way of example, I recovered two cylindrical brass reading lights that were complete with bulbs; a bathroom shelf that was made of black glass; various brass accoutrements; and four bottles on whose plastic caps was stamped "Hiram Walker." Hiram Walker makes an assortment of liqueurs. The paper labels had long since dissolved in seawater, so I could not determine what kind of liqueur the bottles had contained.

On another dive I penetrated fifty feet along A Deck. I counted at least ten sinks among the debris, and one or two urinals or bidets (I didn't look too closely).

Perhaps the most exciting dive was the one on which I entered the bottommost deck, and ended up going in farther than I wanted to go. I found myself in such a huge compartment that I could see no bottom and no bulkhead ahead of me. The only thing that I knew for certain was that I didn't want to be there. I made a quick and tactful retreat. Afterward, I studied the deck plans, and determined that some of decks had collapsed, and I had somehow found my way into the garage.

In 2011, Jitka Hamakova and I recovered drinking glasses, a brass holder for one of the glasses, and a silver spoon; the handle of the spoon was adorned with the crown logo and the word "ITALIA."

On a subsequent dive I discovered one of the vessel's wine cellars or storage compartments in the forward side of the break. I counted more than one hundred bottles on a ledge that was the size of a walk-in closet. The external pressure at 220 feet had forced most of the corks into the bottles. I retrieved three of these bottles; the rest I left for other divers.

One of the bottles still had the cork in place; the contents were uncontaminated by seawater. I don't know what kind of wine the bottles contained because the paper labels were gone. But the bottom of each bottle is embossed with "THIS BOTTLE IS MADE IN ITALY."

These newly accessible passageways will continue to yield artifacts for many years to come.

I first dived on the *Andrea Doria* in 1974. In 2011, Marcie Bilinski accompanied me on my milestone dive that was my 200th descent to the *Andrea Doria*. I should have celebrated afterward – especially as I brought back a full bottle of wine from the above-mentioned wine compartment. Instead, I groaned in agony.

For the previous several months I had been suffering from sciatica: a medical condition in which a pinched nerve causes excruciating pain in the back or legs. I had a couple of bad bouts on the boat that only strong pain killers ameliorated. While climbing up the ladder after my 200th dive, my sciatica kicked in and sent stabbing twinges of pain down my left leg. I was barely able to climb onto the swim platform without help.

Dave Console dragged me onto the deck and pulled off my tanks and other gear. Then I stretched out flat on my back, groaning in misery: a discomfiting rather than a triumphant return from a momentous dive. I could not bend at the waist or move in any way that did not cause agonizing pain. I had to have my drysuit stripped off me. Then I crawled into the cabin like a wounded cripple. I celebrated the event by swallowing a pain pill.

I pray that my 201st *Doria* dive will be more fun and less ignominious.

Explosive Correction

To err is human, as the saying goes. Everyone makes mistakes and I am no exception, even though I try harder than most people not to. I would like to put one of my

Leftover from the previous war.

mistakes on record.

In the 2002 edition of *Shipwrecks of Delaware and Maryland*, I wrote about munitions that had been found on the destroyer *Jacob Jones*. I described gun shells whose warheads had nosecones that were "interesting because the fuses were adjustable for amount of armor penetration; they are made of finely machined bronze, and are etched with lines and numbers."

Phil McGrath informed me that what I mistook for armor-piercing nosecones were in fact time-delay fuses for anti-aircraft shells. Rotating rings enabled the timing element to be adjusted. The numbers referred to seconds of delay between the moment of firing and the actual burst. The gunnery officer had to estimate the altitude of the target, correlate the muzzle velocity of the projectile with the number of seconds required to reach the estimated altitude, and adjust the timing rings according.

This was the naval version of flak. The nosecone possessed a threaded base so it could be screwed onto the top of a projectile as needed, or unscrewed and replaced with a nosecone that detonated on impact.

You learn something new every day, and so do I.

Unfortunate Omission

When I revised *Shipwrecks of Delaware and Maryland* in 2002, I expanded the text and added wrecks that were not included in the original volume. I couldn't include every wreck that lay off Delmar – that would require a multi-volume encyclopedia. So I chose the ones that were the best-known sites, and added a couple that had not yet been discovered. The book exceeded my space allocation, forcing me to delete two pages of photos. One wreck that I researched but ultimately left out due to space constraints was the *Lucy Neff*.

In 2005, I received a phone call from Harold Moyers. He had just discovered a wreck off Delaware in 205 feet of water. He described the condition and lay-out of the wreck, and read information off a builder's plaque that Steve Gatto recovered. Five minutes into the conversation, I said, "That sounds like the *Lucy Neff*. Let me check my files."

I pulled out my *Lucy Neff* folder. The Lloyd's data sheet matched perfectly with what was stamped on the builder's plaque. Positive ID.

Lucy Neff as the *W.P. Ketcham*. (Courtesy of Bowling Green State University.)

Montgomery Identification

As I have written elsewhere, most shipwrecks are identified not by the recovery of a singular item such as a bell or plaque on which the name of the vessel is stamped, but by a preponderance of evidence. Here is a recent example.

In *Shipwrecks of New Jersey: South*, I wrote about an unidentified wreck that was known locally as Max's Wreck. I compared the historical account with the wreck's location, description, and condition, and suggested the possibility that it could be the *Montgomery*.

This merchant vessel was purchased by the Union Navy for service in the Civil War. After the cessation of hostilities, she was returned to merchant service. In January 1877, the *Montgomery* sank after a collision with the *Seminole*.

The historical location was close to the actual position of Max's Wreck. The wooden hull and machinery matched the description of the vessel's construction. The degree of collapse was consistent with that of a wreck that had lain on the bottom for more than a century and a quarter.

The clincher to the vessel's identity came in 2009, when Gene Peterson found a brass pump in the wreckage. He and Harold Moyers, skipper of the *Big Mac*, secured three liftbags to the pump – and were unable to lift it! Attached to the pump was a long length of lead pipe which was buried in debris and entangled in a net. They had to cut the artifact free before the liftbags floated the pump to the surface.

Stamped on the 100-pound pump were the words "U.S. Navy Yard, New York." This does not make identification absolutely positive, but it certainly adds a corroborative if not definitive piece to the puzzle: one that is consistent with the history of the vessel's wartime service, when repairs and maintenance were conducted by the Navy department.

Additionally, Moyers recovered a bottle that was embossed "Karl Hutter Lager." The manufacture of this rare bottle is contemporary with the *Montgomery*.

Hail to the *Champion*

Not all my faithful readers will be familiar with the wrecks of the *Champion* and *Admiral Dupont*, especially my international readers. Both were paddlewheel steamers, and both sank off Cape May, New Jersey: the former in 1879, the latter in 1865.

The remains of two paddlewheel steamers are known and dived off Cape May. Due to their relative positions, one is called the Offshore Paddle Wheeler, and one is called the Inshore Paddle Wheeler. Because the similarities between these two wreck sites outweigh their differences, neither has been positively identified as the *Champion* or *Admiral Dupont*. The mystery of which wreck is which has persisted for years.

I covered these wrecks in *Shipwrecks of New Jersey: South*. I made an exhaustive comparison between each vessel's statistics, and I detailed everything that was known about the sites at the time of publication. The sum of the evidence led to inconclusive identifications – although I personally favored the Inshore Paddle Wheeler as the *Champion*, and the Offshore Paddle Wheeler as the *Admiral Dupont*.

The depth of the Inshore Paddle Wheeler is 105 feet; that of the Offshore Paddle Wheeler is 150 feet.

Enter Rusty Cassway and Brian Sullivan, owners and operators of the Research Vessel *Explorer*, which was dedicated to the exploration of shipwrecks that lay off Cape May. For more than a decade they have been compelled to identify the paddlewheel steamers. They started their search for an identifying artifact by scanning the debris of the Inshore Paddle Wheeler; then by digging or by fanning the sand; then by using a scooter to move larger quantities of overburden; and then by using an airlift to enable them to excavate deeper into the seabed.

Their dedication resulted in the rescue of a number of artifacts such as a brass Derringer, powder flasks, shot, and forks. But none of these items helped to identify the wreck. Then came the momentous occasion.

Rusty and Brian built and installed a water dredge on the *Explorer*. This facilitated the removal of great quantities of sand. They and their cohorts excavated a hole that was six feet in depth. It appeared that they were unearthing a luggage compartment, for they found personal belongings such as gold rings and bracelets.

In June 2010, the *Explorer* departed from Cape May with a group of dedicated divers who planned to take turns at operating the water dredge. In addition to Rusty and Brian were Sam Demore, Andy Florey, Steve Gatto, Bruce Leinan, Bart Malone, Lou Sarlo, and Tom Packer.

Bart suggested rather fervently that after setting up the dredge on the bottom, they needed to secure a mesh bag over the discharge end of the exhaust hose, in order to filter the spoil. The mesh bag allowed silt and mud to escape, but solid objects that were smaller than the mesh were captured. Every so often the mesh bag was retrieved and the spoil was spread on the deck for examination.

As Brian, Steve, and Tom were going through the spoil, Tom plucked what proved to be a brass luggage tag out of the spoil.

On the brass was stamped "CHAMPION" and "195." Case closed!

Congratulations to Rusty, Brian, and the rest of the gang who positively identified the Inshore Paddle Wheeler as the *Champion*.

By inference, the Offshore Paddle Wheeler should be the *Admiral Dupont*. I guess they'll have to start working there with the dredge, in order to confirm the inference.

Another Boston Tea Party

My New England readers, and others who have cosmopolitan interests, might have read what I wrote about the destruction of a minesweeper in Boston Harbor. To recapitulate, the *YMS-14* was sunk by collision with another warship during World War Two. The wreck lay unmolested until I featured it in *Shipwrecks of Massachusetts: North*.

Marcie Bilinski and I discovered the site where the remains of five depth charges lay exposed among rocks and kelp. I photographed the depth charges, and used one of the photos to illustrate the back cover of the book.

I joked about how official heads would turn when they discovered that inert explosive charges lay only one hundred yards from the main shipping channel, which was plied on a regular basis by supertankers that transported liquid natural gas. In a knee-jerk reaction, those official heads turned way too far: more like a victim of possession and exorcism than a cool-headed administrative figure.

The U.S. Navy took it upon itself to demolish the wreck – without authorization from the Massachusetts Board of Underwater Archaeological Resources.

The largely eroded depth-charge remnants could not have exploded on their own. Nor could they have been of any use to terrorists. Explosive material deteriorates over time, the same way in which food rots and medicine goes bad – by means of chemical breakdown.

Marcie and I conducted extensive surveys of the wreck during the summer of 2010. If I claimed that the Navy blew the wreck to smithereens, I would be understating the case. Hardly any smithereens remain to mark the site.

Fortunately, Marcie had accurate GPS coordinates, else we might have thought that the wreck had been blasted to oblivion and hauled away to the scrap yard. Only by searching for hours at the end of a line reel were we able to locate what used to be the site of an historic landmark that now hardly exists.

Navy divers detonated so many pounds of explosives

This East Coast shipwreck not only has depth charges from World War Two, but has some stowed in the launching rack on the fantail. Because government officials read my books, I will not reveal the name or location of this wreck unless ordered to do so by the presiding judge in a court of law . . . unless I choose to take the Fifth Amendment.

around the depth charges that the wreck now looks like a moonscape. The seabed was unearthed by the blast, large boulders were shattered and the pieces were tossed great distances, and marine life was obliterated.

One bronze rudder post is completely missing. The other one was laid down horizontally by the explosion, and a deep pit was gouged out of the rocky substrate beneath it. The bottom contours are so altered that the broad patch of sand that extended outward from the depth-charge area is gone; the seabed is now a debris field littered with shattered rocks.

If there is any saving grace to this travesty, it is that some of the timbers of the wooden hull have been exposed by the removal of overburden. That is small recompense for the destruction of a fascinating shipwreck.

You can thank the Navy for demolishing an important piece of America's past.

There is irony to this situation. Had the witch-hunters at the Naval Historical Center caught an American citizen removing so small an item as an iron bolt from the blasted wreck, they would have sicced the Naval Criminal Investigation Service on him – as they have done in the past – for stealing what they perceived to be government property. Go figure.

Icy Dicey Diving

I recently completed a series of three presentations in New York and New Jersey. Each and every time during the question and answer period, I was asked, "Have you been diving recently?" (Or words to that effect.)

Generally, I spend most of my winter months in exercising my keyboard and doing research for forthcoming books, but this time I was able to inform my audiences about diving on the *Weetamoo* (1902 – 1926), in Lake Sunapee, New Hampshire.

Because the wooden-hulled excursion vessel lies in only 70 feet of water, it is not normally considered to be a challenging dive. In this case, however, cutting through 15 inches of ice added a fillip that is absent in warmer weather.

Although I kept my real hat on my head when I was over the ice, I took off my figurative hat to Jeff Downing for a masterful job of organizing the event. Jeff is a scuba instructor. This particular event constituted the in-water (and under-ice) portion of an ice-diving course that he was teaching to Tom Howarth and Brian Campbell.

Also participating in the cold-water dive was Joe King. Although Joe is a veteran with more than two hundred ice dives under his frozen weight belt, this was the first time that he ever dived under the ice in a drysuit. All his previous ice dives were made in a wetsuit. *Brr-rr-rr!*

Early in my career I made several ice dives in a wetsuit – only because I didn't yet own a drysuit. Wetsuit ice diving is an experience that I do not care to repeat. I leave that to polar-bear toughies like Joe.

Support personnel consisted of Kathy Downing, Marcie Bilinski, and Christa Howarth. Kathy kept a camp-stove fire going under a large pot of beef stew. Marcie and Christa tended lines. I've never had tenders who were more tender.

I couldn't help but make comparisons between this ice dive on the *Weetamoo* and my previous ice dive the year before on the *Lady of the Lake* (1850 – 1895) in Lake Winnipesaukee. At that time I had only one fellow diver: Dave Cunningham. The *Lady of the Lake* lay in 30 feet of water about a quarter mile from the nearest boat launch and parking lot. We had to drag or tow our tanks and gear to the wreck site. Dave brought a plastic sled that made the transfer of equipment easier than it would have been otherwise.

The *Weetamoo* lay more than a mile from the closest parking lot and launching ramp. Jeff furnished an all-terrain-vehicle and the trailer that was used to transport it. After driving the ATV off the trailer, he then unhitched the trailer from his pickup truck and hitched it to the back of the ATV. We loaded tanks, gear, and people onto the trailer for an effortless drive to the wreck site. Two trips were required to transport everyone and everything.

In Lake Winnipesaukee, Harold Dutton single-handedly wielded a chain saw with a 20-inch bar to cut through 18 inches of ice. In Lake Sunapee, Jeff and his students used a gasoline-powered augur and a hand-held tree saw to drill and carve a hole in the shape of an equilateral triangle. Each leg of the triangle measured four feet in length.

To locate the *Lady of the Lake*, we walked toward a vertical block of ice that the Finatics Dive Club of Atkinson, New Hampshire erected over the wreck the week before, when they conducted their annual ice-diving event. Club member Keith Kelly told me where to look for the frozen marker.

To locate the *Weetamoo*, Jeff used a hand-held GPS receiver, and coordinates that he and I had confirmed when we dived on the wreck the previous summer. The numbers were so accurate that after pushing the triangular ice block under the surface, we spotted the bleach bottle that served as a subsurface marker by the edge of the hole.

Jeff forced a stake into the ice next to the hole. He secured a line to the stake, and gave me the reel to secure to the rope beneath the bleach bottle. This was only a backup precaution. Each diver had a rope clipped to a D-ring on his harness. A tender paid out rope as the diver swam away from the hole and around and into the wreck, then drew in the rope as it slackened during the diver's return and approach to the hole. Constant tension ensured that entanglements did not occur.

On the *Lady of the Lake*, Dave showed me where a school of foot-long fish congregated inside the hull between two hatchways. The hull was intact but the superstructure had been razed and the machinery removed prior to scuttling. In essence, the *Lady of the Lake* is a giant barge whose greatest asset was a full-length swim-through. Age is also an attraction, as the hull was taken out of service before the *Weetamoo* was even put on the drawing board.

The *Weetamoo* had also been scuttled, but the su-

Ice diving on the *Weetamoo*. Note the hand augur in the foreground. Instead of a chain saw, this hole was cut by drilling holes in the corners of the triangle, then wielding a tree saw to connect the holes.

perstructure and machinery were left in place. The wooden wreck is almost perfectly intact. The hull stands upright on a muddy bottom whose coating of silt quickly stirs into an opaque cloud at the slightest touch or errant passing of a fin. Silt also covers the horizontal surfaces of the wreck. Divers are cautioned to employ the frog kick or some other anti-silting propulsion technique when maneuvering in, on, and around the site.

The wreck appears much as it does in topside photographs. The hull has settled into the lakebed to within three feet of the windowsills. Engine-room entry and egress are facilitated by the absence of glass in the windows. The boiler and engine rise out of the silt that has accumulated inside the machinery compartment. This compartment extends for most of the length of the hull: from the aft end of the wheelhouse to the fantail. The overhead or ceiling is nearly intact, with only a few missing planks. These missing planks are more noticeable from above, while swimming over the top of the wreck. The odd-shaped cylindrical items that litter the top, and which may be found on the lakebed next to the hull, are sections of ornate posts that once supported a safety cable that surrounded the top passenger deck.

The closet-sized wheelhouse protrudes upward like a pompadour. It is shaped like the home plate on a baseball diamond, except that the forward point is squared off, or blunt. You can enter the wheelhouse from a doorway on either side. From inside the wheelhouse, you can proceed aft down a stairwell into the machinery compartment, or up a set of steps onto the top passenger deck. The wheelhouse windows are paneless (groan!).

The stem is located about ten feet forward of the wheelhouse. The wood is preserved so well that the grain can be seen beneath the silt.

Nameboards used to adorn the exterior planks above the wheelhouse doorway lintels. These have been recovered and are on display in the museum (closed in winter) across the street from the lake's main boat launch (not the boat launch that we used for the ice dive). A reproduction nameboard has been placed above the port doorway lintel.

Visibility on the bottom tends to be in the range of ten feet or less, and may be very dark – almost like a night dive. Due to the lack of disturbance when the lake is frozen over, the vis on our ice dive approached fifteen feet and was not nearly as dark – although frosted ice reduced the amount of ambient light that reached the bottom.

In case of a summertime silt-out, a diver can simply ascend a few feet above the swirling cloud, then proceed in clear water to the mooring line, or all the way to the surface if decompression is not required. On an ice dive, a diver needs only to follow his lifeline to the hole.

The mooring line is secured to a vertical plank that separates two windows on the starboard side of the wheelhouse. You can easily swim around the perimeter of the wreck and return to your point of origin in just a few minutes.

Although the *Lady of the Lake* is more than twice the length of the *Weetamoo* – 125 feet compared to 55 feet – its barebones hull lacks the intricacies of its smaller brethren. There is more to see and do on the *Weetamoo* than on the *Lady of the Lake*. But I would dive on both of them again in a heartbeat – winter or summer.

There's not much more to say except that the water temperature was 35 degrees. *Ouch!* Even the fish were sluggish.

Bell of the Ball

A unique event occurred at the home of Mike and Lynn Boring on January 15, 2011: a concatenation of bells. Not church bells, not sleigh bells, not Christmas bells, but shipwreck bells.

The event began simply as a single bell transfer, then grew to mammoth proportions over the course of two short weeks. First, some background information for those of you who are unfamiliar with the history of the bell that initiated the event.

On a week-long expedition in 1985, seven wreck-divers recovered the stern bell from the *Andrea Doria*. These seven divers were Mike Boring, Kenny Gascon, Artie Kirchner, John Moyer, Bill Nagle, Tom Packer, and this author. We all shared ownership of the prized artifact.

It was not possible for all of us to display the bell at the same time at our individual homes, so we forged an informal agreement to share possession of the bell. This agreement has worked ideally for twenty-five years. One person might have the bell for a year or two, then another person would take it for six months or more. There were never any arguments among us. After all, the bell would not have been recovered if we had not all worked together in the first place. The full story is told in my book, *Andrea Doria: Dive to an Era*.

Occasionally the bell was displayed at museums and conventions. It is a most peripatetic bell.

The most recent possessor of the bell was Mike Boring. When Artie Kirchner professed an interest in possessing the bell for a while, he and Mike agreed that Artie could pick up the bell from Mike's house in Virginia. Artie lives in New Jersey. They set a date for the pick-up.

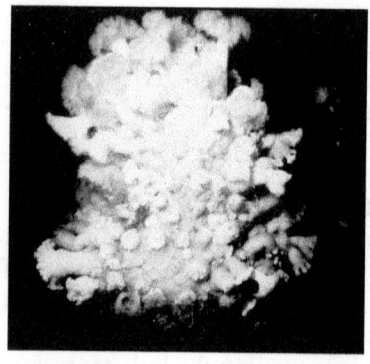

Mike sent a group email to let friends and fellow divers know about the occasion. He invited everyone to pay a visit to his house, and to bring a recovered bell if they had one to display. News spread like wildfire, from one group email to other group emails. Within days the *Andrea Doria* bell became the centerpiece of a major assembly of bells, of people who had recovered bells, and of long-time friends and dive buddies who had not seen each other for years.

To switch metaphors, the *Andrea Doria* bell was like a snowball rolling downhill, gathering more snow and growing larger as it sped toward the bottom of the slope.

The number of people who promised to attend grew exponentially. Mike was overwhelmed by the response to an extemporaneous get-together. Suddenly he found himself throwing a large-scale party.

A bell party.

A real-live carillon without the belfry.

Mike prepared for the celebration by buying a couple of pork shoulders. He asked prospective attendees to bring drinks, side dishes, and desserts. He wound up with a huge smorgasbord of everything from soup to nuts. (Some might contend that the visitors were the nuts.) He also asked at-

tendees to bring sleeping bags if they planned to stay over. Most did. Although every room in the house was packed with overnighters, there was no frigging in the rigging. (At least, none that I was aware of).

The final count was 30 bells and I don't know how many people from all over the eastern seaboard. The official estimate was between forty and fifty.

For me, the highlight of the evening was a gathering around the *Andrea Doria's* stern bell: a gathering that consisted of five of the seven divers who recovered it. Only Bill Nagle and Kenny Gascon were absent. Bill's son Andrew was there to take the place of his father.

Also on display was the *Andrea Doria's* bridge or crow's-net bell, which was recovered seven months earlier year by Carl Bayer and Ernie Rookey. Carl assumed the honor of bringing the bell to the bash.

Even without gongs, the otherwise quiet neighborhood fairly rang in accord with the chiming and the tinkling and the tintinnabulation of such a wonderful and historic display of shipwrecked ships' bells.

Thanks to Mike Boring for throwing a once-in-a-lifetime party. Its likes will likely not happen again.

I have five bells to my credit. These pictures show how they appeared when I first saw them. Counterclockwise from upper left: Andrea Doria, Bow Mariner, Sebastian, Manuela. For the story of bell number five, turn the page.

A Whopper of a Bell

The bell party moved me to reflect upon my unique underwater adventures, particularly with regard to the recovery of bells. I realized that I had participated in five successful bell recovery operations (as well as some others that were not successful because the bell in question could not be located). Four of those bells were on display at the bell party.

It almost goes without saying that I wrote about the recovery of the *Andrea Doria*'s stern bell in *Andrea Doria: Dive to an Era.*

I wrote briefly about the team effort to recover the *Bow Mariner*'s bell in *Shipwreck Sagas*. Harold Moyers organized the expedition, and we used his boat, the *Big Mac*, to reach the wreck. He currently has the bell on display in his home.

I described my discovery of the *Manuela*'s bell, and the concerted effort to recover it, in *Wreck Diving Adventures*. This bell resides permanently on the hearth of my fireplace.

My solo discovery and recovery of the *Sebastian*'s bell is told in two books: first in Book Two of *The Lusitania Controversies: Dangerous Descents into Shipwrecks and Law*, and again in *Shipwrecks of Massachusetts: South.* This bell also resides permanently on my hearth, so that it and the *Manuela*'s bell straddle the fireplace.

The story of the fifth bell has never been told . . . until now.

I started diving in Nova Scotia in 1979. Thereafter I organized annual pilgrimages to Halifax throughout the 1980's, until I turned over the organizational torch to Gene Peterson, who has run the trips ever since. Gene started by going on my trips, then I started going on his trips. My most recent trip was last year (2010).

The logistics of these trips was sometimes complicated. The way they were organized deserves some comment. Also, some of the interesting and amusing incidents that occurred on those trips deserve some description, especially as I have never written about them; so indulge me. After all, this *is* a book about reflections. So let me take the long-winded route, and reflect. In this manner you can understand how much effort (and enjoyment) preceded the recovery of the Nova Scotia bell, so that the event does not come off as merely a chance discovery.

Like life, every adventure is a journey, not a destination.

Getting There is Half the Fun

The distance from Philly to Halifax is about a thousand miles, and takes some twenty hours to drive. Carpooling (or truckpooling as the case may be) is a practical necessity.

This reminds me of a joke that I created and used to tell, about the abject fear that certain individuals felt when approaching a tunnel or underpass in a car full of riders. Psychiatrists studied the symptoms but never reached any conclusion as to what caused the sudden and unnatural anxiety attacks that were experienced by their patients while driving through an overhead environment. They named this weird mental anomaly "carpool tunnel syndrome."

Now that I've gotten that humor out of the way . . .

Standard operating procedure was to meet at a specified time and central location, then form a convoy and drive straight through from morning throughout the night, in order to avoid the cost of interim lodging. Sometimes we slept in the vehicles overnight or camped on the gravel shoulder by the roadside. In those days, you were allowed to do that in Maine and Canada without fear of police intervention. Our goal was a campground outside of Halifax, called Juniper Park (alias Five Islands Lake), which was owned and operated by Ken Doyle.

These travel arrangements were not always convenient for all participants, so sometimes vehicles went solo and converged at the campground. On one solo venture, Dave Poponi and I found ourselves crossing the Canadian border (from Calais to St. Stephen) well after dark. There was a dearth of gas stations in New Brunswick and Nova Scotia, and those that existed were closed after midnight. Most of those provinces can be called wilderness areas with occasional towns that roll up their sidewalks at sundown.

To make a long and anxious story short, we ran out of gas at 3 o'clock in the morning about twenty miles short of our goal. We could easily see the lights of Halifax in the distance. Dave steered his stalled van onto the narrow tree-lined shoulder in a typically desolate spot. We tossed our sleeping bags onto the gravel in front of the van, using the van as a buffer from a possible rear-end collision, and slept soundly until dawn. The only disturbances were the slipstreams from passing tractor-trailers.

In the dawn's early light, we spotted a red brick building in the grassy separation zone between the northbound lanes and the southbound lanes. Unbelievably, there was a public phone booth in front of the highway maintenance building. Dave called for help on the pay phone. In due course a tow truck arrived with five gallons of gasoline in a jerry jug. We reached the campground just as the rest of the group was preparing for departure, so we didn't even miss the morning dive (although we were well-nigh exhausted from taking turns at the wheel the previous day and night).

On one of Gene's trips, I was returning with Jon and Judy Hulburt when a moose meandered onto the road in front of us. We stopped and waited for it to move, but it did not appear to be in any hurry to do so. Not ones to miss a photo op, we climbed out of the van and approached the moose to take some pictures. Eventually it stopped ignoring us. It lumbered into the forest. I chased it into the woods to get some close-up from behind the protection of the trees. Then we (the moose and us) continued on our separate ways.

On another one of Gene's trips, our four-vehicle convoy was proceeding northward in New Jersey when we encountered a toll plaza on the Garden State Parkway. Commuter traffic was in full swing. Every toll booth was swamped by a long line of vehicles. Our convoy got separated into different lanes that were all mobbed and crawling at different speeds.

Not to worry. For such an eventuality, Gene had supplied each vehicle with driving instructions and a walkie-talkie with a five-mile range. Lynn DelCorio and I were driving together. By the time we paid the toll, everyone else had gone through the plaza and was out of sight ahead of us. Lynn was driving, so I grabbed the walkie-talkie and called for help. I could not get an answer on any frequency; they were out of range.

I pulled out the driving instructions. Instead of continuing north, they called for us to take I-287. That didn't make sense. According to my road atlas, the interstate led either east or west: east onto Staten Island, west toward Piscataway. What was Gene thinking?

I threw down the instruction in disgust. By this time I had been going to Nova Scotia for twenty years. I knew the way by heart. I told Lynn to proceed north on I-95. I figured on picking up Gene's route farther north, then catching up with the convoy at a predetermined waypoint later that afternoon or evening.

We reached Connecticut a couple of hours later. As I was taking in the scenery, I spotted Gene's van. *He was behind us!* I called him on the walkie-talkie and told him to look at the van that was a hundred yards in front of him. He speeded up, then pulled alongside of us, glaring with a grimace of disbelief.

It turned out that I-287 swung west then north around the heavily populated areas that surrounded Newark, then east across the Hudson River into New York State – a route that was longer than the direct route that Lynn and I had taken, but that was generally faster because of better traffic flow. We all stayed together once we had regrouped.

On two of my trips, I selected dates that dovetailed with wilderness canoe trips in Quebec. The first time I did this was in 1980, but it didn't work out exactly as I had planned. The run down the Mistassini River measured some 200 miles in length and took three weeks to paddle. Afterward, six members of the group returned to Pennsylvania, while Walt Daub and I drove to Carrabassett, Maine, to visit his daughter Faron and her husband Tom Fahy, and to paddle with them on some local whitewater rivers.

I had previously dropped off my dive gear at Jim Murtha's house. He, Andy Weaver, and Art White were driving together to Halifax and were supposed to either pick me up along the way, or meet me at the campground if Walt couldn't drive me to someplace on their route through Maine, and I had to hitchhike instead.

In the event, I got ill in Maine after contracting giardiasis from drinking infected water from the Mistassini River. The gestation period between imbibing the single-celled animal *Giardia lamblia*, and the onset of debilitating symptoms, was ten days. I was weak after two days of fever and constant nausea, vomiting, and diarrhea. Walt took me home early. I recuperated fast. I ended up going to Jim's house and turning the threesome into a foursome.

The next time I scheduled such a maneuver was in 1982. This time the river was the Moisie. We started paddling in Newfoundland, ran more than 300 miles of placid lakes and fierce whitewater, and finished at Sept-Iles three weeks after we started – none the worse for wear except for black fly bites.

We then drove southwest along the north shore of the St. Lawrence Seaway. My canoeing partners dropped me off at the ferry dock at St-Simeon. They continued on to Quebec City and thence to the States, homeward bound. I took the ferry across the seaway to St-Patrice. I arrived at dusk with my backpack on my shoulders. There I was supposed to meet Kathy Warehouse.

Kathy lived in Maryland. She had never been to Maine or Nova Scotia, so in addition to diving in Halifax, she was eager to see some of the sights along the way – and didn't mind seeing some of the sights that were *out* of the way. I had given her my house key on a weekend dive trip prior to my departure for the wilderness. She stopped at my house in Philly, loaded my pre-packed dive gear into her pickup truck, then proceeded northward to our rendezvous at St-Patrice.

The ferry dock was a rinky-dink facility outside of town. Only one backwoods road connected the wharf to St-Patrice. Yet somehow we missed each other.

She told me that she was there when the last ferry arrived, but didn't see me disembark. I hung around the dock until I was the only person left; I never saw her. (Oh, for cell phones.)

She presumed that I had missed the last ferry of the day, and hoped that I would catch the first ferry in the morning. She drove into town and found lodging in a motel.

When she didn't appear by dark, I started to walk along the road, hoping to run into her (and not vice versa). I gave up hope when it started to rain. The forest was dense on both sides of the motorway. I beat through the wet underbrush and spent the night in the woods without a tent – although I did have a waterproof bivy sack for my sleeping bag.

I packed my meager belongings at first light, donned my raingear, shouldered my backpack, and hiked toward town in a light but constant drizzle. I wasn't on the road for five minutes when I spotted her pickup truck coming toward me. It was a reassuring encounter for both of us.

On another one of my trips, two divers were traveling in a van and planned to meet us at the campground in time for the first day's diving. For reasons that will soon become obvious, I will refrain from mentioning their names. When they reached the Canadian border after sunset, the customs agent did not whisk them through after a few seconds of questioning. Instead, he told them to pull over so their vehicle could be inspected.

What followed was the nightmare that you always

hear about but seldom encounter. Customs agents made them empty the van of every last bit of dive gear, camping equipment, and personal belongings. Agents inspected everything with the proverbial fine-toothed comb: they went through their luggage, scrutinized their packs and gear boxes, examined their cameras, and went so far as to open every film canister.

One of the agents ejaculated "Ah, *ha!*" when he discovered small white tablets in a film canister. He was demonstrably dejected when he moved into better light and read "Aspirin" on every tablet. It was a bitter pill for him to swallow. Reluctantly the customs agents let the pair off the hook and told them to get on their way.

Then came the laborious task of reloading the van with more than a ton of tanks, boxes, packing cases, and miscellaneous items. The Canadian customs agents did not offer to help.

All during the inspection, one of the divers was literally shaking in his shoes. He told me that his legs were twanging like guitar strings, and his hands were quivering so badly that he had to keep them in his pockets so his nervousness didn't show. Turns out that he had a bag of marijuana in his pocket. The customs agents inspected their vehicle; they did not frisk their persons!

As soon as they were out of sight of the customs stop, the diver dumped the marijuana out the window. I asked him why he got rid of it after the fact, when he was home free by then; there wouldn't be any more inspections. He said he didn't care. He was so scared of getting caught with the goods that he didn't want to have anything to do with illegal drugs.

During another border crossing on one of my trips, Gene Peterson and John Moyer had their van packed all the way to the ceiling with dive gear for two and camping gear for four, plus their girlfriends Joanie and Marie. They spent hours in the hot sun unloading and reloading the van. They were not importing any contraband. Gene and John figured they got the overhaul treatment because they wore long hair and looked like hippies. So much for stereotyping.

I often ran two trips back to back. I went to Halifax as a passenger with a group on the first week's trip, then returned to the States with a group on the second week's trip. In this particular case, I returned with Gene and John, Joanie and Marie. It was a tight fit but we were all friendly people.

Because I had short hair, Gene and John suggested that I drive the van when we crossed the border. I did. When I stopped at the customs station, the agent asked me how long I had been out of the country. I said two weeks. He said, "Welcome back," and motioned for me to proceed. Gene and John were understandably annoyed.

This particular trip terminated early because a hurricane swept the Nova Scotia coast and blew out the remainder of our diving plans. The five of us decided to utilize the time to camp and hike in Fundy Provincial Park for three days before returning home.

Gene and Joanie slept in one tent; John and Marie slept in another; I slept in a sleeping bag under the stars. We pooled our food and drink.

On our first evening in camp, a mistake occurred during the preparation of macaroni and cheese. Both Joanie and Marie added salt to the concoction without knowing that the other was salting it too. The combination made the side dish inedible. After dinner, the uneaten macaroni and cheese was left in the frying pan on the picnic table.

Raccoons raided our campsite late that night. I woke up when I heard them clattering around the cooler, which was crammed with grub that was supposed to last for the next couple of days. I had a speed-zip on my army surplus sleeping bag. When I spread my arms, the mummy bag unzipped in a flash. I climbed out of the bag, jumped to my feet, and chased the raccoons away before they decimated our food supply. The raccoons had tipped over the cooler but hadn't had time to get away with any comestibles.

In the morning we learned that the frying pan was empty and the macaroni and cheese was gone. The raccoons had eaten it all. Considering how much salt it contained, we joked about finding that the creeks had gone dry when the affected raccoons drank all the water to assuage their unnatural thirst; or about reading headlines that announced the discovery of a band of raccoons that had died of dehydration.

That night I took extra precautions. I placed the cooler on the table, made sure the lid was snapped tight, and collected a bunch of stones that I placed strategically around my down sleeping bag: my clever arsenal of ammunition to fend off marauding raccoons.

Sure enough, raccoons ransacked our campsite again in the middle of the night. They couldn't open the cooler lid because the closure was snapped tight. So instead, the shrewd buggers shoved the cooler completely off the table. The lid was jarred open when the cooler struck the ground. The crash woke me up. I tossed stones at them from the comfort of my sleeping bag, and chased them away. Then I got up, reclosed the lid, and, after searching for a bit, placed heavy rocks on top of it.

I crawled back into the warmth and security of my sleeping bag. I figured that the raccoons were scattered for the night. I figured wrong.

One bold raccoon returned with a vengeance. I was snuggled deep in dreamland when I felt a sharp and painful pinch on my earlobe. When I opened my eyes, I saw that a raccoon had sunk its needlelike teeth into me . . . counting coup, as it were. I let out a yell that woke up the rest of the gang, and that put the raccoon to flight.

Gene and John called out, asking what was the matter. I leaped out of the bag, gathered a handful of stones, and shouted, "The son of a bitch bit me." I chased that raccoon all across the campground and into the trees, throwing stones as I ran. But it easily outdistanced me.

On the good side, the raccoon wasn't rabid; it was just resentful.

Being There

I detailed the discoveries of the *Zoe* and *Kolkhosnik*

in *Wreck Diving Adventures*. There is no need to repeat those stories here. I've had numerous other adventures in Nova Scotia that, while not as poignant or dramatic, possessed an appeal that was perhaps more humorous than adventurous.

In the early days, dive boats in Halifax were rare to nonexistent. We made most of our dives from shore, sometimes humping our dive gear as far as half a mile to a put-in site – twice: double tanks on the first trip, then drysuits and accessories on the second trip. During RNT (residual nitrogen time, or "sit" time) between dives, we humped the used tanks back to the vehicles, then humped a full set to the put-in site for the second or repetitive dive. It then took two trips to get our gear back to the vehicles. This kind of diving was not for the weak-willed or faint of heart.

In addition to diving on wrecks that lay close to shore in the harbor, we also did some bottle dives: either in the Dingle in the Northwest Arm, or off Fort McNab.

A shore dive to the *Clare Lillie* required considerable rock-climbing skill. The way was long and steep, the rocks and roots were slippery, and the boulder field made for precarious footing. Not only that, but the surge in the water could bash you to pieces against the wreckage.

After one such dive, Gene Peterson put rocks in the feet of Eric Garay's drysuit while the latter was humping his tanks up the cliff face. John Moyer had the same idea without knowing what Gene had already done, so he slipped some more rocks into Eric's drysuit. Eric had secured straps to his gear box so he could carry it like a pack. He struggled up the crags under the load, but he never complained.

Gene was so aghast at the way Eric was sweating and gasping for air when he reached the top of the cliff, that he was afraid that Eric might have a heart attack. Gene took the drysuit that was draped across the gear box, and hauled it the rest of the way to Eric's car. Then he confessed to his misdemeanor. Upon hearing Gene's confession, John then confessed that he had compounded the misdemeanor into a felony.

Eric accepted the joke with equanimity. But that night, rocks mysteriously appeared in both Gene's and John's sleeping bags.

On another trip, Bill Schmoldt surfaced in evident excitement because he found a compass binnacle. He sent it up on a liftbag. When we hauled in the liftbag, we found hanging beneath it not a binnacle, but a urinal! He took quite a bit of ribbing for the rest of the day.

That night we went to a restaurant for dinner. At one point Tom Conley excused himself to use the restroom. When he came back to the table, he told Bill that he had just left a whole room full of binnacles. From that time on, Schmoldt's new moniker was Binnacle Bill.

Sometimes a diver got into the water without first defogging his mask. Some divers used a store-bought liquid that the rest of us claimed was nothing more than saliva from a bunch of minimum-wage workers who spent the whole day spitting into a tub, the contents of which was then drained and bottled in plastic squeeze tubes. Be that as it may, it was common practice that a diver with an unrinsed mask would hand it up from the water to someone in the boat for a quick cleansing with defogging solution; or, as was more often the case, for a shot of spittle.

Bob Belak had a trick when he was asked to do this. He quickly chewed up an Oreo cookie and spat the soggy mess into the diver's mask.

Tom Conley once rolled off the boat without rinsing his mask. It fogged immediately. He doffed the mask and held it up for rinsing. When Bob reached for the mask, Tom yanked it away, and yelled, "Let Gary spit in it."

I did. After the dive, Tom raved about how fog-free and crystal clear his mask had been under water. For the rest of the trip, my saliva was the official defogging solution – for everyone.

On a shore dive to the hospital ship *Letitia*, Andy Weaver lost buoyance control in his drysuit. He suddenly popped to the surface – upside down! The feet and legs of his drysuit pointed skyward like overinflated balloons.

From shore I could see that his kicks were ineffectual, and that he might very well be drowning. Down-exhaust regulators do not breathe well when they are inverted, because water pours into the exhaust tee; in fact, they do not breathe at all when they are inverted – you have to tilt your head sideways or slightly upward to purge the water before every breath. That is why I use side-exhaust regulators.

Andy's situation was serious. I was still wearing my drysuit. I quickly donned my fins, mask, and snorkel, then charged into the breaking surf. Andy was bobbing only fifty feet from the rocky coastline. I reached down and grabbed his outthrust hands. He squirmed as I pulled. After a fierce struggle and by working together, we were able to get his upper body parallel to the surface. I depressed his drysuit's exhaust button and purged his drysuit of excess air.

Andy's fins were still on the feet of his drysuit, but his feet were no longer *in* the feet of his drysuit. His fins flopped uselessly. He looked like a person with two broken ankles. I had to tow him to shore and pull him partway onto the rocks. He doffed his tanks and crawled out of the water on his hands and knees.

On another occasion, as I was climbing up the stern ladder of a boat, Bob Belak spoke gruffly and disparagingly about Mike Caudle. He pointed to where Mike's drysuit legs protruded vertically from the water like a pair of fat tubular pillars. There were no fins on the feet.

Bob said, "Would you go pull it in?"

I was no stranger to body recovery, but I was aghast that Bob was so callous about the death of a fellow diver. It was with great trepidation that I swam out to tow my deceased friend to the boat.

The joke was on me. Mike did not have a liftbag for retrieving artifacts. He had taken an old drysuit and cut it in two at the waist. He then affixed straps to the bottom portion so he could fill the legs and pelvic cavity with air, in order to lift heavy objects to the surface.

Most divers think of shore dives as being shallow. Such is not the case in Nova Scotia, where the bedrock slopes precipitously both above and below the surface. On a wreck like the *Letitia*, which slammed against the rocks perpendicular to shore, the forward wreckage lies in only a few feet of water, while the stern wreckage lies at a depth of 150 feet. Thus a shore dive can easily become a decompression dive.

On wrecks like this, my routine was to explore the deep end first, work my way shallower, and decompress while examining the wreckage at decompression depths. During decompression, I also stabbed flounder which I later cooked over the campfire.

In addition to catching flounder, I also caught wolffish, although not by stabbing because their bodies were roundish and rotund rather than flat. I caught them by hand; or rather, by hands (plural).

Wolffish average two to three feet in length, although they do grow larger. They like to hide under rocks and, since the advent of mankind's maritime excursions, in wreckage. Much like their lookalike ocean pouts, they ignored passing divers. Unlike ocean pouts, they became wildly aggressive when molested. They went from sedentary mode to attack mode at the slightest touch.

Because wolffish feed largely on shellfish such as clams and mussels, their strong jaws are fitted with massive teeth. These teeth are blunt rather than sharp because they are used primarily to crush their prey and to crack their shells. Wolffish also sport pharyngeal teeth for mastication before swallowing.

In the "flight or fight" school of thought, whereas a flounder will dart away after an unsuccessful attempt at capture, a wolffish will attack. I was fully aware of this behavior, but I had developed my own technique for dealing with it and for capturing the fish. I grabbed the fish by the tail and one pectoral fin simultaneously, so it couldn't bend its body to bite me; then I steered it into a mesh bag. Wolffish were not as tasty as flounder, but they were a welcome change from canned food.

After explaining my capture technique to Jon Hulburt, he professed an interest in capturing the technique on film. So we dived together for a photo shoot in an area that wolffish were known to inhabit. We found a piscine model without difficulty. Although the wolffish in question did not volunteer its services willingly, I drafted it for the occasion.

When Jon indicated that he had his camera and strobe ready, I seized the wolffish by the fins. Naturally it squirmed and wiggled. Unfortunately, it squirmed and wiggled harder than I had anticipated. A moment later I lost my grip on the pectoral fin. Now I was holding an angry wolffish by the tail. The wolffish instantly bent its body double, lunged at me, and sank its formidable dentition into my forehead. My quarter-inch hood offered scant protection. I felt as if I had been pole-axed.

A wolffish does not bite and cling like a Gila monster; it bites and lets go. Then it bites again. And again. And again . . .

I couldn't simply release the wolffish, because then it would be free to wreak additional vengeance. I didn't dare let go of the tail, because that was the only hold I had on it. I couldn't get another hold on the pectoral fin because of the fish's rapid and unpredictable antics. The wolffish lunged again and slammed its teeth into my faceplate, partially dislodging my mask in the process. Now a thin stream of water spurted across my face and into my right eye.

There was only one way to protect myself from further onslaught. When the wolffish lunged at my face, I yanked back hard on its tail. This device temporarily straightened out its body. As soon as it came at me again, I whipped its tail the other way. In this strange fashion I kept the irate creature at bay. I felt like a mad conductor who was swinging his baton in cadence with the orchestra during the finale of the William Tell Overture. I was too preoccupied to think about Rossini or the Lone Ranger.

Finally, when I thought the wolffish might be dizzy enough to give me a moment's respite, I flung it aside and swam in the opposite direction. Jon was on his own.

I escaped with deep indentations in my scalp but no bloody puncture wounds. Jon got away unscathed. After that debacle, I lost my appetite for wolffish.

After a shore dive on the *Isleworth*, most of my group went out for lunch. Two people stayed behind to guard the gear that was spread across the rocks at the put-in site: myself and a woman who shall remain nameless in order to protect the reputation of at least one of the guilty parties.

The air temperature was mild, and the sunshine created a comforting warmth that was certain to dry the undergarments that were spread out on the rocks in a crazy patchwork quilt of riotous color. The spot was isolated from the road by a curvy quarter-mile trail that meandered over rocks and down into gullies. A couple of hundred yards away, a solitary house was perched atop a tall cliff that overlooked the gently rolling swells that washed the coast.

I don't remember whose idea it was, but as we basked in the warm sun after eating lunch, I believe I was the one who suggested that the woman remove her clothing so I could take some pictures of her in the nude with the ocean in the background. She had a lean athletic body of which she was inordinately proud. I knew that she had posed for at least one girlie magazine, because I had seen her picture in print: a full-page full-frontal nude.

She was game for it. She removed her bathing suit and struck a number of poses as I shot half a roll of film or more. Probably more.

After the impromptu photo session, we both donned our undergarments, drysuits, and tanks, then went for our second dive of the day before the rest of the gang returned from lunch. We were under water during the subsequent fireworks with a local wild woman and the Royal Canadian Mounted Police.

When we emerged from the water, Eric Garay gave us the details of what transpired when the gang arrived at the trailhead after lunch. The local woman claimed to have seen "all kinds of nudity" that was being photographed. She called the RCMP's. An officer was duly dispatched to the scene of the alleged crime; he arrived in a car, not on horseback. The woman started shouting about how she was offended by the excessive display of skin.

Eric took charge of the defense. He explained to the officer that we were divers from the States, that we changed from street clothes to long-johns to wear under our drysuits, that perhaps the local woman saw us (the female diver and me) changing clothes before a dive, and so on, and so on . . .

Of course, Eric had no idea what was going on or what the local woman actually saw. He only surmised that she had misinterpreted events. He managed to calm down the woman and smooth-talk the policeman into accepting his probable scenario. He promised that henceforth we would be discrete when changing clothes in the open. The woman was somewhat mollified. The policeman was confident that the situation was resolved. Everyone went on his and her happy (or unhappy) way.

Eric and the others were understandably shocked when the woman and I admitted that I had indeed taken pictures of her au naturel.

Bellzapoppin'

On one particular trip that I organized, in 1987, my driving companion was Lynn DelCorio. Lynn used to live in New Jersey, but he moved to Key Largo where the air and water were warmer and more suitable to his tastes. He was self-employed as a tropical fish collector. Every day he scoured the reefs to capture rare specimens for sale to pet stores and aquariums.

In August of that year, he drove to his parent's house in New Jersey. I picked him up in my van, along with his dive gear and camping equipment. The twenty hour drive to the campground outside of Halifax was exhausting but thankfully uneventful. There we rendezvoused with the rest of the group.

We habitually got our tanks filled at the Timberlea Dive Shop. Steve Giza, the owner of the shop, had a friend who owned a couple of boats in Canso. His friend – whose name I failed to record and cannot remember –

was a commercial diver, fisherman, lobsterman, and a lot of other things that were either licensed or unlicensed. In order to earn a living, he had to be a jack of all water trades.

What he was *not* was a charter boat operator. His boats were not licensed for passenger service; nor was he personally licensed to carry passengers for money. No big deal. In all my years as a Nova Scotia trip leader, I never found a boat that was licensed for passenger service, or was operated by a licensed skipper. This didn't mean that the boats weren't safe or that the skippers weren't competent, only that licenses were absent. I chartered them anyway.

Things are different nowadays, but that was the way it was at the time.

Steve made arrangements for us to dive with his friend in Canso. For ease in reading, I will arbitrarily call his friend Bob (because he went up and down).

Canso is a sleepy village on a headland that juts into the Atlantic Ocean about 160 miles east-northeast of Halifax. You could drive there in two and a half hours if Halifax and Canso were connected by an interstate (or interprovince) highway. But they are not. The circuitous route is more the 200 miles in length, and takes nearly five hours to travel. Oh to fly direct like a seagull.

After a week of diving off Halifax, we broke camp at Juniper Park and packed our dive gear and camping equipment for the excursion along the coast. Darkness fell shortly after we pitched our tents in a Canso campground.

This was a fortuitous time to be in northern latitudes, for the intensity of sunspot activity reached an uncommon peak. Consequently, the Earth was showered with beta particles, or free electrons, that were emitted by grand old Sol. These electrons struck the magnetosphere that surrounds the planet, then skittered along the lines of force to the magnetic poles. The great accumulation of negatively-charged particles interacted to create a spectacular auroral display that was visible as high as thirty degrees above the horizon. A green shimmering curtain covered the entire northern quadrant. It was a fantastic light show that only nature could devise.

The next morning we learned the bad news. Bob had two boats: the *Dantina* (a steel-hulled power boat that was outfitted with a wheelhouse and an A-frame with medium lift capacity), and a work barge. The barge had recently sunk in a navigable waterway.

Bob's problems were manifold. The loss of the uninsured barge created a large financial deficit, in addition to which he no longer had a platform from which to conduct his commercial diving operations. The Canadian Coast Guard determined that the barge was a menace to navigation and had to be removed – quickly. If Bob didn't have the barge raised in short order, the Coast Guard would hire a contractor to raise it for him – and charge Bob for the cost of the barge's removal.

Bob had a better idea. He and the divers who worked for him were capable of preparing the barge for lift. Bob could then borrow or rent a crane and pumps that were necessary for the task. But in its present condition, the weight of the barge exceeded the lifting capacity of the only floating crane that was in the area. In order for Bob to do the job himself, he had to reduce the barge's weight by removing several tons of ballast rock.

So he made us a deal. This charter fee was the strangest method of payment I have ever made. He would take us diving for two days without charge, if we would dedicate one day to removing ballast rock from his barge. He and his divers had already started the job by erecting a ramp that stretched from a cutout in the hull to the seabed thirty feet away. They had removed a few rocks, but didn't have the manpower to complete the removal before the Coast Guard got antsy about their progress, and contracted the job to a commercial salvor.

We talked it over among ourselves. We agreed.

So that I don't have to relate this part of the Canso adventure as an anticlimax, I will relate the end of the story now. After diving for two days, Bob took us to where his barge lay on the bottom. The depth of water was 44 feet. We took turns working inside and outside the barge. The inside divers picked up a roundish boulder from the bilge, carried it to the cutout in the hull, and deposited it on the ramp. The slope of the ramp was not steep enough for the boulder to roll downhill on its own; it had to be pushed. So the outside divers shoved the boulders to the bottom of the ramp, then picked them up and tossed them onto the ever-growing heap. When the ballast pile grew too high, Bob changed the position of the ramp so that it terminated at an adjacent location on the seabed. In this manner we built a lozenge-shaped mound of boulders.

If this process sounds easy, take my word that it wasn't. The ballast boulders were larger than cantaloupes, perhaps the size of honeydew melons. Their weight offset my neutral buoyancy so much that I couldn't swim with a rock in my hands. In fact, when I picked up a rock from a horizontal position, it was difficult for me to get vertical. I had to push up to arm's length with the rock still in place, shuffle my knees forward, then lean back and heft the rock up to my chest.

Now I was vertical but kneeling and top heavy. I had to move forward fast by pushing with my fin tips on the boulder field. I either bounced along on my knees, or I attained a semblance of off-balance by kicking with my fins faster than the weight of the boulder tilted me onto my face. If I fell over before I reached the cutout in the hull – a distance of twenty to thirty feet – then I had to reattain verticality and proceed forward faster than my uncontrolled fall.

When I worked outside, I had to grab each boulder as it was placed at the top of the ramp, and manhandle it all the way to the bottom, whereupon I had to lift it and toss it high onto the ever-growing heap. This was a laborious process that got harder as the pile of boulders grew taller – until we shifted the base of the ramp a few feet to the side.

We worked in this manner for an hour, took a topside break, then worked for another hour and a half. That night, we all complained about pain and muscle strain in our forearms and triceps.

Anyway, back to the beginning. It turned out that Bob didn't actually know of any wreck sites. He knew only where some ships were thought to have struck the rocky coast. His presumption was based solely on local lore, not on any hard-fast evidence or documentation. On the *Dantina*, he took us to a remote outcrop that couldn't be reached from land without boulder hopping hundreds or thousands of yards from the nearest dirt road.

We spread out along the rocky bottom to explore the shallows for wreckage. No one found anything that even remotely resembled a shipwreck: no wooden beams, no steel hull plates, no debris, nothing. I saw little more than bare rock, and not even much in the way of marine life. The one saving grace was that the visibility was good.

Bob returned with a couple of lobsters. He was surprised that no one else had caught any crustaceans. He asked if we had spotted any bugs.

I told him that I had seen several, but thought that Canadian law made it illegal for scuba divers to catch them. Bob said that was true as far as it went, but because he had a commercial lobster license, he could allow it, except that we couldn't take them back to the dock where an observant coastguardsman might not look askance. Instead, we could slip into a secluded cove that was inaccessible from land, where he could boil them in a pot of seawater over a two-burner propane stove that he always kept onboard for such occasions.

The next day I was part of a threesome, my two buddies being Lynn DelCorio and Miles Wagner. Lynn and I were supposed to keep an eye on Miles because he had only recently been certified. This was his first diving season. As a neophyte he was understandably enthusiastic about tagging along with two long-timers. He was also exuberant about everything that he saw and did under water. Being new at the game, he was also a little chary and, in the event, underbold, especially when it came to encounters that were too exotic for one with his limited experience under water.

As we worked along a rock shelf, Lynn managed to distance himself from Miles and me. By exploring separately, we hoped to have a greater opportunity of discovering wreck remains.

Now that Bob had given us the go ahead to catch lobsters, in addition to watching for wreckage, I peered under rocks and inside cavities for tasty specimens of *Homarus americanus*. I didn't look for very long before I spotted a veritable monster in the alcove of an overhang. Two mammoth claws guarded the entrance with all the belligerent stubbornness of King Leonidas and his three hundred Spartans when they protected the mountain pass from King Xerxes and his overwhelming Persian army at the battle of Thermopylae.

Each serrated claw was larger than my head. The carapace and tail were the size of a loaf of bread.

In the past, I had caught two lobsters that weighed in at eighteen pounds, and one that tipped the scales at twenty-one pounds. This one clearly outweighed my largest previous catch. I estimated that it grossed in excess of twenty-two pounds.

Despite the enormous size of the beast and the wide open claws, it looked like an easy catch because there was plenty of space on either side of the body to reach in and grab the lobster behind the business end of its armored defense system. I thought this would be a great experience for a novice diver to enjoy, so I backed away from the opening, flashed the beam of my light into the interior, and signaled for Miles to go for it.

Miles's eyes grew to the size of silver dollars. He shook his head and retreated as if a swarm of angry hornets was after him. He had never caught *any* lobster before, much less a record breaker that could have gone ten rounds with a kraken – and won the duel. No amount of coercion would convince him to grasp the rare opportunity to grapple with the catch of a lifetime.

I tilted my head and raised an eyebrow at Miles. He kept shaking his head. So it was up to me to take the bull by the horns; or in this case, the lobster by the tail.

I got in position to make the grab. Quick as an arrow I thrust my right hand past the lobster's massive claw. I clutched it by the knuckle that was closest to the carapace and yanked the lobster out of the hole as fast as I could. It came out sideways, scooting its tail like a fast-acting party blower. I seized the tail, spun the lobster around, then quickly gripped it by the base of each claw so that the top of the carapace faced me.

I held the creature at arm's length. I expected Miles to open his bug bag – something that a Jersey diver would do automatically. He backed away as I moved toward him. He didn't want to be anywhere near that lobster, and especially he didn't want to be near the business end of the lobster.

I argued by making harsh facial expressions.

Eventually he overcame enough of his trepidation to show me that his bug bag was too small for such an oversized lobster. I used body language to indicate the wire-frame bug bag that was clipped to my weight belt. Miles got the message. He relieved me of the mesh bag, opened it wide, and approached me with extreme caution and arms extended to their fullest.

As soon as I lowered the tail through the opening, I discovered that the lobster was holding its claws too far apart for me to fit them past the metal hoop. A big tussle ensued as I forced the claws closer together. I didn't dare lose my grip. It was touch and go as to who was going to be the stronger. After a prolonged struggle, I managed to get the two giant claws inside the bag – but then I couldn't close the hoop. I had to shake the bag up and down in order to knock the beast to the bottom of the bag. Then I closed the hoop and locked the hasp.

I made Miles take the bag. He was diving with a single tank, whereas Lynn and I had doubles. After Lynn rejoined us, Miles went to the surface with the lobster, while Lynn and I continued our dive.

Once again to avoid anticlimax, after the dive Bob did as he had promised. He drove the boat to a secluded cove, cranked up the stove, and set the water to boil. Although he had a large pot on board, the pot was not big enough to fit a lobster of this size. We had to cook it piecemeal: a claw at a time, and another time for the tail. We used our sledge hammers to crack the shell. No one had utensils, so we munched and lunched on lobster by taking meat by the handful. It was gross and scrumptious at the same time.

After everyone at his fill, we had about eight pounds of cooked meat leftover. We put that in a plastic bag, and packed it with ice in the cooler that held the lunch that we never touched. It made an appetizing dinner.

Back under water, Lynn and I were disenchanted because we saw no sign of wreckage. We moseyed along half-heartedly with our expectations ebbing. We didn't hold any expectations of finding anything worthwhile. We found ourselves exploring an underwater rock wall. The plateau lay at a depth of 30 to 40 feet. Over the ledge, a sheer cliff face dropped down to a sandy bottom at a depth of 78 feet. Visibility was fifty feet or better, thus enabling us to swim along the edge of the plateau and see all the way to the seabed.

We poked our light beams into every crack and cranny on the ledge, and glanced over the precipice for any sign of wreckage or debris on the seabed.

Then we spotted it!

Or them.

What I saw – or rather, the way I interpreted what I saw – threw me into a paralyzing state of confusion and apprehension.

Caught on the lip at the top of the cliff was a sunken German mine leftover from World War Two. Lying on the seabed directly beneath it was a ship's bell from an ancient Viking sailing vessel.

The mine was a dented globe that measured three to four feet in diameter. Stubby prongs protruded from the rusted iron surface.

The bell lay on its side with the hanger in profile. The bell was so big that it looked like it belonged in the belfry of a cathedral rather than on the forecastle of a sailing vessel. The hanger was shaped like an giant oxbow. The bell and its hanger were the only objects in view on the

Catch of the day. I have a firm grip on the monster lobster. Miles Wagner is standing behind and above me.

sand. There was no other wreckage of any kind.

I was so stunned by the improbable convergence of two such exceptional and disparate artifacts that I was momentarily unable to employ rational thought. My eyes and my mind danced incomprehensibly from one to the other to the one. The mine bothered me to distraction. Could the explosive charge still be active? Would the mine detonate if I mishandled the prongs? And how coincidental was it that this mine came to rest on a ledge above the only visible remains of an ancient sailing vessel? The incongruity was disturbing to say the least.

While I was trapped in a reversing cycle of imponderable contemplations, Lynn dropped straight down to the seabed to examine the bronze bell. Eagerly he waved for me to come down. Reluctantly I backed away from the German mine, feeling as much trepidation as Miles felt earlier when I confronted him with the business end of a colossal lobster. As I settled on the soft sand next to Lynn, it required uncommon mental strength to ignore the mine that hovered overhead like the sword of Damocles, and to concentrate on what Lynn was trying to communicate to me by means of seemingly inane gestures and hand signals.

He pointed up and he pointed down; he pointed up and he pointed down. Slowly I began to make the connection. I ascended 40 feet to the "mine." Upon close examination the truth slowly dawned on me. The "mine" was actually the airtight base of a navigational buoy. The "prongs" were the stubs of the metal supports for the heavy-duty frame from which a warning bell had been suspended. The "ship's bell" was a navigational bell that clanged a warning to mariners who were approaching a dangerous rock or shoal, or who were veering out of a channel.

My two overlapping visions coalesced into one coherent image of a floating marker.

I started to breathe easier. Now I could focus on the task at hand.

I pulled out a 200-pound liftbag. Lynn and I worked together on securing the liftbag to the bell. Then we each used the purge button of our regulators to fill the liftbag to capacity. The bell didn't budge.

By now we had been under water for fifty-two minutes. I was wearing a decompression computer that took into account my multi-level profile; according to its calculations, I did not yet have a decompression obligation. Lynn was relying on Navy Tables, which was based on a square profile, so he had a decompression penalty to serve.

We were each carrying a decompression reel: a section of broom handle or wooden dowel, around which was wrapped a couple of hundred feet of quarter-inch sisal line. Instead of heading back for the anchor line, we each deployed a reel, tied our lines to the bell's hanger, and unreeled line as we ascended: Lynn so he could have vertical stabilization for his decompression stops, I in order to have a direct line to the bell. We exchanged "okay" signs as I made my departure.

When I surfaced, I saw that the boat was anchored

a couple of hundred feet away, bobbing and rolling on the surface chop. Instead of cutting my line as I usually did, I swam toward the boat and unreeled more line as I proceeded. I was out of line by the time I reached the side of the boat. I shouted for Bob to take the reel and tie the line to a cleat. The line was stretched so taut that he was barely able to do as I instructed. Now we didn't have to relocate the bell on the bottom; the sisal line ran directly from the boat to the bell.

I couldn't keep the excitement out of my voice as I explained what we had found, and that the bell was so heavy that a 200-pound liftbag wouldn't lift it. I had another 200-pounder in my gear box, but I wasn't sure that I had enough air remaining in my tanks to make another dive and fill the second bag. I asked Miles to go with me. He was only too glad to help.

I explained exactly what we would do: use the liftbag's snap hook to clip it to the other liftbag's snap hook, put our regulators under the mouth of the liftbag, then press the purge button and exhaust air into the second liftbag until it lifted the bell off the bottom.

Although Lynn was still decompressing when we entered the water, I calculated that he must be pretty close to completion by now. In the event, either we accomplished our task faster than I anticipated, or Lynn chose to hang longer than I expected. As a result, the liftbags surfaced before Lynn surfaced.

The situation was what I would call an "oops." But it was a small oops.

Lynn's decompression line was tied to the bell so he could maintain constant depth. The raising of the bell made his line go slack. The loss of vertical orientation meant that he had to exercise precise buoyancy control in order to stay at his decompression depth. I figured that he could do a free-floating deco for a few minutes, and I was right.

Miles and I returned to the boat. Lynn surfaced a minute or so later and signaled that he was okay.

Meanwhile, as soon as the liftbags burst to the surface, Bob started pulling in the sisal line that was secured to the bell. In short order he had the bell in position astern of the boat. By that time Lynn was climbing up the ladder, wearing a grin that threatened to split his face apart.

We were fortunate to be on a commercial dive platform. Had the boat not been outfitted with an A-frame and block and tackle, we never would have gotten the bell on board. It was way too heavy to lift by muscle power. Bob wasted no time in rigging tackle to the A-frame. He lowered a hook to me in the water. I secured the hook to the bell. Then Bob used mechanical advantage to lift the massive bell clear of the surface.

That was the easy part. The A-frame was angled aft so that the bell hovered about three feet astern of the transom. In order to position the bell on top of the transom, we had to swing it like a pendulum by means of ropes. Timing was the essence of success. Lynn and I swung the bell, Bob gradually let out rope until the base of the bell swung over the transom and just barely missed hitting it. Once we had a good swing going, Bob suddenly released the tackle precisely at the moment when the bell reached the end of its arc above the transom.

Much like a baseball batter sliding into home base, the bell plunked down hard, but safe. Bob pulled in the slack until there was just enough tension on the rope to keep it taut. Gradually, Bob released tension as we inched the bell inboard. When the bell fell off the inside of the transom, Bob tightened the tackle; then he slowly let the rope slide through the pulley and lowered the bell until it rested on the deck.

Lynn and I took a moment to rejoice and to catch our breath.

A superficial examination of the bell revealed that five capital letters were embossed on the outer rim: USLHS. This was the abbreviation for United States Light House Service. This begged the question: what was an American bell buoy doing off the coast of Nova Scotia. I didn't have an answer then, and I still don't have one today. All I can say is that it was a long way for a navigational buoy to drift before coming to grief upon a friendly but foreign shore.

Back at the dock, we used the A-frame and block and tackle to offload the bell. We procured a couple of balks of lumber whose cross section measured four inches by four inches. Bob lifted the bell and then lowered it onto this pair of six-foot lengths of wood. Four pall bearers lifted the contraption by the corners, and manhandled the bell – along with its makeshift pallet – into my van.

In New Jersey, we transferred the bell to Lynn's pickup truck. He drove it to his home in Key Largo. He had a glass tabletop cut to size, and the bell became the base of a unique coffee table. It has graced his living room ever since.

Afterward, I did some research on bell buoy bells. The dimensions of the bell that we recovered matched the height and diameter of the standard buoy bell.

The weight was given as 375 pounds!

The bell table is too heavy to move. Lynn has to vacuum around it.

Lynn DelCorio and the whopper of a bell.

Robinson Crusoes of St. Paul Island

Toward the end of my tenure of organizing dive trips to Nova Scotia, I expanded my horizons first by going to the southwest coast of the province, then by going northeast to Canso. After Gene Peterson took the torch, he decided to travel even farther afield: to the northernmost point of the province, and beyond.

August of 1998 found ten of us carpooling (or, more accurately, truckpooling) for the long haul from New Jersey to Cape Breton. In addition to Gene and me, the group consisted of Mike Benson, Jim Brightly, Lynn DelCorio, Franz Dietl, John Galvin, Greg Modelle, Dennis O'brian, and Andy Pierro.

Cape Breton was not our ultimate destination. It was only the staging area for a diving expedition to St. Paul Island: a picturesque but uninhabited isle in the Gulf of St. Lawrence some 15 miles northeast of the mainland. The island measures some four miles in length and slightly more than one mile in width at its widest point. You could walk around the perimeter in a day if there was a beach to tramp or a trail to follow, but there are neither.

The island is an irregular block of granite whose jagged coastline is dangerous to approach in all but the smoothest sea. The area is renowned for stormy weather and unpredictable fog. Hundreds of vessels and thousands of lives have met their end on the coastal rocks of St. Paul Island. Mariners who were lucky enough to survive shipwreck generally starved to death afterward. Although seals might occasionally hunt in the near-shore shallows, no land mammals of any kind inhabit the island – not even mice.

Seabirds frequent the naked outcrops. Insects hide in the weeds. Mosquitoes are legion. The vegetation is inedible by humans. Fresh water is available from two inland lakes – except in winter when these lakes freeze over. The best that shipwreck survivors could hope for was to be rescued before they suffered a long and lingering death.

There is one word that best describes Cape Breton: remote. I saw more moose in Cape Breton than people. There are no dive shops. Charter boats don't exist. There is no *St. Paul Aggressor*. There are no motels, hotels, or bed-and-breakfast lodging. There is not even a campground. Visitors have to make like a turtle and bring their own carapaces and plastrons.

Even if there are no moose crossing signs, moose always have the right of way.

Diving visitors have to bring everything they expect to need, and even things that they don't expect to need. They also have to bring their own compressor. Because there are no docks on the island, they have to bring their own landing craft. In addition to dive gear and backups they have to bring tents, cots, sleeping bags, food, water, stoves, cookware, utensils, and so on, and so on, and so on . . .

Because of my extensive outdoor experience in backpacking and wilderness canoeing, Gene asked me to take responsibility for purchasing freeze-dried meals for ten people for a week. No problem.

We took a roundabout route to the island. First stop was Halifax, where we rented two compressors and a pair of inflatable boats from Neil Connors, the owner of Connors Diving Service (for commercial divers) and Divers World (for recreational divers). Neil also provided a trailer to transport the inflatables. Jim Brightly carried the compressors in the back of his flatbed truck. Jim also towed the trailer. Gene supervised a shopping spree for groceries that we would need during our stay on the island.

In order to blend in with the locals, we took the opportunity to brush up on our Canadian English while doing our chores in Halifax. It was important to pronounce "out" and "house" as "oat" and "hoce," (or "hose," in which the "s" has an "s" sound instead of a "z" sound), otherwise the indigenous folks would know that we were out-of-towners. "Filet" rhymed with "millet."

Most important of all, every sentence had to end with "eh?" This "eh?" is equivalent to "right?" in the States. Thus one might declare, "I am a scuba diver, eh?" Or, "We are going to dive on St. Paul Island, eh?" As the saying goes, "When in Canada, do as the Canadians." Or was that Rome and the Romans?

In any case, after our chores were done we proceeded to Cape Breton, eh? For a dive boat Gene had made arrangements to charter the *Misty Dawn*: an antique wooden-hulled commercial fishing vessel that was old enough to have been a rumrunner during the era of Prohibition. Old as she was, though, she was clean, well kept, well maintained, and lacked all trace of fishy odor.

The skipper was Kelly Fitzgerald. The mate was his brother John Fitzgerald. John had been the St. Paul Island lighthouse keeper from 1970 to 1972. Now he was unable to walk without his cane.

The *Misty Dawn's* dock was equipped with a hoist for lifting baskets of fish. We used the hoist to load tanks and the compressors onto the boat. Everything else was manhandled from dock to deck with very little slippage.

Fresh food was stowed in the fish hold where it was packed in shaved ice that was generally used to preserve fish during multi-day trips. After all our personal gear was loaded, we stacked the inflatables on top.

The crossing took three hours. Upon arrival at St. Paul Island, the first order of business was to establish base camp. The *Misty Dawn* anchored in a protected area that was called Atlantic Cove. The inflatables were launched and tied up alongside her. The outboard motors were clamped to transom boards. The process of transporting the camping gear commenced.

Several guys disembarked on the only strand of beach that we could find among cliffs that dropped thirty feet straight down to the crashing waves. This pebbly strand measured no more than twenty feet wide, and extended only ten feet from the base of a sloped cliff face. The stevedores scrambled up the rock, secured ropes to some bushes, then used the ropes to climb up the rock with camping gear in hand or worn over the shoulders in knapsacks.

Some guys remained on the *Misty Dawn* to hand food, water, and camping gear over the gunwale and down to the boat handlers. The handlers then shuttled the inflatables back and forth until everything was landed. This physically exhausting operation made the beachhead assault on Iwo Jima look like a cake walk, except that no one was shooting at us. Dive gear remained on the *Misty Dawn*.

The boat anchored in the cove overnight. Captain Kelly and brother John stayed onboard. The rest of us went about setting up camp.

A grassy plane that was bigger than a football field offered ample space on which to pitch the tents. There was plenty of room for everyone to spread out. A kitchen area was established close to shore. Food and water were stored next to the propane stove that served for outdoor cooking. As far as campsites go, this was one of the better ones in my experience. I thrived on the isolation.

Two abandoned buildings in various stages of collapse were perched on the hill above our campsite. At one time a radio station was maintained there, and life-saving personnel lived on the island for weeks at a time. The other end of the island sported a lighthouse. The keepers had long since been replaced by automation.

Note the *Misty Dawn* across the cove.

The next day – August 9 – we started diving. First we used the inflatables to reach the *Misty Dawn*. Then the *Misty Dawn* took the boats in tow as we proceeded around the island to search for suitable dive sites. At the conclusion of each day's diving, we returned to Atlantic Cove and split the various camp chores among the participants. Some stayed on the boat to run the compressor and refill tanks. Others went ashore to prepare dinner. Jobs were rotated so that no one had to work harder than anyone else. After the tanks were filled, the fillers went ashore, tied up the inflatables, and relaxed by an open fire that was fueled with driftwood that the cooks had collected from the rocky shore.

We followed this routine for three days running.

The water temperature was 48° below the thermocline, and between 54° and 64° above. Visibility averaged thirty feet. We dived on five sites, two of which were on different sections of a wreck that was known as the *Norwegian*. The wreck was little more than a debris field of twisted and broken metal; the hull had been widely dispersed by storm surge and current.

We did not find wreckage at the other three sites, but the live bottom was colorful and picturesque. Lobsters were plentiful. I caught nine by myself, and many more were caught by other divers. We steamed them as a supplement to our freeze-dried dinners.

August 11 ended like any other day. We gathered around the fire, ate a leisurely dinner, told ribald jokes, reminisced about the day's adventures, and made plans for the morrow. Dark clouds rolled in after nightfall. Wind speeds gradually increased.

Aboard the *Misty Dawn*, Captain Kelly and brother John prepared for the storm by battening down the hatches. In camp, we pounded extra stakes into the ground, and placed huge boulders on the tent tie-downs. Ropes were used to secure tarps over the foodstuffs and loose kitchen items.

I was sleeping in Gene's family-sized tent with Gene and Lynn. I read a book by flashlight until my eyelids grew too heavy to keep open. I drifted off to sleep.

I am a sound sleeper. Through rain, through hail, through sleet or snow, I slumber as peacefully as if I were tucked in my warm cozy bed at home. I was not consciously aware of the arrival of the tempest. I did not hear Gene tiptoe out of the tent. What shattered my pleasant dream state was Gene yelling at the top of his lungs, calling all hands on deck because the inflatables

Tent city before the storm.

were being smashed against the rocks.

Everyone turned out in extremely short order in answer to this clarion call. By now the wind was whipping across the campground with ferocious abandon. Rain fell in sheets. Through the pitch black night I heard waves crashing violently against the shore. Gene illuminated the scene with his powerful dive light. When I reached the edge of the drop-off and looked down at the frothing sea, I was reminded of Edgar Allan Poe's description of "A Descent into the Maelstrom."

The small spit of gravel was gone: buried under a couple of feet of swirling seawater. The inflatables looked like rollercoaster cars as they pitched up and down, crashing from side to side into each other, and pounding their bows and sides against the rough-hewn cliff face.

Andy and John were the first to scamper down the rocks; they nearly fell into the surf and were almost carried away to sea. Gene climbed down and stood knee-deep in water. All three of them grappled with the inflatables at the bottom of the cliff. Gene was shouting orders, one of which was to haul in the ropes. Along with several others at the top of the cliff, I grabbed a rope and started hauling an inflatable up the rocks. Any moment I expected a sharp granite edge to puncture the pontoons. The inflatable was heavy, especially as it was half filled with water.

Someone – I don't remember who – climbed partway down the cliff to grab the inflatable's life rope. Once we got the boat partially upright, most of the water drained out over the transom. This action lightened the load considerably. Somehow we dragged the boat high enough that it was clear of the breaking waves. To secure the inflatable, we buried an anchor in the middle of the meadow, then tied off the painter so it wouldn't fall back into the raging sea.

Now we pitched in to save the other boat. Those of us at the top of the cliff kept tension on the rope while those down below tried to keep the boat from banging against the adjacent cliff face. Compounding the problem was the weight of the outboard motor. Now I saw that John was standing chest deep in the violent surf at the stern of the boat. With superhuman strength and an incredible feat of balance, he lifted the motor off the transom board and carried it through the waves to the submerged beach. Then he climbed up the cliff with the motor in hand. He wore only shorts and sandals.

Without the weight of the motor, we still had to struggle to pull the boat up the rocks. We hauled away until the stern was clear of the surf, then tied off the rope so the boat wouldn't slip back down and get battered to ribbons against the rocks. We left the boats in that position: high if not necessarily dry.

All of us were cold and exhausted from our exertions, but John suffered the most because of his complete immersion. He was shivering uncontrollably as he dried himself off; then he crawled into his sleeping bag. Quite a while passed before he regained his normal body temperature.

Everyone was soaked. We all retreated to our respective tents, toweled down, donned dry clothing, and snuggled in our sleeping bags. After this nighttime escapade we thought the worst was over.

We thought wrong.

In the gray gloom of an overcast dawn, we discovered that the *Misty Dawn* was missing. We had no way of knowing what catastrophe had overtaken her. Speculation ran riot but did nothing to appease our tortured minds. In consideration of gale-force wind, worst case scenarios seemed the most likely.

We would have been stranded even if the *Misty Dawn* appeared on the horizon. Huge swells and high rollers surrounded the island. The waves that crashed against the cliffs in the cove mounted twelve to fifteen feet in height, and sent wind-blown spray some twenty feet into the air.

Some wag – it might have been me – yelled, "Surf's up!"

The scene reminded me of the monstrous combers that attracted surfers from around the globe to Hawaii's sandy beaches. No surfer could have survived these breakers because they broke against solid granite. Some waves struck the cliff so fiercely during the day that green water – not spray – was hurled onto the grassy plateau. We had to re-establish the kitchen farther back from shore.

The wind was unkind to the tents. Gene's tent was fitted with expedition-strength fiberglass poles. Yet extreme gusts nearly flattened the tent; one pole smacked me in the head as it flexed.

Greg's tent was completely discombobulated; it

looked as if it had been run over by a steamroller. By morning, Greg was soaked to the skin.

A number of tent stakes had pulled out during the nights. Rainflies flapped in the torrential downpour. The affected tents had to be repitched. Rocks that had been used to weigh down the tie-downs had abraded the wildly vibrating lines, which then parted. Franz and Dennis put rocks *inside* their tent, in the corners, to keep the floor from flapping.

Gene made certain that the inflatables were still secure. Other than that, there was little that we could do except drink coffee and eat breakfast. In order to get out of the rain, we all retreated to the two buildings at the top of the hill. Despite the lack of windows – and some of the walls – a few of the rooms were dry if a bit drafty. We huddled in corners out of the chilly wind. I was happy that I had brought a warm jacket to wear.

The title of this chapter alludes to Robinson Crusoe. It would have been more appropriate to allude to Alexander Selkirk. I chose the allusion in the title because practically everyone has heard of the fictional character, whereas few have heard of the real-life person on whom Daniel Defoe based his novel.

The primary difference between Crusoe and Selkirk – aside from the former being fabricated and the latter being factual – is that Crusoe was marooned on an island as a result of shipwreck; Selkirk marooned himself voluntarily because he did not trust the seaworthiness of the vessel on which he was the pilot. A secondary difference, and a major one with respect to our unanticipated situation, is that Crusoe had to endure twenty-seven years of solitude before he was rescued. Selkirk was rescued after four years of isolation.

We were trapped on the island. It was impossible to launch the inflatables against mountainous waves. Even if we could have launched one of them, we did not have enough gasoline to reach the mainland. The extra gasoline cans were on the *Misty Dawn*.

How long we would be marooned on St. Paul Island was a great unknown. Nonetheless, no one was scared;

the group was cheerful; we accepted the situation and dealt with it as best we could. We were more concerned about the survival of Captain Kelly and brother John than about ourselves.

The light drizzle passed. We returned to the campsite, did some chores, and pretty much took it easy or went exploring. We found a gravesite around the headland but not much else. I had brought an ample supply of books with me, so I spent much of the day reading in the tent.

That evening we had a cookout on the rocks above the reach of the heaving sea. Around sunset we started a huge driftwood bonfire. We sat around on rocks or folding chairs and told jokes, jokes, and more jokes. We were not uncomfortable or in dire straits.

Gene found that by standing on the stoop of one of the buildings on the hill, he could get patchy service on his cell phone. He was unable to reach the skipper of the *Misty Dawn*, who lived in Cape Breton only fifteen miles away, but he managed to get through to his wife in New Jersey. He apprised Joanie of the situation, and asked her to get in touch with the skipper via landline. Failing that, he asked her to notify the Coast Guard of our predicament.

This form of communication was sporadic at best. Gene soon lost the signal and was unable to reacquire it; then the phone's battery died. But at least we were secure in the knowledge that people who were landside were aware of our difficulty. It is interesting to note that Gene's cell phone was an old analogue model; a couple of other people with digital cell phones could not obtain sufficient signal strength to make a connection.

With Gene's phone dead, and none of the others operational, we had no knowledge of the fate of the *Misty Dawn*.

Being marooned was not as bad as it sounds. Historically, shipwrecked sailors generally landed with nothing or little more than the clothes on their back. They then faced privation without water, food, or shelter. We had none of the comforts of home, but we had all the

Note the outboard motor halfway up the cliff face. The other inflatable is to the left of the one that is shown; from this angle it is hidden by the projecting outcrop.

comforts of a well-stocked camper, without much cause for complaint. After all, we had expected to camp pretty much as we were doing.

We spent our second day marooned pretty much the same as we spent the first: reading, exploring, joking, and watching the surf. About lunchtime we made an unfortunate discovery: we had plenty of food for several more days, but we were desperately short of drinking water. There hadn't seemed to be any reason to land all the water jugs on the day of arrival, so some of them were left on the boat for later transfer. Now we had enough water for dinner but not for breakfast.

Gene had found a stream during a hike across the island. We gathered containers and made plans to replenish our water supply in the morning.

That night we built another bonfire. Although the surf had not gone down very much, we did not see as many whitecaps in the distant ocean. It was still impossible to launch the inflatables, and it was uncertain that a fishing vessel could enter the cove without fear of coming to grief. We expected to be marooned for at least another day.

The wind died down somewhat overnight. A shift in the direction helped to lay down the seas in Atlantic Cove. Large swells rolled offshore, but the cove was now protected and our tiny beachhead was, if not calm, at least no longer in the surf zone.

Gene organized the water party. I donned raingear and shouldered my pack in preparation for departure. Before we took our first step, Gene made a last-minute call on his handheld VHF radio. Much to his surprise, he received a reply! The boat had to be close because the range of the radio was less than five miles.

Then someone shouted, "There's the boat!" (Or something similar.)

I looked seaward. Sure enough, the *Misty Dawn* was entering the cove. A group cheer was sounded.

Lynn DelCorio took notice of the change in expression on my face. "You look disappointed."

He was right. I *was* disappointed, but I didn't know that it showed. Being stranded on an uninhabited island appealed to my sense of adventure. I would have been content to suffer a little privation before being rescued.

One of the inflatables being launched through heavy surf. The boat had to be pushed into water that was deep enough to lower the outboard motor without damaging the lower unit by smashing it against the rocky bottom. Note the *Misty Dawn* on the other side of the cove, where the water was deep enough for her displacement hull.

As far as I was concerned, the greatest adventure ended as soon as the *Misty Dawn* appeared. I was the only one in the group who felt that way.

We lowered one of the inflatables to the narrow strand. Waves crashed against the rocks but not so bad that the boat could not be launched into the surf. Gene went to confer with the skipper. When he returned, he told us to break camp and pack our belongings. We were leaving the island and returning to the mainland.

It took several hours to do as he directed. I was alone in being sorry to leave the island.

On the boat, Captain Kelly told his story to us. The *Misty Dawn* had to pull anchor during the height of the storm because the boat was being pounded by the waves and her anchor was dragging. The direction of the wind was straight into the cove. The skipper ran around the island and tried to hide in a lee cove, but the surge was so bad that the boat was in danger of being dashed against the rocks by the backwash. So he made a headlong dash for home, nearly foundering in the process. Later, twenty-foot seas prevented him from crossing the gap between Cape Breton and St. Paul Island. He planned to come and get us as soon as it was possible to do so. Otherwise the Coast Guard would have to come to our rescue.

Captain Kelly told us that we had time to make a dive before crossing the strait to Cape Breton. He suggested that we dive on a nearby headland called Sovereign Point, or Money Point, where the British sailing vessel *Sovereign* was supposed to have sunk with a cargo of Mexican silver dollars.

Maximum depth was 30 feet. Because the bottom was above the thermocline, the water temperature was a pleasant 61°. The granite seabed consisted of channels and narrow grooves with pockets or depressions that were partially filled with sand. The idea was to fan away the sand in order to expose heavy objects that had settled in the bottom of the depressions. I stayed underwater for 105 minutes. I found some bronze sheathing nails but no silver dollars. I also caught three lobsters.

Then came the fearful crossing to the mainland. The seas measured ten to twelve feet in height. The fishing vessel managed the seas quite well, but not so some of the passengers. More than one person puked over the side; others were barely able to refrain from vomiting. Sheets of salt spray inundated those who were forced to stay on the exposed after deck. This went on for four miserable hours. We were all exhausted upon reaching the dock.

The St. Paul Island diving adventure was over. And what a great adventure it was!

Addendum

Gene did not give up on St. Paul Island. We returned three years later, in August 2001. This time he chartered the fishing vessel *Meg & Kel*, Captain Scott Fitzgerald (Captain Kelly's son). This time the trip was strictly a land-based operation.

The Fitzgeralds let us sleep in the loft above the fish house. Every morning we left the dock at oh-dark-hundred, made the three-hour passage to St. Paul Island, made two dives, and returned by nightfall, whereupon we had to fill tanks for the next day's trip.

Compared to the previous outing, this one was far more exhausting because of the round-trip travel time, and a lot less exciting because no wilderness camping was involved. On the positive side, we made a number of dives on the recently discovered wreck of the *Clymene*: a nineteenth-century sailing vessel whose hull and rigging lay scattered in depths that ranged from 50 feet to 140 feet. The photographic opportunities on the *Clymene* were spectacular. There were deadeyes galore.

Rescue and Redemption

Accidents happen.

They happen on the highway, in the home, at work, and during recreational activities.

Most accidents are minor, resulting in cuts, scrapes, bruises, burns, or other trivial injuries that can be treated by the hurt individual or, in many cases, ignored. These types of injuries don't go away; they heal.

Serious nonlethal accidents may require immediate hospitalization or at least examination and treatment by a doctor.

Accidents that happen under water are generally fatal. This is not to say that divers don't survive from getting cut on sharp metal hull plates, or being bitten by bergalls or trigger fish, or getting pinched by crabs and lobsters, or being stung by jellyfish. I have suffered all these indignities without being close to death.

The Sting

My most painful such accident occurred from the sting of a Portuguese man-of-war. The incident occurred off Miami, Florida, on a trip with Billy Deans and Tom Mount. I was wearing a lightweight wetsuit, but because the water was warm, I was not wearing a hood or gloves. I was the last passenger to jump off the stern of the boat. As I was swimming forward along the starboard side, a wave shoved me toward the rolling hull. In order to keep from being clunked on the head, I extended my left arm and placed my hand against the painted hull at the waterline.

Unseen by me, the current swept a Portuguese man-of-war between my body and the boat. The long tentacles wrapped around my naked hand. The pain from the stinging cells was immediate and intense. It felt as if the back of my hand had been stabbed by a thousand hatpins or sewing needles.

I jerked my arm back reflexively but the pain didn't stop. The large purple air bladder floated past my eyes. The pain was so penetrating that my hand and fingers quickly became paralyzed. My fingers swelled and stiffened. The back of my hand inflated like a balloon; the skin was scarred with jagged red welts.

I drifted back to the ladder. Because I could not close the fingers of my left hand, I had to hook my elbow over the rungs. Two crewmembers remained onboard. Between clenched teeth, I told them that I had been stung and asked them to take my camera rig. Then they helped me climb the ladder.

I collapsed on a bench. They helped me out of my harness and pulled my tanks away from me. I didn't have the strength to stand. I leaned back while one of the mates examined my hand. He took a sharp knife and used it as a scraper. He dragged the blade edgewise across the skin. In this manner he scraped off the clinging nematocysts. The pain from the venom was so powerful that I didn't feel the sharp edge of the knife. The mate then poured seawater on my hand.

The pain did not subside. It grew worse.

My hand felt as if it were on fire; as if the blue flame of a blowtorch were being held against my skin, continuously and without surcease.

I was so distracted by pain that I was only vaguely aware that the mates were preparing to dive. They had stayed onboard to watch the boat while the rest of us went diving; their turn came after the others returned. They asked me if I planned to proceed with my dive. I shook my head. There was no way that I could make a 200-foot dive in my condition.

They reasoned that as long as I was not going back into the water, they may as well make effective use of my presence on the boat. They hastily donned their gear and jumped overboard.

I was alone. I lay down on the deck and rolled back and forth, groaning in agony. My situation worsened.

The venom was slowly moving up my arm, increasing the extent of excruciating pain. I groaned louder in order to keep from screaming. I was on the verge of losing consciousness.

The venom crept past my elbow, along my upper arm, and into my shoulder. Now I was afraid that if the venom spread across my chest, it would paralyze my heart. There was no one to help me if it did.

Miraculously, the venom stopped spreading shortly after it encompassed the left side of my chest. The awful pain persisted, but by that time I was fairly confident that I was going to survive the poisoning. I was still lying on the rolling deck when my fellow divers returned after a run time of an hour and a half.

By that time I was able to sit up. I was weak; my left arm hung limp and useless at my side. I was quiet on the ride back to the dock. Onshore, someone gave me diphenhydramine: an over-the-counter antihistamine that is generally prescribed for coughs, colds, and allergies; it helps to suppress the symptoms of the venom, and alleviate the pain. It also causes drowsiness.

I was "looped out" for the rest of the afternoon and evening. The next morning, I started the long drive home to Philadelphia. I felt sluggish, my hand was still swollen and partially paralyzed, and angry red welts scarred the back of my hand. I could not grip the steering wheel with my left hand; it dangled in my lap. More than a week passed before the swelling finally subsided, the welts faded, and I regained the flexibility of my fingers.

If you want to know what the sting of a Portuguese man-of-war feels like, hold your arm over a Bunsen burner for a couple of hours.

All Adrift

Other than the times when I was left at sea as a result of a broken anchor line, I was the rescuer instead of the rescued. Most of these rescues involved swimming from the boat to tow an exhausted diver back to safety. I have lost count of the number of times that I have performed this obliging function.

Other times I lent a helping hand – or knife – to cut monofilament off an entangled diver. On a couple of occasions I have had to pass my regulator to a buddy who was experiencing mechanical difficulties. Once I found a pair of divers who were lost inside a wreck, and escorted them to an exit point and thence to the anchor line because they were almost out of air. It all goes with the territory.

I might hold the record for going adrift at sea. I can think of five such incidents: on the *Andrea Doria* (recounted in *Andrea Doria: Dive to an Era*), on the *John Morgan* (recounted in *The Technical Diving Handbook*), on an unidentified wreck while diving off the *Kiwi* (recounted in Book One of *The Lusitania Controversies*), on the *Ethel C.* (not previously recounted), and on the *Ocean Venture* (not previously recounted).

The *Ethel C.* incident was the least stressful of all of them. I was the last diver on the bottom when the hook pulled out of the wreck. The current was so strong that tying a decompression line to the wreck appeared inadvisable. Because the depth was 185 feet, I was facing a fairly long decompression. I sent up a liftbag on quarter-inch sisal from my Jersey wreck reel, then slowly ascended the line to conduct my decompression.

I was drifting along under calm seas when a shadow loomed overhead. Larry Keen on the *Gekos* had not had any difficulty in locating me. The water was so clear that I could recognize the faces of people who peered over the railing. I lay back horizontal, facing upward, spread out my arms and legs, and made an exaggerated motion of sweeping my right arm out to my side and placing my hand on my head: the diver's okay signal. I saw people laughing and cheering. Keen cut off the engine and drifted nearby until I surfaced.

The *Ocean Venture* incident was a bit more nerve-racking. Once again the current was overly strong; it was accompanied by light chop and occasionally breaking waves. It was calm under water. My buddy was Barb Lander. I had dived on the *Ocean Venture* a number of time throughout the years. This was Barb's first time.

I led her around the wreck until it was time to return to the anchor line. Despite ambient light visibility that measured better than thirty feet, the wreck was so spread out that I veered off course and lost my way while passing over a large stretch of sand that separated one section of wreckage from another. I couldn't find the anchor line.

Before we reached the point of imminent danger – where air was too low and decompression was too long – I made the call to send a liftbag to the surface. Neither one of us wanted to do a remote decompression because it seemed unlikely that we could swim against the current to reach the boat if we surfaced anywhere but directly forward of the bow. The best we could hope was to catch the trail line.

This is where many divers make the big mistake of believing that the anchor line lay just beyond the limit of visibility, and that another few seconds of searching was all that was needed to find it. I am reminded of Bernie Chowdhury and his fiasco on the *Northern Pacific*.

The way Chowdhury told the story, he left a stage bottle secured to the anchor line. The bottle contained oxygen that he intended to breathe during his ascent in order to accelerate his decompression. When his planned bottom time expired, he returned to where he believed the grapnel was hooked, but couldn't find it. At that time he had more than enough air in his tanks to conduct a remote decompression without the oxygen in the stage bottle. Instead of instituting an emergency procedure – sending a liftbag to the surface with a line tied to the wreck, or making a controlled ascent and doing a drift decompression – he chose to keep looking for the anchor line and stage bottle.

He swam all the way to the opposite end of the wreck. This was a considerable feat when you consider that the hull measured more than five hundred feet in length. He did not see the anchor line at the other end, either. So he swam back around the hull, and continued to do so until he ran almost completely out of air. Then he ascended to the surface without doing any decompression at all, his penalty by this time being more than two hours.

He yelled and waved for help, and was towed to the boat, where he suffered a severe case of the bends: both pain and paralysis. He was lucky that he didn't die on the spot. Captain Bill Nagle, owner of the *Seeker*, called the Coast Guard for helicopter evacuation. Chowdhury was treated in a recompression chamber, after which he showed significant improvement. After a stay in the hospital and months of follow-up therapy, he ultimately made a nearly full recovery.

Once you lose your orientation under water, the only way to get reoriented is to find a recognizable location from which to trace a path. The grapnel was hooked high on the wreck, which has a relief of more than thirty feet. He must have passed underneath it during his frantic peregrinations.

Chowdhury was a cave diver with little wreck-diving experience. Cave-diving techniques differ from wreck-diving techniques. For one thing, the cave-diving mindset of always returning to the entrance is not a wreck-diving protocol of always returning to the anchor line. For another, a wreck-diver generally keeps his sling bottle with him when he explores away from the anchor line. That way he doesn't *have* to return to the grapnel in order to collect his decompression gas. Chowdhury may have believed that he had to return to the anchor line, but a wreck-diver would have considered other options.

The trick in such a situation is in knowing when to cut and run; that is, when to quit searching and employ an alternative measure. Divers other than Chowdhury have been unable to make a reasoned decision to take affirmative if undesirable action; some have paid the ultimate price for their equivocation.

Barb and I might have found the anchor line a few seconds later. And then again, we might not. I weighed our remaining air against our increasing decompression penalty at 160 feet, and calculated that persistent meandering was not worth the risk. We deployed a liftbag, inflated it, and sent it to the surface clipped to the nylon line of a wreck reel.

The top current was much stronger than the bottom current. As soon as the liftbag hit the surface, and I unreeled some extra line to tie to a piece of wreckage, the slack was ripped out of my hands. Furthermore, I was hauled along the bottom with incredible celerity.

I finally managed to wrap the reel around a protruding piece of wreckage. I made two or three wraps in order to take off the strain. Then I cut the line. As the saying goes, "If you can't tie a knot, tie a lot." I was no master knot maker so I tied a square knot followed by a long string of half hitches.

Barb and I ascended to our first decompression stop. We had some difficulty in gripping the thin line which, because so much of it had been yanked off the reel, did not rise vertically to the surface but extended downcurrent at an acute angle. Our fingers kept sliding up the line so that we had to constantly reposition our hands. Despite the rough seas, we didn't bounce much because the waves washed over the liftbag, so that most of the vertical wrench was absorbed. This was one of the advantages of a liftbag decompression.

The current pushed against us hard. Our combined drag was severe. Nylon line that measures one-eighth inch in diameter may have a greater breaking strength than quarter-inch sisal, but it does not have the same resistance to abrasion. The line chafed against encrusted metal, and parted. We went adrift long before we completed our decompression.

Because our tanks were more empty than full, they contained more reserve buoyancy than I cared to have. We made ourselves heavy so we could hang beneath the liftbag. We drained our buoyancy compensators, and we let as much air out of our drysuits as possible. The result was slight negative buoyancy that prevented us from breaching.

We hunkered down for the long haul. Once we completed our decompression, we would be so far astern of the boat that there was no way we could swim upcurrent to the ladder, or even to the trail line. We would have to drift on the surface in worsening seas until the boat could pick us up. But the boat could not be detached from the anchor line until all the divers returned. All that time, we would be drifting farther and farther away.

Barb and I both carried signal mirrors and strobes to call attention to our location. If we were still adrift after dark, we had dive lights to indicate our position.

We were nearing the end of our decompression when I heard a high-pitched whine in the distance. The Doppler effect told me that the sound was approaching. This was not the deep-throated roar of the *Miss Lindsay's* diesel engines or slowly spinning propellers. It was the sound that was made by a smaller and faster boat.

Suddenly I saw a silhouette zoom overhead. Just as suddenly I was yanked to the surface when the line I was gripping was pulled upward. I swung like a pendulum under the white hull of a boat. My body struck fiberglass and my fin tips came to within inches of the propeller. I increased my grip and bent my knees to avoid being shredded by the churning blades.

My negative buoyancy was lost when the air in my drysuit expanded from the explosive ascent from 10 feet. My head popped to the surface. I reached up and grabbed the gunwale so I wouldn't get sucked under the boat and into the propeller.

I spit out my regulator and yelled as loud as I could, "*Stop the engine! Stop the engine!*"

I saw four fishermen with wide-eyed looks on their faces: looks that could have graced a cod after death. They didn't seem to understand what was happening. Only one of them reacted at all to my sudden appearance: the one at the throttle. His reaction was less than instantaneous. He pulled back the handle and switched off the engine. Friction brought the boat to a stop.

Barb was pressed against my side away from the engine, angrily screaming words to the effect, "*Let go of the bag!*" She may have added a few choice expletives for emphasis.

The liftbag was deflated so that letting going of it wouldn't improve our situation. The men on the boat had done a high-speed pick-up by racing alongside of the liftbag and snatching it from the water.

I glanced at my computer and saw that it was three minutes away from clearing decompression. I didn't like breaking my ceiling, but I knew that the computer was conservative enough that I could miss a few minutes of decompression without getting bent.

Probably.

This hope did nothing to quell my anger. Or Barb's. She was equally as familiar with the computer's conservatism, but espoused the same prohibition against breaking decompression. We held onto the plunging gunwale as we discussed our options. The fishermen were awkwardly silent. Our situation was incomprehensible to them. They knew nothing about decompression or the danger of terminating it early, and it was impossible for us to explain it to them so they could understand our attitude.

I don't remember who spoke or what words he used, but someone explained that they had received a radio call from the *Miss Lindsey* to retrieve the floating yellow bag. They thought that they were doing a favor for the skipper – which they were. They had no idea that there were divers under the bag. In retrospect I cannot blame them for their ignorance. But at that moment I was too upset about nearly becoming chop suey, by being strained through the blades of their underwater Cuisinart, to be mollified. Neither was Barb.

The fisherman said that they would transport us to the *Miss Lindsey*. As we did not seem to be getting bent, we took their offer. The *Miss Lindsey* was at least a quarter of a mile away: too far for the fishing boat to tow us, as our arms would probably give out along the way. Nor did the boat have a ladder.

We instructed the fishermen on how to help us get on board. We removed our weight belts and held them up for someone to take. We inflated our back-mounted buoyancy compensators, unplugged the drysuit inflator, and doffed the tanks. They floated. We pushed them upward as the fishermen hauled them over the gunwale. Then they pulled us into the boat.

The demeanor onboard was solemn. Barb and I tried to break the ice by thanking them and by apologizing for our outburst. Considering what the fishermen did for us, I don't think that we expressed adequate sincerity. I have always felt regret that I did not treat them with greater respect and consideration.

The fishing vessel drew astern of the *Miss Lindsey*. Barb and I donned our weight belts and tanks, thanked the fishermen again, and rolled overboard. We grabbed the trail line, pulled ourselves forward, and climbed the bouncing ladder to the safety of the deck.

Captain Mike Hillier then related the course of events from his perspective. He saw the liftbag pop to the surface. He assumed that someone had sent up an artifact. He couldn't go after it because divers were decompressing on the anchor line. When he spotted the passing fishing vessel, he called it on the radio, informed the skipper of his restricted maneuverability, and asked him to fetch the liftbag for him. The fisherman and his buddies happily complied.

All's well that ends well, as another saying goes. I suppose that Barb and I had little cause for complaint. But I could have done with a little less anxiety.

Upside Down and Dirty

Perhaps the strangest underwater rescue of all time was the rescue of Dean Ziegler.

I was on a fortnight trip to the Great Lakes when this incident occurred, in Lake Huron, off the Thumb of the Michigan peninsula. I was diving from the *Viking* with Alan Jensen (owner and skipper), Martha Heil (Alan's nondiving fiancé), Joyce Hayward, and Dean. In consort with us was the Mohrman family boat *Slip-N-Away*; onboard were Bud (father), Barb (mother), their two sons Phillip and Brian, and Buzz Anderson (friend of the family and Bud's employee).

Bud dropped a grapnel onto a wreck whose identity

I took this picture of the *Viking* on the morning prior to departure for the *Foot*. Martha Heil is standing on the left. Alan Jensen is crouched on the deck, adjusting his tanks. Note the swim platform and the raised ladder.

at that time was uncertain. Supposedly it was either the *Foot* or the *Commodore*; Alan is sure it was the *Foot*. Alan positioned the *Viking* close to the stern of the *Slip-N-Away*. Bud tossed a line to Alan so he could secure it to a bow cleat. The current was negligible. With the *Viking* streaming off the *Slip-N-Away's* stern, we all planned to use the *Slip-N-Away's* anchor line to descend to the wreck.

Bud secured a traverse line from the bow of the *Slip-N-Away*, and let it out until it passed the side of the *Viking*, so that we on the *Viking* could pull ourselves to the anchor line. Alan deployed a tag line that returning divers could grab if they drifted past the boats, or if they surfaced downcurrent of the boats. He also deployed a weighted decompression bar.

I was first in the water, diving alone. I checked the hook to make certain it was secure. The maximum depth was 142 feet; the bottom temperature was 42°; visibility was a couple of feet with a dive light, and zero without one. No ambient light reached the wreck.

As I glanced around the grapnel, I saw nothing but flat wooden decking with no discernible features. In some places the deck planks were separated from the supporting timbers, enabling me to see a couple of feet down into the hull, or perhaps into the bilge. It appeared as if the sides of the wreck had fallen outboard long ago, and that the top deck had fallen straight down into the hold during the evolution of collapse.

The thin layer of silt was easily stirred into a cloudy soup of mote-sized particles.

I secured my wreck reel to the anchor chain. I let out line to get away from the haze that surrounded the grapnel and the lifting and falling chain. Visibility improved to about eight feet. I worked my way across the wreck in search of distinctive features to photograph. I didn't find any, but I switched on my photo strobe anyway, and took a few pictures of the grain in the planks and the white caulking that extruded between them: the most noteworthy features I encountered.

I held the reel tightly as I worked my way around the wreck. I was less than halfway into my dive when I felt someone tugging on my arm. Joyce motioned for me to come with her.

I shook my head and turned away. I wanted to take some more photographs.

She grabbed me again, more forcefully this time. She waved frantically for me to follow her. The firm expression on her face matched her wild gesticulations. I figured that I had better see what she was fussing about. Perhaps the grapnel was in danger of coming loose – although I didn't see why Dean, her buddy on this dive, couldn't deal with the situation. He was strong and capable, and should be able to reset the hook without any help from me.

She followed my line to the grapnel. I reeled in the line as I followed her. When she reached the grapnel, she pointed upward as a signal for me to go to the surface. Then she followed a different line-reel line and disappeared from sight with a couple of hard kicks. I didn't know that this was Buzz's line.

I was puzzled by her bizarre behavior. The grapnel was secure, and I wasn't ready to terminate my dive. So I unreeled my line again and proceeded away from the anchor line.

I didn't get far before Joyce reappeared at my side. Now she forcibly tugged me back toward the grapnel. I did not have any presentiment of danger, but the realization was slowly dawning on me that something was amiss else she would not have been so insistent. Joyce was not given to moments of irrational action.

Reluctantly I followed her back to the grapnel. She showed me a different line-reel line. She spread her arms with an expansive gesture, then pointed to the surface. Now I began to get the picture. Because I knew that she and Dean had planned to dive together, I interpreted her hand signals to mean that Dean's drysuit had overinflated, and he had soared to the surface.

This meant that Dean was bobbing above us on the gentle lake swells, perhaps unable to swim to the boat, and that topside personnel might have had to toss off the anchor line in order to go after him.

Alan planned to wait until we were decompressing before he left the boat in Martha's care and went diving. I didn't know what the Mohrmans had planned as far as who was diving first and who was staying topside to tend their boat.

In any case, there was a potentially serious situation in the works. It behooved us to do whatever we could in the matter, either by assisting in the rescue or by not becoming a hindrance to those who were in a position to conduct the rescue.

Joyce could not have helped her buddy by following him to the surface, for then there would have been two divers adrift and suffering from decompression injury. She took the most reasonable course of action under the circumstances: she gathered the divers who were on the bottom and made them curtail their dive. I didn't know at the time that she had retrieved Buzz between the two times that she had come after me. Because of the poor visibility, all she had to do to locate anyone was to follow line-reel lines. I was the last diver on the bottom.

Joyce and I ascended. I had to do a 20-foot stop, but Joyce continued up to 10 feet. There she encountered Alan coming down. Joyce would not let him pass, and motioned for him to return to the surface. Alan did so and swam back to the *Viking*.

I had just reached my 10-foot stop when Bud and Barb came down the anchor line. Again Joyce wouldn't let them pass; she made them turn around. They followed her instructions even though they didn't know the reason for her persistence. Bud and Barb surfaced and returned to their boat.

By this time Buzz was nearly done his decompression, his dive having been shorter than Joyce's. He surfaced next.

Joyce surfaced a few minutes later. I was left alone in the water to complete my decompression.

Joyce climbed onto the swim platform of the *Slip-N-Away*. There she explained the situation to Buzz and the Mohrman's on the stern of their boat, and to Alan and Martha on the bow of the *Viking*. Then she slipped into the water and returned to the *Viking*.

Alan dashed to the flying bridge. He soon spotted a floating glove, and then he saw bubbles breaking the surface not far away. He immediately went into rescue mode. He told Martha to get out the oxygen kit while he pulled up the lines.

By the time I surfaced there was a frenzy of activity. I handed my camera rig to Martha, then climbed up the ladder and swung over the transom onto the deck. Martha told me to stay in my dive gear. Joyce quickly reiterated the circumstances for my benefit.

Dean deployed a line reel when he reached the grapnel. He led the way across the wreck away from my line. Joyce followed close behind him. They were about ten minutes into the dive when Dean bumped his hand – the one that was holding the line reel – on an upward protruding board. This caused him to drop the reel. The unchecked line unspooled and the reel fell through the decking. He nose-dived down to catch the reel.

When Dean tipped downward head first, the air in the chest cavity of his drysuit rushed up into the legs and feet, ballooning them and lifting his lower extremities off the bottom. The fins felt "funny" on his feet. He immediately disregarded the reel, curled into a ball, and tried to right himself the way he had been taught, and the way he had practiced in the quarry. The practice method didn't work because, due to the extra-large pockets of the fins, the fins had slipped sideways off the hard-soled foot of the drysuit.

He scooped water with his hands. Joyce tried to help by pulling down on his legs. But each time she grabbed his legs and Dean attained a nearly horizontal profile, Dean's tanks banged into her and knocked her away. Dean was now breathing hard and close to being overcome by exhaustion. He suddenly erupted off the bottom upside down, and disappeared from Joyce's view in a flash.

Joyce found herself alone in a swirling cloud of silt that made it impossible to see. She knew that Dean would burst to the surface in a matter of seconds. She figured that the boats might have to break away from the anchor line in order to go after him. She also knew that he had a decompression penalty against him, and that his skyrocket ascent to the surface would likely result in a bad case of the bends – assuming that he didn't die from embolism or pneumothorax.

She located Dean's reel line and followed it back to the grapnel. Then she followed the other two lines in order to retrieve the divers at the end of them.

Oddly, no one topside had seen Dean break the surface. Now everyone was scanning the horizon for him. He was nowhere to be found, so where could he possibly be?

To me, the obvious scenario was that his drysuit seals burst from overexpansion. The drysuit then filled with water whose weight dragged him back down to the bottom. I saw this happen when Jon Hulburt and I sent Jerry Rosenberg's body to the surface from a depth of 170 feet, on the *Sommerstad*. (See Book Two of *The Lusitania Controversies* for details.)

By now, Dean had been missing for nearly twenty minutes. He could not possibly have drifted out of sight because there was hardly any current. Was he pinned to the bottom in a flooded drysuit? In that case he shouldn't be very far away from his abandoned reel.

Alan pointed to the spot where bubbles were breaking the surface. Were these exhaled bubbles, or were they bubbles being purged from a free-flowing regulator that had dropped from the mouth of a drowned victim?

Everyone on the boat was acting and communicating at once, with each person taking the role for which he or she was best suited.

Alan started the engine. Martha pulled the line from the *Slip-N-Away* off the cleat. Joyce assembled the oxygen kit in preparation for use. I unclipped unneeded accessories from my person: sling bottle, line reel, and backup light. Martha cleared a spot on the starboard gunwale. I shuffled to the clearing and awaited Alan's command. Alan maneuvered the boat alongside the bubbles. I put one leg on the gunwale. Martha steadied me. Alan shouted "Go!" I rolled overboard and hit the water on my back.

I twisted under water like a cat in midair. As soon as I was facing downward I purged air from my drysuit. I fell through a stream of tiny bubbles in clear surface water where visibility extended to twenty-five feet, and where the temperature above the thermocline stood at a balmy 62°.

The first thing I noticed was that the bubbles were not rising in a steady stream, but were rising in groups that were well separated from each other. I knew at once that Dean was exhaling. I also knew from the spacing of the bubble groups that he was breathing slowly. Not only was he alive somewhere beneath me, but he was not breathing like a panic-stricken diver. I was puzzled.

Because I descended through the middle of the bubble stream, my downward view was somewhat obscured. It came as a shock to come upon Dean abruptly at a depth of 60 feet. He was upside down and holding on tight. The feet and legs of his drysuit were so bloated that they reminded me of an African native with a bad case of elephantiasis.

Dean's predicament was so bizarre that for the moment I could not make sense of what I was seeing. But first I let him know that help had arrived. I squeezed his upper arm twice. He let one hand go of the hose he was gripping to give me the okay sign. I checked his gauges and saw that he was low on air but not dangerously so.

Now I examined the situation closely. Dean's feet were up and his head was down. Dean's tanks were not on his back; they were beneath him, connected to his drysuit by the inflator hose. He was holding onto this inflator hose with both hands. He was breathing from one of his two regulators. A pair of thin lines extended down from the inflator hose of his buoyancy compensator to form a narrow inverted V.

To be clear, Dean's rig consisted of two inflator hoses: one for his drysuit and one for his buoyancy compensator. He was gripping the drysuit hose. The buoyancy compensator hose was stretched taut by the inverted V-shaped line that extended all the way down to the lake bed.

For the reader to understand Dean's unusual position, it will be helpful at this point to describe how he got into this predicament. As Joyce had already told me, and as Dean later confirmed, he reached down into a hole in order to retrieve his reel. The head-down attitude forced air into the legs of his drysuit. The shift in buoyancy raised his legs higher than his head. The slight reduction in the depth of the air caused it to expand ever so slightly, but enough to yank him off the bottom before he could catch himself by grabbing onto the wreck. Once the cycle of expanding air commenced, there was no stopping it.

At this moment Dean consciously thought of his wife Diane. He fully expected to die or to be seriously hurt, perhaps with some permanent disability. Silently he apologized to Diane for making a fatal error.

He ascended out of control. The air in his lungs was also expanding exponentially, so he exhaled as hard as he could. He rose higher and faster until he was jarred to a sudden stop. He felt no sensation of movement. He knew that he was not on the surface. So where was he? All he could determine was that he was upside down.

Now comes the ironic part that Joyce didn't see and that Dean couldn't understand. As he leaned down into the hole, the corrugated inflator hose of his buoyancy compensator slipped under the line-reel line. When he was catapulted upward, the slender line was snared by the mouthpiece of the oral inflator, which projected an inch or so from the manual inflator/exhaust assembly.

The line-reel line snagged on a piece of wooden wreckage. The reel lifted but the housing jammed against the bottom of a plank. The reel free-spooled until it reached the end of the line, which was knotted onto the spool. This tenuous hitch abruptly halted Dean's uncontrolled ascent, and was responsible for maintaining his precarious perch.

Viewed another way, the line-reel line stretched from the anchor chain across the wreck to a piece of wreckage on the edge of the hole a foot or so away from the reel, thence up some eighty feet to the inflator/exhaust assembly of Dean's buoyancy compensator, thence down some eighty feet to the reel that was wedged under a plank in the hole. The chances of this contrived situation ever happening were slim to none, and Slim left town. But there you have it.

Dean did not know what mechanism had caused the stop of his ascent before reaching the surface. He couldn't see his surroundings because his mask had flooded. He tried to clear the mask but it kept flooding, perhaps because the skirt was folded or because it was resting on the material of his hood. He ran a finger around the perimeter of the mask in order to free the skirt from the hood. While doing so, he accidentally knocked the regulator out of his mouth.

At this point he was in what he called a "frenzied state." The exhaust T of his down-exhaust second stage kept filling with water. He choked as he tried to inhale. He pressed the purge button, but only partway because the regulator might free-flow if he kept the purge mechanism open too long.

Now he thought about his three children; about how he was not going to quit fighting for his life because they needed him. He purged, inhaled, and choked several times before he cleared the water out of the exhaust T. Once he started breathing regularly again, he calmed down and tried to think through his predicament.

The first order of business was to breathe slowly and deeply.

He wanted to know how much air remained in his tanks, but his mask was still flooded so he was unable to see. He also did not know how deep he was.

His next thought was to stab the legs of his drysuit with his knife. But first he inflated his buoyancy compensator so he wouldn't sink when the air escaped from his drysuit.

Before he unsheathed his knife, he stretched his hands toward his feet to determine how far he could reach: barely "below" the knees. The drysuit was so taut that he couldn't bend or buckle his body as if he were doing a sit-up. Cutting holes in the drysuit that far up the legs would not let air escape from the feet. Scratch that plan. A leaking drysuit would only make is situation worse.

His next plan was to prepare for being rescued. He trusted the divers in the group, and he knew that we would make every effort to save him. So he wanted to be ready to go when the time came to go. He wasn't wearing a weight belt; he didn't need one for diving in fresh water.

His rig consisted of double tanks, two regulators, a back-mounted buoyance compensator, a stainless steel back-plate, and harness webbing with a waist buckle. Dean figured that when rescue arrived, he should be ready to let go of his harness and scream for the surface

Dean Ziegler owned his own boat, the *Ziggy II* (both shown above). He had it with him on the day of the accident, but instead of making a three-boat convoy, we decided to go with Alan Jensen and Martha Heil on the *Viking*.

on a single breath. Working blind, he unhooked his waist belt with the intention of holding onto a shoulder strap with the crook of his elbow. As soon as he doffed the backplate he realized his mistake: the drysuit had so much buoyancy that the harness was yanked out of his hands; or rather, his buoyancy yanked him out of the harness. He suddenly "fell" upward.

Worse, he forgot to disengage the drysuit inflator hose. His "fall" was abruptly brought short. Fortunately he had a seven-foot hose on his regulator, or else the mouthpiece would have been wrenched out of his mouth, and he would have drowned on the spot. There was so much pressure on the inflator hose that he could not disconnect it from the drysuit valve.

Dean had run out of self-rescue options. He was snared in midwater, literally hanging by a thread and by a low-pressure hose. There was no telling when that hose might rupture from the tension, or when the valve would rip out of the drysuit, or when the line-reel line would chafe through on the wreck or snap apart from the tension. He held onto the inflator hose close to the valve, breathing slowly in order to conserve the remaining air in his tanks.

This was how I found him.

Now I had to figure a way to get him to the surface without killing him in the process.

Naturally I tried to flip Dean around by pulling down on the gigantically swelled feet of his drysuit. I got nowhere with this; I could not even budge the legs. In terms of lift capacity, the positive buoyancy must have measured in the scores of pounds, if not in the hundreds.

Next I thought about stabbing the feet or legs of his drysuit in order to let the trapped air escape. This would work, but then his drysuit would flood and he would sink to the bottom like a torpedoed freighter. If I held onto him after doing so, I would probably be dragged down with him. Then I might have to furnish buoyancy for both of us in order to lift him to the surface. The complexity of helping him to don his tanks after we crashed to the bottom in a cloud of silt seemed insurmountable. Such an attempt could very well develop into a double fatality if we got entangled in the line-reel line during any part of the maneuver.

I remember the time that a diver (whose name I can't recall) got inverted during his ascent of the anchor line from 150 feet on the *Lillian* in April. He was fortunate enough to have kept his grip on the line before his legs inflated to monstrous proportions. He was then able to extricate himself from a nearly untenable position by pulling his knife from its sheath with his free hand, and stabbing himself in the legs to release the air. After he righted himself, he partially inflated his drysuit and completed his ascent.

I also remember the pain in his eyes when I later reached him at the 10-foot decompression stop. His drysuit was flooded with 39° water. His body shook like a leaf in a gale as he decompressed for forty-five minutes. I was shivering, and my drysuit wasn't flooded! The saving grace in that situation was that he maintained his grip on the anchor line when he stabbed his drysuit.

The only option that I could figure that was viable – and I dreaded to even consider it – was to cut the line-reel line.

I did not reach this decision lightly. I thought about it long and hard; then I thought about it longer and harder. But I couldn't think about it forever. Every breath reduced our supply of air. Every moment of strain on the low-pressure inflator hose brought it closer to the breaking point. Ultimately, cutting the line was the best solution that I could envisage in the time that was available.

I surveyed the layout in preparation for taking this drastic measure. The line was draped over the buoyancy compensator's mouthpiece: not the rubber part but the extension to which the rubber part was cable-tied. (Alan later examined this area closely. The running line had sliced halfway through the thermoplastic molding.)

The corrugated hose was stretched to its limit; it was nearly as thin as a straw. I now noticed that the base of the hose had been torn from the material; the ruptured bladder was deflated and would no longer hold air. The fact that the inflator/exhaust assembly of the buoyancy compensator was firmly connected to the first stage of the regulator by means of a low-pressure inflator hose, was all that was keeping the situation static.

The status quo could change in an instant. If the inflator hose of the buoyancy compensator pulled apart, Dean would take off for the surface – but the ruptured hose might rapidly spew out what little air remained in his tanks. He would have no air to breathe and no air to inflate his drysuit. He would then plummet to the bottom with no air at all.

Dean's life hung tenaciously by the strength of two low-pressure hoses that were under a great deal of strain and that could split at any time. I had to take decisive action, and I had to take it fast before the delicate balance of the situation changed for the worse. The horns of a dilemma were never sharper.

Reluctantly I pulled my knife from its sheath. I ascended the contraption of articulated dive gear. I squeezed Dean's arm twice and held the knife under his mask. He gave me the okay sign. I presumed that he would interpret what I intended to do.

What I didn't know was that Dean's mask was flooded so that he couldn't see. I had never made eye contact with him because his mask faced down, and I was distracted by assessing the situation in haste. Dean did *not* know what I intended to do. He told me afterward that he simply expected me to do whatever it was I had to do. He steeled himself for the worst.

I descended to the line. My knife was ready to do its deed. Yet I was short on resolve.

I hesitated.

I ran scenarios through my mind, but I was unable to conceive of any other approach that had a greater opportunity for success.

I positioned the knife by the line. I looked up and observed Dean's breathing pattern: deep inhale, long slow exhale, deep inhale, long slow exhale, deep inhale, long slow exhale . . .

I sliced the line just as Dean completed an exhale.

I wanted his lungs to be empty when he vaulted for the surface. If I cut the line on an inhale, he might not be able to expel the air fast enough to keep from embolizing.

Dean rose like an artillery shell on a 90° trajectory. One moment he was there; the next moment he was gone. I lost sight of him through the mass of expanding bubbles.

During Dean's rocketlike ascent, air gushed out of his mouth so fast that he felt as if he were vomiting. Expanding air spurted out of his other end as well. He lost consciousness momentarily before he reached the surface. His mask was ripped off his face.

Alan had moved the boat away from the bubbles; he waited nearby. Suddenly he heard a big whoosh of water. Then Dean rose full length into the air "like a Polaris missile."

Dean flopped down with a "splat" onto the surface and started to regain his senses. He opened his eyes. He was floating right-side up. He rolled over, wrapped his arms around his tanks, and hung on feebly face down.

Alan knew that Dean was still breathing because he saw bubbles erupting periodically from his regulator. He expertly maneuvered the boat alongside the bobbing body. Dean felt himself moving but could not understand how. Martha snagged him with a boat hook. At first she had difficulty dragging him because the hook kept sliding over his drysuit without catching on anything. His drysuit was so overinflated that he resembled the Michelin man, or the Stay Puft marshmallow giant in *Ghostbusters*. Martha pushed and maneuvered his body toward the stern of the *Viking*.

Phillip jumped into the water from the *Slip-N-Away*. He helped to push Dean toward the stern.

Still face down in the water, Dean grabbed onto the swim platform. Alan and Martha jumped down to the swim platform and grappled with him. Phillip disconnected Dean's inflator hose from his drysuit, thus freeing him from his tanks. He then swam the tanks to the *Slip-N-Away*.

Alan and Martha rolled Dean onto the platform so that he was facing up. They wrestled him to a sitting position with his back against the transom. They got their hands into Deans armpits, and heaved. Dean managed to get one heel onto the metal grating. With Alan and Martha lifting, and Dean pushing with one leg, they all got up to a standing position and then fell over the transom onto the deck, like three earthworms in a tangle, with Dean on top.

Dean rolled off of Martha. "Give me oxygen and don't cut my suit."

Alan and Martha propped Dean against the starboard side of the cabin. Alan did a quick neurological examination. Dean had feeling in all his extremities, and he felt no numbness or tingling. Joyce covered Dean's nose and mouth with the plastic mask from the oxygen kit.

I did not follow Dean to the surface. I knew that there were enough support people on both boats to handle the topside situation; I had confidence in their ability. My presence wasn't necessary. Besides, I had to decompress, else we might end up with two patients instead of one.

Although I had attained a depth of only 60 feet, this repetitive dive came immediately after a decompression dive that was followed by only a couple of minutes of surface interval. With regard to the concentration of nitrogen in my bloodstream, this five-minute dive was equivalent to a continuation of my previous dive.

I made a slow controlled ascent to 15 feet, and hovered there for five minutes before surfacing. I was close to the boat. I swam to the ladder and climbed aboard. As soon as I stood safely on deck, Alan gunned the engine and headed for the dock.

Once the boat was underway, Alan called the Coast Guard and requested an ambulance to meet us at the dock.

Dean was shivering from his cold-water immersion. The next step was to get him out of his flooded drysuit and into warm, dry clothes. Joyce helped out of the drysuit (without cutting it); Martha got his street clothes. Together they got him out of his soaked undergarments, and into his street clothes and a jacket.

Dean still was not showing symptoms of decompression injury. However, he felt so cold and was shivering so violently that his hypothermic condition might have masked either pain, tingling, or numbness.

The demand regulator was not delivering oxygen properly. Later it was learned that Joyce had assembled the unit incorrectly, so there was leakage where the regulator fitted into the mask. She then attached the full-face mask to the unit. This worked well, but the constant-flow mechanism consumed oxygen faster than the demand regulator. Dean emptied both bottles before we reached the dock. He wanted more oxygen but there was none to be had. The regulator was still on my swing bottle, which contained nitrox-73 for accelerated decompression, so I gave that to him.

Dean was still asymptomatic when the *Viking*

reached the dock at Harbor Beach. Joyce bundled him into the waiting ambulance. She made sure that he had his wallet. The ambulance transported him to the local hospital. The emergency room doctor had no experience with decompression injury; the hospital was not equipped with a recompression chamber. The doctor would not prescribe oxygen for Dean because he did not believe it was necessary. Nor would the doctor consent to call the Divers Alert Network to obtain advice from medical specialists in diving accidents. He performed a cursory examination and had an X-ray taken of Dean's chest. He did not see any abnormalities.

Joyce called the hospital from a dockside pay phone. She spoke with the attending physician. When she learned that he was not prescribing any treatment, she explained in a voice that was calm yet firm but constrained, how important it was to consult with a hyperbaric specialist. He refused to do so.

Joyce couldn't tolerate the doctor's ignorance. Her wrath was raised even more by his condescending attitude. She insisted that Dean be flown to a hospital that was equipped with a recompression chamber, and that was staffed by doctors who knew how to treat victims of diving accidents. The closest one was the Henry Ford Hospital in Detroit. The doctor refused.

Alan encouraged Joyce to call the Divers Alert Network on her own. She did. She explained the situation to the DAN hotline doctor. She asked the DAN doctor to call the Harbor Beach hospital and speak with the attending physician. The DAN doctor not only did that, but he arranged for helicopter evacuation for Dean.

An ambulance transported Dean to a helipad, which was located about a mile from the hospital. The Life Light helicopter pilot was knowledgeable about the transportation of diving accident victims. He told Dean that the ride would be bumpy due to the necessity of flying low; a large decrease in atmospheric pressure could either cause the bends, or aggravate a pre-existing but asymptomatic condition of the bends. This happened to me in the 1980's.

I was diving off North Carolina from the *Gekos*, Captain Larry Keen. I made two dives on the *Tarpon* at a depth of 140 feet. We left the site immediately after my repetitive dive. Two hours later we pulled into the dock. We scrambled off the boat and drove straight to a nearby airfield, where Larry was keeping his four-seat airplane. We took off at once and headed for Delaware. The purpose of the flight was to take our girlfriends home. We hoped to return to Ocracoke before dark.

Larry took the plane up to 10,000 feet. The thin air at that altitude made for efficient fuel consumption. No sooner had he reached his planned flight altitude than I felt a tingling sensation in my elbows and knees. My fingers and toes went partially numb. I diagnosed the problem immediately – I was getting bent.

When I first alerted Larry of my condition, he thought I was joking. I had to convince him that I was serious. I told him to bring the plane down until I felt relief. He did. The tingling sensations went away. We had to fly no higher than 5,000 feet.

Dean arrived at the Henry Ford Hospital asymptomatic. By that time, Dr. Portelli, the attending hyperbaric physician, had contacted the Divers Alert Network, and consulted with their diving accident specialists. By that time, too, Joyce had spoken with Dr. Portelli and briefed him about the conduct of their dive, including depth and bottom time as they related to decompression penalty.

Dr. Portelli conducted a full examination, including X-rays and a CAT scan. Dean showed no neurological dysfunction other than slurred speech. The doctor thought that this might indicate a stroke or heart condition rather than decompression injury.

Afterward he called Joyce to confer with her. The doctor didn't know Dean's normal speech pattern because he had never met him before. He wanted to know if Dean's slurred speech was abnormal. It was, but after discussing this point at length with Joyce, he decided that Dean's lips were still numb from his brush with hypothermia. Alan and I had been listening to all of Joyce's conversations; we concurred with the doctor's assessment.

Then the doctor explained why he was not prescribing recompression: the CAT scan disclosed a small hole in Dean's left lung. The hole itself was not serious, and would heal by itself in time: perhaps in less than twenty-four hours. But if Dean were to be recompressed, some of the inhaled high-pressure air would escape through the hole into the pleural cavity. During subsequent decompression, as the pressure in the chamber was slowly decreased, air that was trapped in the pleural cavity would expand, and would likely collapse the lung.

The doc promised to keep Dean under close observation. Should he manifest symptoms of the bends, then recompression would become a treatment option. But as long as he was asymptomatic, and the slurred speech was the result of a severe drop in body temperature, recompression could prove more harmful than helpful.

After Dean left for the hospital, we loaded his dive gear into his van. Joyce Hayward and I went south to dive on another boat for which we had made prior arrangements. She drove my van; I drove Dean's van and towed his boat. I took this picture of Joyce on the day after his accident. Dean was supposed to dive with us that day.

Joyce agreed with the doc's wisdom and reasoning.

The doctor then had Dean anesthetized so he could perform a painful operation. He inserted a tiny tube through the skin into the pleural cavity. Vacuum was applied to this tube in order to suck out any air that might escape through the hole in Dean's lung into the pleural cavity. This ensured that pressure would not mount in the pleural cavity and collapse the lung.

Once Dean's core temperature returned to normal, he was able to control his lips in order to speak without a lisp. This confirmed the doctor's diagnosis that Dean was not suffering from decompression injury. In fact, his long stay at 60 feet had served to reduce the concentration of nitrogen in his bloodstream, in effect decompressing him. Had he not been snagged on his line-reel line, he might very well have suffered from the bends; or he might have embolized by going all the way to the surface in a single burst of speed.

In retrospect, Dean's exceptional predicament actually saved him from a serious medical side effect of rapid decompression.

Dean was put on oxygen therapy for twenty-four hours. He remained tubed for two days. Then he was under close observation for three more days.

Dr. Portelli released Dean five days after his admission. Dean felt fine, but the doctor recommended that, because of the tiny scar on his lung, he not dive for two to three months, in order to give the wound sufficient time to heal thoroughly.

Dean has suffered no aftereffects. He has continued to dive.

DAN paid all of Dean's transportation expenses, and made up the difference between the actual cost of hospitalization and the amount that his health insurance company paid. DAN also paid for Dean's lost equipment: his line-reel, mask, and dive knife.

What did he learn by this experience? Later, he practiced and learned how to clear his mask upside down.

As I stated in the previous section, all's well that ends well.

Survival Mode

The Dean Ziegler incident provides much food for thought with regard to prevention, rescue, and survival; perhaps, even, a cornucopia of thought. The outré circumstances and possible outcomes can be parsed into an infinite number of variations.

In retrospect, it is easy to see that certain equipment modifications would have had a great effect on the situation. Had Dean worn ankle weights, it is likely that he never would have lost control of his attitude. The weights would either have kept his legs down in the first place; or, if his legs billowed anyway, they would have enabled him to regain his upright vertical attitude.

A line-reel that cannot free-spool would have prevented Dean's uncontrolled ascent. Most line-reels are fitted with a locking screw that keeps the spool from unwinding accidentally; once the locking screw is loosened, the spool is free to unwind unless the user exerts pressure against the spool with a finger or thumb.

I use a Manta line-reel. Its unique design incorporates a spring-loaded hand grip that prevents the spool from unwinding unless the user squeezes a bar that acts as a release mechanism. The spool locks in place as soon as the user stops squeezing the bar.

A side-exhaust regulator can be breathed in any position because an exhalation diaphragm closes automatically when the diver stops exhaling. Thus the second-stage air chamber cannot fill with water. Such a regulator would have prevented Dean from nearly drowning.

I cannot adequately stress the roles that everyone played in the search, rescue, and post-rescue treatment. Everyone interacted with everyone else in ways that were helpful. These interactions were truly greater than the sum of the individual actions. There were no slackers. Just because not every person had a hand in the eventual outcome, does not imply that those people did not willingly take their part; it means only that the part that some people took was preempted by another person, largely as a matter of luck and random placement rather than vigilance and accomplishment.

Buzz Anderson's performance exemplified the processes of creative thinking and affirmative action. After he learned about Dean's uncontrolled ascent and subsequent disappearance, he returned to the anchor line and descended to the bottom. From there he followed Dean's line-reel line to the place where it was snagged on the wreck, and beyond. When he started to ascend the line, it went slack in his hands.

Had I not cut Dean free when I did, Buzz would have found the line stretched taut. He then would have ascended, would have seen that Dean was caught upside down, and would have been the one to cut him free. In the event, Buzz's quick-thinking action did not achieve its goal only because of the timing.

The foremost hero in this rescue operation was Dean himself.

In most underwater fatalities, an individual is overcome by events which are beyond his ability to control. In this case, Dean did everything within his power to extricate himself from a difficult situation that he could not comprehend. When all else failed, he shifted into what I call "survival mode."

Survival mode is an attitude that is the diametrical opposite of sustained and uncontrolled panic.

Dean did not panic. This doesn't mean that he wasn't scared. Fear is a normal reaction to a life-threatening situation. A person can be scared and still conduct himself rationally and intelligently. When Dean's attempts to free himself proved fruitless, instead of struggling uselessly and wasting precious air, he entered a state of calm that was close to divine. He relaxed. He breathed deeply and slowly. He hung on tightly. He exerted as little energy as possible. He awaited rescue. He had faith that his friends would come to his aid.

Not everyone has survival mode. The Rouses are a case in point.

Chris Rouse Senior and his son Chris Junior, better known as Chrissy, generally dived together. They were exploring the *U-869* – at a depth of 230 feet – when

Chrissy became entangled or trapped by a fallen object while penetrating the pressure hull. His father wouldn't abandon him. After a great deal of effort, both of them managed to get Chrissy free. By that time they had long exceeded their planned bottom time.

Because they were primarily cave divers, they followed cave-diving protocol and left their bottles of decompression gas at the anchor line. (A wreck-diver would have kept his bottles with him, or left them at the point of entry.) They attempted to locate the anchor line, failed, then screamed for the surface without doing any decompression after half an hour on the bottom.

They surfaced forward of the boat, then swam or drifted past the anchor line and alongside the hull. They were hauled up the ladder. Chris died on the deck. Chrissy died later in a recompression chamber. (For a description of these events, see *Shadow Divers Exposed*.)

The Rouses were clearly stricken with panic. They ignored steps that they could have taken to avoid, or at least to ameliorate, decompression injury.

As they both had some air remaining in their tanks, they could have made a controlled ascent to their first decompression stop, then followed their decompression profile until their tanks were empty.

They could have gone back down the anchor line and either shared decompression gas with a diver who was decompressing, or breathed from a sling bottle that was not in use.

They could have shouted for someone on the boat to give them spare tanks and regulators, then gone down the anchor line to their decompression depth and conducted a full decompression.

Instead of exercising any of these readily available options, they simply gave up. They meekly accepted death rather than fight for survival. This is the quintessential difference between Dean and the Rouses. Dean acted rationally under extraordinary circumstances, and survived. The Rouses acted without reason, and died.

Dean possessed a will to survive that the Rouses did not possess.

Yucatan Caves and Mayan Cenotes

Underground Commencement

My interest in caves goes all the way back to my childhood. There were no caves where I grew up in northeast Philadelphia, but there was a substitute that was nearly as exciting and as challenging to explore: the storm drains.

I was but a lad of ten short years when I first ventured underground. It was not a tremendously long excursion – certainly no more than thirty feet – but it whetted my appetite for more of the same. I described my early adventures in darkness in Book One of *The Lusitania Controversies* (subtitled "Atrocity of War and a Wreck-Diving History"); there is no need to repeat the information here. Suffice it to say that by the time I graduated from high school, I had explored many miles of concrete storm drains, and had read dozens of nonfiction books about speleology and spelunking.

I also read the most well-known novel about cave exploration: *A Journey to the Center of the Earth*, by Jules Verne. Reading Verne's novel inspired me to write my own novel about cave exploration. I was only sixteen years old when I penned (quite literally) my version under the same title. It ran to 76,000 words.

The title of the Verne novel was a misnomer, for his protagonists descended only slightly more than one hundred miles beneath the surface of the planet. In my version, my protagonists actually reached the center. For comparison, I published both versions between the same covers, and reproduced the artwork from Verne's original 1874 edition. The book can be ordered from my website: http://www.ggentile.com.

After my discharge from the Army, I put storm drains behind me (well, for the most part), and started

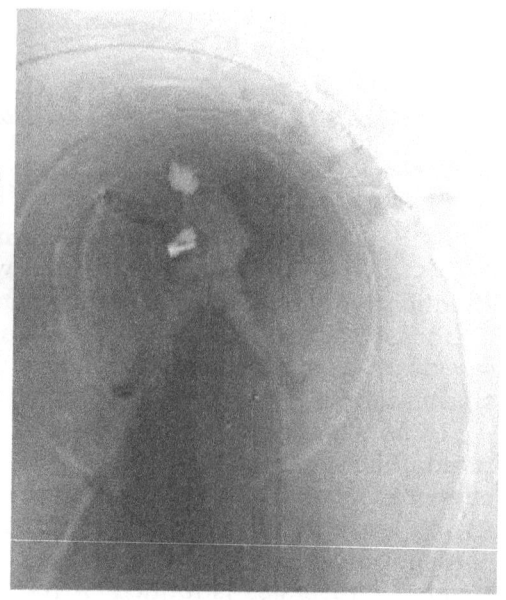

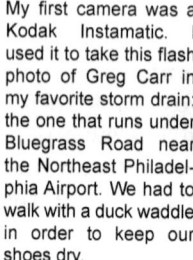

My first camera was a Kodak Instamatic. I used it to take this flash photo of Greg Carr in my favorite storm drain: the one that runs under Bluegrass Road near the Northeast Philadelphia Airport. We had to walk with a duck waddle in order to keep our shoes dry.

exploring real caves, caverns, and abandoned mines in Pennsylvania, New Jersey, Maryland, Virginia, and West Virginia. The State geological survey books that I had purchased in my teenage years provided maps and details about locations. Woodsmanship learned in the Boy Scouts and in jungle warfare school enabled me to read topographical maps and follow compass bearings (nowadays called orienteering).

I solicited some of my friends to accompany me on these underground excursions. We scoured the countryside for entrances that were often well concealed. We didn't have much in the way of equipment. We slept between blankets on the ground in the woods. We illuminated the caverns by means of carbide lamps and dull flashlights. We climbed and we crawled; mostly we crawled.

The highlight of my dry-cave exploits was Laurel Creek Cavern, in West Virginia. The entrance measured 10 feet high and 40 feet wide. The tunnel maintained highway dimensions for half a mile – and there were cowpats that far inside! Hats off to those audacious

When Steve noticed that I was no longer behind him, he waited patiently until I caught up with him and gave him the okay sign.

On another scooter run, I was leading the return when I spotted a gray lead weight in the silt at the bottom of the main tunnel. I slowed down to retrieve it. The "weight" turned out to be a Beuchat Aladin Pro decompression computer! I was ecstatic at my good luck in finding such a valuable piece of equipment. I perfunctorily checked my gauges . . . and discovered that one of my two computers was missing!

The computer I found was my own. The factory-furnished strap had broken, and the computer had dropped off my gauge panel on the way into the cave. I never would have found the computer if it had fallen off during a wreck-dive.

Back to the fossils . . . I wanted to shoot photographs, Steve wanted to test a reconditioned scooter. So we split up. I stayed in the entrance tunnel and shot a roll of film. Steve zoomed between the "lips" into the long and convoluted interior.

The so-called "lips" was a restriction at the end of the entrance tunnel, where the cavern turned sharply to the right. After I exposed thirty-six frames of film, I wandered around the entrance tunnel to see if there was anything significant that I had missed. Then I had a bright idea. Under the lower lip was a small alcove. I swam into this alcove, switched off my light, and rested in total darkness.

After a while I saw a faint glimmer of light passing between the lips. I looked up, spotted the headlight of Steve's scooter, then ducked back into concealment. I held my breath so as not to exhale any bubbles. Just as Steve passed overhead, I reached up and clamped both hands around one leg. I startled him so badly that his entire body shook and shivered like a vibrating tuning fork.

We remained good friends nonetheless. For years afterward, I made periodic treks to Florida in order to dive with him in his favorite caves. Because he was a certified

bulls and cows. Or perhaps they just wanted to escape the summer heat.

(Note: in *The Lusitania Controversies*, I mistakenly gave the dimensions of the opening of this cave as 40 feet high and 110 feet wide. In fact, those were the dimensions of a great interior chamber.)

My fellow cavers on this trip were Greg Carr, Kenny Enright, and Tom Gmitter. Instead of pitching tents, we laid our sleeping bags inside the entrance on dry ground next to the flowing creek. We got wet even though we were sheltered from the weather because condensation dripped constantly from the ceiling. We were not bothered by cattle. We spent three days exploring the cavern's vast and extensive interior.

The cave that changed the course of my life was Blue Hole, in Virginia. This was where I encountered an underground river that was 50 feet deep. Al Dubeck, Tom Gmitter, and I lowered an inflatable raft 90 feet into a sink hole into an underground river, and paddled half a mile upstream. When the ceiling curved down to water level and prevented farther passage, I determined to take a diving course in order to continue my exploration.

I knew that dive courses were given by the YMCA (Young Men's Christian Association). I found the local

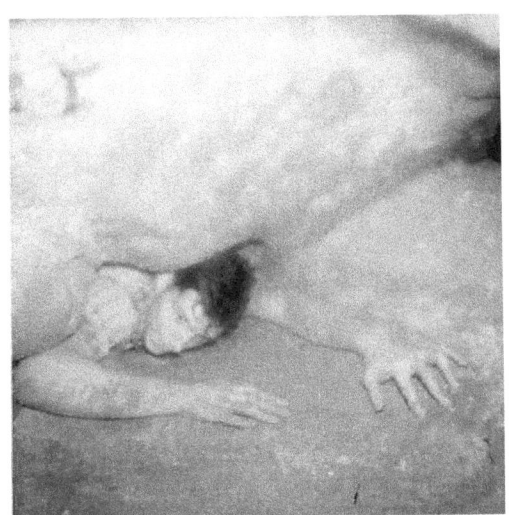

Tight squeeze! This picture was taken in Nestle Quarry Cave, West Virginia, with my Kodak Instamatic camera and flash. I generally wore a hard-hat with a carbide lamp affixed to the front, but it wouldn't fit through this narrow crevice.

branch in the phone book, called, and signed up for the next course. (For more details on both these caverns, read Book One of *The Lusitania Controversies*.)

Florida Cave-Diving Adventures

I started cave-diving the year after I received my open-water certification. At that time, cave-diving certifications did not exist. Undaunted by my lack of knowledge and experience, I dived in a handful of caves in Florida, albeit without penetrating beyond the light zone. I was never able to convince any of my fellow divers to lower a raft and dive gear 90 feet down the sink hole that was the entrance to Blue Hole.

Then I got distracted by the exploration of shipwrecks, and put cave-diving on the back burner for a couple of decades. I finally received my cave-diving certification in 1991. My instructor was the redoubtable Steve Berman. I described some of my cave-diving adventures in Book Two of *The Lusitania Controversies* (subtitled "Dangerous Descents into Shipwrecks and Law").

It is worthwhile at this point to note the difference in definitions between dry-caving and cave-diving factions. In dry-caving, a "cave" is a hollow or overhang such as a troglodyte might inhabit, with sunlight being visible from the farthest reaches of the interior; a "cavern" refers to an extensive system of tunnels or rooms where no outside light ever reaches. In cave-diving the definitions are just the opposite: a cavern resides within the light zone, whereas a cave is an extension that is totally void of light.

My exploration of Florida caves was only half-hearted. I was not overly entranced by miles and miles of wet rock. Perhaps it reminded me too much of the drab and unadorned concrete walls of the storm drains. Dry caves had the advantage of being decorated with flowstone formations: stalactites (from the ceiling), stalagmites (from the ground), and columns (from the ceiling to the ground). But submerged Florida caves were barren and lacking in esthetic appeal – at least for a photographer.

The main attraction to adherents of Florida cave-d was generally length of penetration.

The only subjects that I found of photographic i est in Florida caves were fossils. Steve Berman sho me where fossil shells were exposed in the entrance nel of Ginnie Springs. I wanted to photograph them wanted to make a scooter run.

During a previous scooter run that we did togeth Steve was passing around a curve ahead of me when canister light suddenly blacked out, leaving me in to darkness. I stopped the scooter while I fumbled with t light switch. It took only a few seconds to switch t light back on, but when I did, I found myself in unfami iar surroundings, facing a blank wall at the end of a tun nel. I was momentarily nonplussed. When I turne around, I saw another blank wall at the opposite end o the tunnel.

The gold line – the permanent guideline that marked the main tunnel – was nowhere in sight!

The situation was impossible. It was as if I had been teleported from the main tunnel to a double dead-end tunnel that measured some thirty feet in length and eight feet in diameter, with no connection to any other tunnel. I wasn't terrified but I was getting there fast as tried to find a rational explanation for this incredible an puzzling circumstance.

My horizontal attitude and natural viewing ang gave me a bird's-eye view of the solid rock floor scanned all four sides of my prison without seeing a means of escape. Eventually I glanced upward. A dor shaped opening pierced the top at one end of the tun I rose into the dome . . . and found myself staring at gold line, which extended left and right.

In a flash I knew exactly how my predicamen curred. The short length of tunnel was positione neath and perpendicular to the main tunnel. Whe light went out and I stopped the scooter, the s slowly settled and curved to the right, taking a t trajectory into the lower tunnel without my feeli sensation of sinking or turning.

cave-diving guide, he was able to obtain permission for us to dive in two of the State's most hallowed caves: Eagle's Nest and Diepolder II.

These caves held the grandeur to remind me of why I got into diving in the first place. What I liked about these caves was not that they were deep, but that they were huge. I had interesting experiences in both of them.

Steve led the way into Diepolder II by sliding down a long slanted tunnel that was a fracture zone. Visibility was poor until we bottomed out in the transverse tunnel at 190 feet. We proceeded into a room that was truly gargantuan. It reminded me more of Carlsbad Caverns than Laurel Creek Cave or Blue Hole. I was enthralled by the immensity of the room, yet was disappointed that it contained no flowstone formations.

Standard practice for cave-diving was strict adherence to the Thirds Rule: proceed into a cave until one-third of your air was consumed, then turn around and breathe another one-third on the way out, leaving one-third for emergency use. Because of my bad lung, I was always the one who reached thirds first, and had to "turn" or "call" the dive. I monitored my gauge faithfully, and alerted Steve as soon as I had breathed one-third of my air.

I led the retreat to the vertical tunnel and during the ascent to our first decompression stop. Thereafter we ascended in tandem to subsequent stops. We separated after we exited the vertical tunnel and entered the broad pool in the middle of the forest. There we conducted the bulk of our decompression in clear water with bright ambient light.

I went to the place where I had stashed a thick hardcover book under a rock at the beginning of the dive. The title was *The Berkut*, by Joseph Heywood. I had started reading it during the decompression phase of a dive several days earlier. I kept the book wet between dives by stowing it in a sealable plastic bag. That way the paper didn't dry out and stick together. Reading kept my mind from boredom during decompression obligations that exceeded an hour.

I was still decompressing at my 20-foot stop, and engulfed in the story, when the book was nearly yanked out of my hands. I glanced up, expecting to see Steve trying to attract my attention. Instead I saw a giant snapping turtle with the tattered spine held tightly in its beak! I was appalled. Turtles didn't read, so why would it want to steal my book? I suspect that the pealing and waving spine must have looked like food to a turtle that was either vision impaired or dimwitted.

I yanked the book back from the turtle's clenched jaws. For a moment it seemed as if the turtle might attack me. We had a staring contest that lasted for several seconds. Then the turtle slowly turned and paddled after other game. Now I looked around and saw that I was surrounded by snapping turtles, none of which measured shorter than a foot in length. I counted at least ten. I tore off the flapping spine and threw it away. Thereafter the turtles ignored me and my deteriorating book.

Steve and I made two dives in Eagle's Nest. This cave is truly spectacular. From the bottom of a pond there extended a vertical shaft that was nearly circular, much like a storm drain pipe that was laid on end. At around 60 feet, this tubular shaft opened suddenly into a huge, bell-shaped ballroom that measured several hundred feet across at its base. Directly beneath the entrance shaft was a mound of loose rock that rose to a depth of about 140 feet. A cathedral could easily fit in this mammoth room.

We descended along the upstream tunnel to a depth of 280 feet, at which point I reached thirds and gave the thumb-up signal to turn the dive. My breathing became labored during the angled ascent. Within a couple of minutes I was breathing heavily. I checked my tank pressure gauge and saw that I had plenty of air remaining. I started to get out of breath. I couldn't understand what was wrong. I felt around the mouthpiece . . . and discovered that the air flow switch on the second stage of my Poseidon Odin regulator was set in the negative position. This position restricted the flow of air. As soon as I pushed the lever to the positive position, air was lit-

bulls and cows. Or perhaps they just wanted to escape the summer heat.

(Note: in *The Lusitania Controversies*, I mistakenly gave the dimensions of the opening of this cave as 40 feet high and 110 feet wide. In fact, those were the dimensions of a great interior chamber.)

My fellow cavers on this trip were Greg Carr, Kenny Enright, and Tom Gmitter. Instead of pitching tents, we laid our sleeping bags inside the entrance on dry ground next to the flowing creek. We got wet even though we were sheltered from the weather because condensation dripped constantly from the ceiling. We were not bothered by cattle. We spent three days exploring the cavern's vast and extensive interior.

The cave that changed the course of my life was Blue Hole, in Virginia. This was where I encountered an underground river that was 50 feet deep. Al Dubeck, Tom Gmitter, and I lowered an inflatable raft 90 feet into a sink hole into an underground river, and paddled half a mile upstream. When the ceiling curved down to water level and prevented farther passage, I determined to take a diving course in order to continue my exploration.

I knew that dive courses were given by the YMCA (Young Men's Christian Association). I found the local

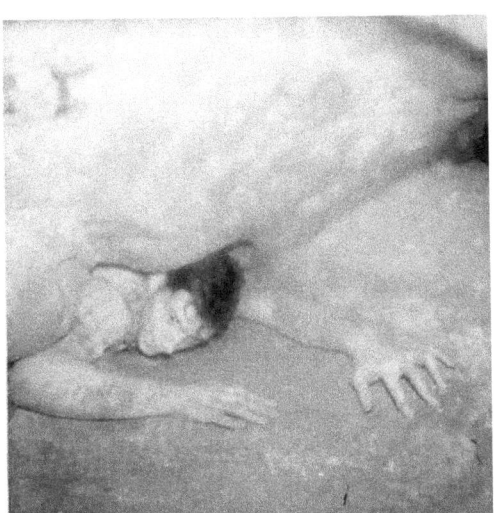

Tight squeeze! This picture was taken in Nestle Quarry Cave, West Virginia, with my Kodak Instamatic camera and flash. I generally wore a hard-hat with a carbide lamp affixed to the front, but it wouldn't fit through this narrow crevice.

branch in the phone book, called, and signed up for the next course. (For more details on both these caverns, read Book One of *The Lusitania Controversies*.)

Florida Cave-Diving Adventures

I started cave-diving the year after I received my open-water certification. At that time, cave-diving certifications did not exist. Undaunted by my lack of knowledge and experience, I dived in a handful of caves in Florida, albeit without penetrating beyond the light zone. I was never able to convince any of my fellow divers to lower a raft and dive gear 90 feet down the sink hole that was the entrance to Blue Hole.

Then I got distracted by the exploration of shipwrecks, and put cave-diving on the back burner for a couple of decades. I finally received my cave-diving certification in 1991. My instructor was the redoubtable Steve Berman. I described some of my cave-diving adventures in Book Two of *The Lusitania Controversies* (subtitled "Dangerous Descents into Shipwrecks and Law").

It is worthwhile at this point to note the difference in definitions between dry-caving and cave-diving factions. In dry-caving, a "cave" is a hollow or overhang such as a troglodyte might inhabit, with sunlight being visible from the farthest reaches of the interior; a "cavern" refers to an extensive system of tunnels or rooms where no outside light ever reaches. In cave-diving the definitions are just the opposite: a cavern resides within the light zone, whereas a cave is an extension that is totally void of light.

My exploration of Florida caves was only half-hearted. I was not overly entranced by miles and miles of wet rock. Perhaps it reminded me too much of the drab and unadorned concrete walls of the storm drains. Dry caves had the advantage of being decorated with flowstone formations: stalactites (from the ceiling), stalagmites (from the ground), and columns (from the ceiling to the ground). But submerged Florida caves were barren and lacking in esthetic appeal – at least for a photographer.

The main attraction to adherents of Florida cave-diving was generally length of penetration.

The only subjects that I found of photographic interest in Florida caves were fossils. Steve Berman showed me where fossil shells were exposed in the entrance tunnel of Ginnie Springs. I wanted to photograph them; he wanted to make a scooter run.

During a previous scooter run that we did together, Steve was passing around a curve ahead of me when my canister light suddenly blacked out, leaving me in total darkness. I stopped the scooter while I fumbled with the light switch. It took only a few seconds to switch the light back on, but when I did, I found myself in unfamiliar surroundings, facing a blank wall at the end of a tunnel. I was momentarily nonplussed. When I turned around, I saw another blank wall at the opposite end of the tunnel.

The gold line – the permanent guideline that marked the main tunnel – was nowhere in sight!

The situation was impossible. It was as if I had been teleported from the main tunnel to a double dead-end tunnel that measured some thirty feet in length and eight feet in diameter, with no connection to any other tunnel. I wasn't terrified but I was getting there fast as I tried to find a rational explanation for this incredible and puzzling circumstance.

My horizontal attitude and natural viewing angle gave me a bird's-eye view of the solid rock floor. I scanned all four sides of my prison without seeing any means of escape. Eventually I glanced upward. A dome-shaped opening pierced the top at one end of the tunnel. I rose into the dome . . . and found myself staring at the gold line, which extended left and right.

In a flash I knew exactly how my predicament occurred. The short length of tunnel was positioned beneath and perpendicular to the main tunnel. When my light went out and I stopped the scooter, the scooter slowly settled and curved to the right, taking a twisted trajectory into the lower tunnel without my feeling any sensation of sinking or turning.

When Steve noticed that I was no longer behind him, he waited patiently until I caught up with him and gave him the okay sign.

On another scooter run, I was leading the return when I spotted a gray lead weight in the silt at the bottom of the main tunnel. I slowed down to retrieve it. The "weight" turned out to be a Beuchat Aladin Pro decompression computer! I was ecstatic at my good luck in finding such a valuable piece of equipment. I perfunctorily checked my gauges . . . and discovered that one of my two computers was missing!

The computer I found was my own. The factory-furnished strap had broken, and the computer had dropped off my gauge panel on the way into the cave. I never would have found the computer if it had fallen off during a wreck-dive.

Back to the fossils . . . I wanted to shoot photographs, Steve wanted to test a reconditioned scooter. So we split up. I stayed in the entrance tunnel and shot a roll of film. Steve zoomed between the "lips" into the long and convoluted interior.

The so-called "lips" was a restriction at the end of the entrance tunnel, where the cavern turned sharply to the right. After I exposed thirty-six frames of film, I wandered around the entrance tunnel to see if there was anything significant that I had missed. Then I had a bright idea. Under the lower lip was a small alcove. I swam into this alcove, switched off my light, and rested in total darkness.

After a while I saw a faint glimmer of light passing between the lips. I looked up, spotted the headlight of Steve's scooter, then ducked back into concealment. I held my breath so as not to exhale any bubbles. Just as Steve passed overhead, I reached up and clamped both hands around one leg. I startled him so badly that his entire body shook and shivered like a vibrating tuning fork.

We remained good friends nonetheless. For years afterward, I made periodic treks to Florida in order to dive with him in his favorite caves. Because he was a certified cave-diving guide, he was able to obtain permission for us to dive in two of the State's most hallowed caves: Eagle's Nest and Diepolder II.

These caves held the grandeur to remind me of why I got into diving in the first place. What I liked about these caves was not that they were deep, but that they were huge. I had interesting experiences in both of them.

Steve led the way into Diepolder II by sliding down a long slanted tunnel that was a fracture zone. Visibility was poor until we bottomed out in the transverse tunnel at 190 feet. We proceeded into a room that was truly gargantuan. It reminded me more of Carlsbad Caverns than Laurel Creek Cave or Blue Hole. I was enthralled by the immensity of the room, yet was disappointed that it contained no flowstone formations.

Standard practice for cave-diving was strict adherence to the Thirds Rule: proceed into a cave until one-third of your air was consumed, then turn around and breathe another one-third on the way out, leaving one-third for emergency use. Because of my bad lung, I was always the one who reached thirds first, and had to "turn" or "call" the dive. I monitored my gauge faithfully, and alerted Steve as soon as I had breathed one-third of my air.

I led the retreat to the vertical tunnel and during the ascent to our first decompression stop. Thereafter we ascended in tandem to subsequent stops. We separated after we exited the vertical tunnel and entered the broad pool in the middle of the forest. There we conducted the bulk of our decompression in clear water with bright ambient light.

I went to the place where I had stashed a thick hardcover book under a rock at the beginning of the dive. The title was *The Berkut*, by Joseph Heywood. I had started reading it during the decompression phase of a dive several days earlier. I kept the book wet between dives by stowing it in a sealable plastic bag. That way the paper didn't dry out and stick together. Reading kept my mind from boredom during decompression obligations that exceeded an hour.

I was still decompressing at my 20-foot stop, and engulfed in the story, when the book was nearly yanked out of my hands. I glanced up, expecting to see Steve trying to attract my attention. Instead I saw a giant snapping turtle with the tattered spine held tightly in its beak! I was appalled. Turtles didn't read, so why would it want to steal my book? I suspect that the pealing and waving spine must have looked like food to a turtle that was either vision impaired or dimwitted.

I yanked the book back from the turtle's clenched jaws. For a moment it seemed as if the turtle might attack me. We had a staring contest that lasted for several seconds. Then the turtle slowly turned and paddled after other game. Now I looked around and saw that I was surrounded by snapping turtles, none of which measured shorter than a foot in length. I counted at least ten. I tore off the flapping spine and threw it away. Thereafter the turtles ignored me and my deteriorating book.

Steve and I made two dives in Eagle's Nest. This cave is truly spectacular. From the bottom of a pond there extended a vertical shaft that was nearly circular, much like a storm drain pipe that was laid on end. At around 60 feet, this tubular shaft opened suddenly into a huge, bell-shaped ballroom that measured several hundred feet across at its base. Directly beneath the entrance shaft was a mound of loose rock that rose to a depth of about 140 feet. A cathedral could easily fit in this mammoth room.

We descended along the upstream tunnel to a depth of 280 feet, at which point I reached thirds and gave the thumb-up signal to turn the dive. My breathing became labored during the angled ascent. Within a couple of minutes I was breathing heavily. I checked my tank pressure gauge and saw that I had plenty of air remaining. I started to get out of breath. I couldn't understand what was wrong. I felt around the mouthpiece . . . and discovered that the air flow switch on the second stage of my Poseidon Odin regulator was set in the negative position. This position restricted the flow of air. As soon as I pushed the lever to the positive position, air was literally shoved down my throat with each inhalation. Soon I was breathing easily again.

On the next dive in Eagle's Nest, Steve filled our tanks with trimix. I made certain that the air flow switch was in the positive position. The dive went smoothly. I had lost none of my admiration for the sheer immensity of the ballroom. I spent my deeper decompression stops in circling the top of the room, poking my nose into every crook and cranny. Then we decompressed in the close confines of the entrance tube.

I didn't have a book with me this time, so once we reached the bottom of the pond, I went exploring. Miniature freshwater flounder lay hidden everywhere; they measured only an inch or two in length, and were quite skittish when I reached out to touch them. They must have mistaken me for a predatory snapping turtle.

Fossil seashells littered the rocky bottom. I fanned away the thin layer of sand in order to expose fossils that were hidden. In no time I collected a large assortment of shells. After a while I glanced around for Steve. He was nowhere in the pond.

When I checked the readout of my decompression computer, I saw that zero decompression remained. I surfaced to find that Steve was already dressed in street clothes, and was nonchalantly waiting for me by his pickup truck. I had been having such a good time in collecting fossils that I did twenty minutes more decompression than was necessary.

I kept diving with Steve until his tragic and untimely death. I miss him sorely.

Which brings us to the subject matter of the present chapter.

Yucatan Bound!

Steve Berman organized cave-diving trips to Mexico, in order to dive in the wondrous caves of the region known as the Riviera Maya, in the Yucatan Peninsula. I knew about these trips, but because of my extensive wreck-diving priorities and my work on my Popular Dive Guide Series, I never took the time to accompany him.

One diver who went on a number of Steve's Yucatan trips was Marcie Bilinski. She was a long-time wreck-diver and cave-diver who lived in Massachusetts. She operated her own boat: a 36-foot Sea Ray which she named *SeaDuctress*. After Steve's passing, Marcie took the torch of organizing annual trips to Yucatan. She was a natural for the job because she knew most of the caves, she was acquainted with many of the people in the local cave-diving community, and she spoke fluent Spanish.

I didn't know Marcie, but I was introduced to her when I started to make contacts in Massachusetts, in order to obtain information on wrecks to cover in my forthcoming book, *Shipwrecks of Massachusetts*. She was indispensible in helping me with my work. She took me to numerous wrecks in Boston Harbor and the outer approaches, and she dived with me in order to help with the survey work.

When she learned that I was a certified cave-diver, and that Steve Berman had been my cave-diving instructor, she suggested that I go on her next trip to Yucatan. When I showed some interest, she made me an offer that I couldn't refuse. No, she didn't put a horse-head in my bed; she offered to use some of her frequent flier miles to obtain a free plane ticket for me.

She traveled by air so much for work that she had racked up hundreds of thousands of frequent flier miles – more than she could ever use for herself. The plane ticket wouldn't cost her anything.

I told her, "Sign me up."

She did.

I have now been on three Yucatan trips with Marcie. For a while it seemed as if the first trip would never get off the ground – quite literally. What follows is my worst air-travel horror story, bar none.

Travel Travails

According to the flight plan, Marcie and the rest of the gang were flying out of Boston. I was flying out of Philadelphia. We were supposed to rendezvous at Washington Dulles International Airport, where we were scheduled to transfer to the plane for Cancun. The schedule called for a one-hour layover between the arrival of my plane at Washington Dulles and the departure of the plane for Cancun. United Airlines operated all flights.

My Philly departure was delayed for forty-five minutes, first by a minor mechanical problem, then by traffic on the tarmac. Because of these delays, by the time my plane reached Washington Dulles, another plane was occupying our assigned gate. All other United Airlines gates were also occupied. My plane was therefore redirected to an American Airlines gate.

United Airlines operated out of Concourse D. American Airlines operated out of Concourse A. Each of these concourses was isolated from the terminal and from each other – much like islands in a 12,000-acre lake. I couldn't run from one concourse to the other; I had to take a bus. The bus operated not on the immediacy of the passengers, like a taxi, but on a schedule. I ran to the bus platform, but then had to wait for the bus to arrive. After it arrived, I then had to wait for the bus's scheduled time of departure. The bus then weaved around airplanes that were either taxiing or docked, taking a circuitous route that was agonizing in its slothfulness.

As the bus finally pulled up to the Concourse D platform, I saw the boarding bridge being retracted from my Cancun plane at the adjacent gate. I ran off the bus as soon as the driver opened the doors. I made the fifty-yard dash to the gate in record time. The plane was sitting idle less than forty feet from the gate. Breathlessly I told the gate attendant that I had to get on that plane.

She informed me nastily that once the doors were closed they could not be reopened because a delayed departure would incur a hefty fine from the Federal Aviation Administration. This was a bold-faced lie! Yet I have been told this falsehood on more than one occasion.

The FAA couldn't care less whether or not a plane disengaged from its gate on time. Flight schedules were not maintained by the FAA, but by the airlines, and for their own benefit. Gates – indeed, entire concourses – were owned or leased by the airlines without FAA interest, approval, or intervention. The FAA imposes no fines or penalties for late departures. Airline policy was responsible for what the gate attendant blamed the FAA.

In addition to all of the above, what good does it do when a jetway is retracted or a plane closes its doors if the plane doesn't back away from the gate and taxi to the runway in preparation for takeoff? That action doesn't qualify as adherence to a schedule.

Whenever airlines want to evade responsibility for company policies, they invoke the FAA. Passengers believe what they are told because they don't know any better. FAA regulations sound more authoritative than absurd company policies.

Three other people arrived behind me. Two women had been on my plane from Philly. One man was on the same bus from Concourse A. We all argued with the attendant to deploy the retractable bridge so that we could board. She kept shaking her head. She refused to call the pilot or anyone else in authority. She just kept insisting that the plane was not "allowed" to open its door once it was closed.

The plane did not move. It sat there for ten more minutes while we kept up a running quarrel with the gate attendant. She was adamant in her refusal to help. Eventually the plane backed away from the gate, turned, taxied to the runway, and then *idled in place for half an hour* before departing for Cancun without all of its passengers. The gate attendant informed us that we were not the only ones to miss the flight. Several other people were on a connecting flight that was still in the air.

The plane arrived in Cancun more than fifteen minutes ahead of schedule.

The only advice that the gate attendant gave us was to go to the reservation desk and try to get on the next plane to Cancun – which, she informed us, was not scheduled to depart until the following day. Although she could have done this from her console, she walked away and left us in the lurch. We had to fend for ourselves.

Before proceeding farther with this manmade horror story, let me back up in order to present two other viewpoints that demonstrate the depths to which the airline stooped to proactively thwart amelioration of the circumstances.

The two women were part of a tour group that was vacationing in Cancun. They were friends with others in the group, all of whom lived in different parts of the country. This was their third trip to Cancun with the same group. As soon as the Philly plane landed, and "approved" electronic devices were permitted to be used, one of the two women switched on her cell phone and called the group leader, who was sitting in the Cancun plane and who was waiting for the rest of the group to arrive. Passengers were still boarding.

When the stream of passengers stopped, the group leader informed a flight attendant that two of the group were on the ground and were on their way to the gate. The group leader asked the flight attendant to inform the pilot of their imminent arrival. The woman and the group leader kept the phone line open between them. By means of this running dialogue, they were able to provide the flight attendant with a continuous report of their progress. Thus the pilot knew exactly when we reached the bus platform, when we boarded the bus, and when the bus left the platform.

At the same time, *my* group leader was in *direct* communication with the pilot and copilot. Because Marcie flew with United Airlines so often for work, she was a high-mileage Gold Star member with special privileges. When the stream of passengers stopped, she informed a flight attendant that she needed to speak with the pilot. Marcie was permitted to enter the cockpit. She explained the situation to the pilot and copilot. By communicating via radio with company officials, they confirmed that my plane had departed late from Philly, but had already landed in Dulles.

Marcie pleaded with the pilot to postpone departure

until I could reach the gate. Both the pilot and copilot said that they wanted to help but they were instructed by a higher authority to close the door. Then they idled the plane forty feet from the gate while they completed their preflight checks.

Marcie saw me through the huge picture window when I arrived at the gate. She watched as I argued with the gate attendant. She pointed me out to the pilot and copilot. Once again they communicated with the tower. Airline officials refused to give permission to open the door of the aircraft and to deploy the retractable bridge, or to let us board on a moving stairway. They ordered the plane to depart as soon as the flight crew completed their preflight checks. Marcie kept the pilot and copilot engaged in ardent conversation, trying to persuade them to let me board the plane – but to no avail. They said that they had to follow instructions; they did not have override authority.

To recapitulate: the flight crew, the air controllers, and company officials knew that the four of us had landed in Dulles and were within seconds of reaching the gate before the plane's doors were closed and the jetway was retracted. The gate attendant knew when we actually arrived. The plane idled forty feet from the gate and sat in place for ten minutes while the pilot and copilot completed their preflight checks. Company officials instructed the plane to depart, with full knowledge that four passengers were standing at the gate. In effect, they ordered us to be left behind overnight. Then the plane sat on the tarmac for another thirty minutes.

At least three of us would have reached the gate on time if the Philly plane had docked at its pre-assigned gate (or any other gate in the United Airlines concourse) because that gate was right next to the gate of the Cancun plane. The docking deviation caused three of us to be late. The seats that we would have occupied remained empty.

I understand and accept complications that are caused by weather. Mankind is subservient to Mother Nature and acts of God. The absurdity of *this* situation is that it could have been avoided; or the issue could have been resolved had those in authority chosen to do so. Instead, company officials made a conscious decision to strand its passengers overnight. Not only did this decision lack ordinary compassion for the plight of the airline's customers, it was a decision that made no sense in terms of business and public relations. A little forbearance would have gone a long way toward ensuring that customer service was a company priority.

In the aftermath, the four of us were left to our own devices.

My personal position was particularly precarious because I didn't know where in Mexico I was going: not only did I not know the name of the condominium, I didn't even know what city it was in. I was depending on Marcie to lead the way after I joined the group. She had arranged the flights, the car rental, and the accommodations. As a result of my separation and lack of knowledge, my anxiety level was high.

We four beleaguered travelers stuck together for mutual support. More than one hundred other displaced passengers were thronged in front of the United Airlines service desk. While the other three stood in line, I grabbed a red help phone and got in the reservation queue. I got help before the other three were halfway to the desk (less than half an hour later). I was able to get a seat on the following day's flight. I got seats for my erstwhile companions as well. I called them to me and gave their names to the reservation assistant. We were fortunate that seats were available on the next day's flight. Otherwise, we might have been stranded for days.

We were stuck in the airport overnight, so next we descended upon a United Airlines help desk to see about our luggage and what sleeping accommodations could be made available to us. In less than short order we were told that our luggage had been placed in a secure holding facility from which it could not be retrieved. I didn't believe that our luggage couldn't be retrieved; I believed that no one wanted to bother to retrieve it. In either event, this left us without toilet articles, personal belongings, and a change of clothes.

(I always used to carry my toothbrush and toothpaste in my vest pocket, but I stopped doing so when toothpaste was banned as a carry-on item.)

The only thing the help desk helpers would do for us was to make reservations at the airport hotel. The airline denied culpability for missing our flight. Therefore we would have to pay for our lodging . . . at more than $100 per room. The two women shared a room and split the cost. The man and I declined; we each went our separate ways.

My close friend Dave Bluett lived not too far from the airport, in Vienna. For the past twenty years, I had stayed at his house whenever I did research in Washington, DC. I didn't know his phone number and I didn't have my address book with me, but by great good fortune he was listed in the directory. And equally as fortunately, he had recently retired and was at home when I called. He picked me up and took me back to his house.

I called Marcie's cell phone. She was still in flight so she did not have her phone switched on. I left a message. She called me at Dave's house later that night, after her arrival in Mexico. The airline debacle caused the whole group to miss the first day's diving, because Marcie had to take the car and drive an hour and a half to Cancun to pick me up in the middle of the day.

You might think that I am ranting unjustly about a situation that can be viewed as an inconvenience. I agree that I am ranting, but I believe that my ranting is justified. This situation was not *just* an inconvenience; it was a *major* inconvenience. And it was one that was created intentionally by apathetic airline employees who could have ordered the doors opened and the jetway extended so that the other passengers and I could board. This action would not even have delayed the plane's departure, as the plane did not back away until ten minutes after our arrival at the gate.

The gate attendant was indifferent to our plight. The flight crew wanted to help but were stymied. The reservation desk assistant was exceedingly helpful. The help desk helpers were supportive and sympathetic, but were not authorized by airline protocol to extend free lodging for the night; nor could they personally get our luggage out of hock. We would have had to complain to the proper authority, but the help desk helpers didn't know who that authority was. The best they could suggest was to check with the people in baggage claim, or with someone above them in the corporate hierarchy.

The real culprits were the airline officials who blindly followed established airline policy instead of responding reasonably to the situation. United was disunited.

Dave drove me to the airport in the morning. My three friends-in-need were also there. The flight went without a hitch.

The heat in Mexico was oppressive. I started sweating immediately. But my separation anxiety ended as soon as I saw Marcie in the crowd. I was never so glad to be back in the fold as I was at that moment.

We had a lot to talk about as we headed southward. Our destination was Puerto Aventuras, a drive of about an hour and a half along the east coast of the Yucatan Peninsula, in the state of Quintana Roo. I decided then and there that I would never again rely on United Airlines – or any airline, for that matter – for logistical support. On my two subsequent cave-diving trips (both with Marcie), I drove to Boston and boarded the plane with the rest of the group. That way, I figured, if United Airlines stranded us, it stranded all of us together.

Although Mexico lies only across the border from the United States, the nation was so different that it could have been on another planet. I don't mean just cultural differences such as language, living conditions, government, art, architecture, heritage, and so on. American tourists might look upon Mexico as a police state.

Uniformed officers thronged the airport. Police vehicles patrolled the streets in swarms. The highway to Puerto Aventuras was guarded by soldiers who carried automatic weapons. Army outposts were stationed along the road. There were periodic way stations where vehicles could be stopped for inspection by heavily armed troops. Some stores had armed guards who kept an eye on vehicles as they entered the parking lot. Constabularies milled and mingled with the crowd in shopping malls.

Yet despite this obvious military presence, civilian life went on as if nothing were amiss; as if the proliferation of men-at-arms was a normal state of affairs. In Mexico, it was. For law-abiding citizens, there was little or no intervention from government combatants. Neither the police nor the soldiers intruded upon the general populace when they were conducting their affairs in a lawful manner.

I quickly noted the difference between a patrolman in Mexico and his counterpart in Venezuela. In Caracas, an overbearing street cop had threatened me with his gun because I wanted to take his photograph. In Quintana Roo, the police ignored me completely. They were there to keep the peace, not to harass the citizenry. I felt safe in Mexico because the police and the soldiers were after criminals, not innocent tourists or honest citizens.

Marcie and I were only halfway to Puerto Aventuras when the engine conked out. She coasted onto the shoulder and let the car roll to a stop. No amount of trying would restart the engine. I lifted the hood and made a perfunctory look at the engine and its accessories, but unless some overt mechanical malfunction reached out and punched me in the face, I was merely going through the motions.

Marcie called Hertz on her cell phone. Hertz promised to dispatch a mechanic from Cancun, but we could not expect help to arrive for at least a couple of hours. We were stranded in the hot sun in the middle of nowhere.

After half an hour or so, Marcie retried the starter and, lo and behold, the engine cranked over. I slammed down the hood and jumped into the passenger seat. We raced for the condominium in Puerto Aventuras. The car got us there, but after we parked and Marcie made a trial restart, the engine refused to crank over.

She called Hertz again and told them that she no longer had any confidence in the car. She wanted a different car. After some argument, Hertz reluctantly agreed to send a replacement. We didn't dare use the car again for fear that it would strand us somewhere else, so we stayed put for the rest of the day. The replacement car was not delivered until 11 o'clock that night.

So far, I wasn't having a good time on this trip. But then we started diving the next day, and the first dive made all my suffering worthwhile.

The Realm of Fantasyland

My introduction to Yucatan cave-diving began on January 19, 2007. My buddies on that first dive were Marcie Bilinski and Butch Amaral. We donned wetsuits to brave water that registered 77° on the thermometer. I wore a lightweight hood but no gloves. This was a far cry from drysuit diving in Florida caves.

Marcie guided us through a system that was known as Chac Mool. I didn't take my camera on the orientation dive. I wanted to observe my surroundings and enjoy the experience.

I logged the visibility as 100 feet, but in fact it may have been greater. The limitations on visibility were straight line of sight and light beam penetration. If we had entered a room that measured 200 feet across, I might well have been able to see the opposite side, and I certainly would have seen another diver's light beam on the opposite wall.

It took only five minutes for Yucatan cave-diving to exceed my expectations. We were still in the light zone when I spotted flowstone formations that adorned a nearby wall. The vertical surface was covered with undulating ribbons that were tinged with orange. A section of ceiling that was farther away was full of sharply pointed stalactites that reminded me of quills on a porcupine's hide, or perhaps the interior of an iron maiden (a Renaissance torture device whose two halves were lined with spikes that pierced a person's body when the

Chac Mool.

halves were closed).

There was no end of wonders to appreciate as we proceeded deeper into the cave. One entire chamber was filled with delicate soda-straw stalactites. Elsewhere, massive blocks of flowstone lay at odd angles on the floor, the result of collapse that occurred when the enormous weight of accumulated limestone exceeded its strength of attachment. It was as if a giant explorer had swept through the room breaking off not individual stalactites, but large conglomerations. Cabin-sized rooms were adorned on all sides with stalactites that were the length of spears, and that were just as pointed.

Maximum depth was 42 feet. During 52 minutes of bottom time, my only moment of anxiety occurred when the guideline dipped beneath the halocline and became difficult if not impossible to see.

A halocline is similar to a thermocline. A thermocline is a horizontal line of demarcation where warm water rests atop cold water, because cold water is denser and therefore heavier than warm water; the two masses of water will not readily mix. A halocline is a horizontal line of demarcation between fresh water above and salt water below. In this case, sodium chloride in salt water makes it denser and therefore heavier than fresh water, so the salt water settles to the bottom and supports the fresh water above it.

Unlike a thermocline, a halocline has a mixing zone that separates the fresh water from the salt water. The mixing zone might be a foot or two thick. Where the fresh water and salt water mix, the turbulence creates a swirling effect that gives the saline solution an "oily" appearance. Visibility is clear both above and below the mixing zone. But anything within the mixing zone – such as a guideline or a fellow diver – appears distorted. When the thin guideline is distorted it becomes nearly invisible. This partial invisibility accounted for my trepidation.

Light beams reflect off the mixing zone when played at an oblique angle. From above, the mixing zone then has every appearance of a highly reflective floor, yielding the impression that one is floating on water in an air-filled chamber. From below, the mixing zone may look like a ceiling. These visual effects were fun to play with once I became accustomed to them. But I never got used to being unable to perceive the guideline.

Chac Mool was a learning experience as well as a bold eye-opener. And this was only the beginning.

The Geology of Cave Formation

Most of the rock that forms the Yucatan Peninsula is limestone. Limestone, or calcium carbonate, is readily soluble. Natural acids in rainwater and groundwater dissolve limestone and wash it away to create a jagged surface that is gouged full of holes, giving it the appearance of serrated Swiss cheese. Geologists refer to this rugged kind of terrain as karst topography.

As acidic water flows along cracks and bedding planes, it dissolves the subterranean limestone to create a convoluted system of underground passageways: a process that is ongoing and self-expanding. This process is called "phreatic action," in which phreatic refers to groundwater. When these passageways grow large enough for a person to enter, they are called caves – or, more specifically, solution caves.

Riviera Maya is a collective name for the vast drainage area that extends from Cancun to Tulum: a distance of approximately 80 miles. Nearly all the rivers flow underground until they reach the Caribbean Sea. Each river is called a "system." These systems are accessed by breakdowns in the overlying rock, where the groundwater is exposed to the air.

In the United States, this breakdown is called a sink hole. In Mexico, it's called a cenote. Cenote is not pronounced with two syllables, as in C note (a hundred dollar bill, short for century note), but with three syllables; the accent is on the middle syllable.

Seawater percolates a considerable distance through porous limestone. This is why salt water is found in the bottom of caves along the coast. The level or depth of this salt water is slightly variable. It is generally found below 35 to 40 feet. Caves in which the water is shallower than 35 feet will not have a halocline.

There are no formations in submerged Florida caves, and there are no caves in Yucatan without formations. This is because formations can't grow in water-filled caves. Formations can grow only in dry caves. Water

The cenote at right is so tiny that a normal sized person cannot fit into it. (Note my shoe for scale.) The cenote at the bottom of the opposite page is large enough to function as a group swimming hole.

that percolates through the rock above a dry cave carries dissolved minerals in solution. When a droplet evaporates from the ceiling, the minerals are precipitated out of the solution. After thousands or tens of thousands of years, these minerals assume definite form in relation to other variables: relative humidity, mineral content, crystal forming tendency, and so on.

Florida caves have always been submerged, whereas Yucatan caves were dry sometime in the past. Formations grew during dry spells, perhaps when the water table was lower, such as during the Ice Age when much of the Earth's water was bound in the form of ice at the poles; or perhaps due to tectonic movement when plates or the landmass was raised. Melting polar ice or the subsiding landmass then depressed the caves to below the water table, at which time they were flooded.

The growth of formations stopped once the caves were inundated. On the other hand, sometimes the water table fluctuated throughout the millennia. In this case the water table stabilized at different levels. The history of stabilization can be seen in stalactites whose bottoms are flattened where they terminated at a previous water level, at which time the dissolved minerals were dispersed in the river, or the precipitation of minerals spread outward to create a flat stub instead of a point.

In this fashion Yucatan caves became a wonderland of submerged formations of endless size and variety.

Cenotes and Man

Cenotes came to popular attention in the middle of the twentieth century, when archaeologists started dredging operations in Mexican sink holes that produced Mayan artifacts. Archaeologists interpreted these relics as sacrificial offerings with religious associations, but much of what they found could just as easily be explained by comparing the beads, potsherds, effigies, and marble-sized metal bells to coins in a fountain or wishing well. It is possible that the recovered items were discarded because they were no longer wanted or had outlived their usefulness: in other words, rubbish.

More funding is available for archaeological digs than is available for the examination of trash dumps, so archaeology was stressed. This is another way of saying that one person's trash is another person's treasure. It is interesting to note that the Mayans disposed of their refuse in water long before ocean dumping became a convenient if questionable method of disposal.

Archaeologists have built a picture of Mesoamerican culture that is based largely on artifacts, stone pictograms, and codices. Yet less than 3% of ancient Mayan ideograms have been deciphered or interpreted, and there is no guarantee that these so-called translations are accurate, or even close to their intended meaning.

The popular myth about the Mayans practicing human sacrifice is just that: a myth. There is no documentation or oral tradition to substantiate the practice. But it sells books and it looks dramatic on film. The only mention of human sacrifice came from conquering Spaniards, who were prejudiced because they looked upon the Mayans as backwards and undeveloped, worthy only as slaves to do Spanish bidding.

After the archaeologists came the cave-divers. Little if any archaeology is conducted in cenotes any more, but the exploration of submerged caves has become a fervid pastime that attracts scuba divers from around the world. Some of these caves have been measured and mapped, some of them have yet to be fully explored, and some remain to be discovered.

Nomenclature Convention

As I mentioned above, an underground river is called a system. Like rivers, systems have been given names. I made my first dive in the system that is known as Chac Mool. This name is Mayan, not Mexican or Spanish, although some systems have Spanish names, such as Dos Ojos. Some systems have English names, such as Ponderosa and Carwash. Some systems have multiple names: one in Mayan and one in English.

Cenotes also have names. If a system has only one known cenote, the cenote is often named after the system. Chac Mool is the name of the system as well as the name of the cenote.

Some systems have more than one cenote. In these cases, each cenote has its own name. One cenote might be named after the system, while the other cenotes will have names that distinguish them from the primary entrance.

The system/cenote nomenclature might read something like this: Sac Aktun/Grand Cenote, or X'Tabay/Chiken Ha.

When talking about dive sites, cave-divers generally disregard the name of the system and mention only the name of the cenote that is associated with it. To my knowledge, the names of systems and cenotes are unique.

Anyone who wants to learn more about cave-diving in Yucatan should obtain a copy of Steve Gerrard's indispensable book on the subject, *The Cenotes of the Riviera Maya*. It is replete with maps, directions, descriptions, and spectacular color photographs.

The Dangers and Disciplines of Cave-Diving

Scuba diving possesses inherent dangers. Cave-diving is more dangerous than open-water diving because there is no direct access to the surface. If you have an equipment failure half a mile inside a cave, you have to deal with the problem on the spot, because the surface is half a mile away. There is no such thing as a free ascent in cave-diving. Snorkels are useless.

For this reason cave-divers rely on backups: two tanks, two regulators, two lights, and at least two divers diving together. Cave-divers also carry more than one line reel.

Local cave-divers have installed permanent guidelines in well-known caves. A guideline may start several hundred feet from the cenote, and may be accompanied by a sign that warns divers who lack cave-diving certifications not to proceed any farther. It is deceptively easy to get disoriented in a cave, or to create a silt-out by kicking mud off the floor.

To ensure that a returning diver can find the exit from the beginning of the permanent guideline, it is necessary first to deploy a personal guideline from the cenote to the tie-off point. The line reel is left in place and is retrieved upon exiting the cave. The practice of having a continuous guideline to the surface should never be violated.

Smaller reels called gap reels are used whenever you want to leave the primary guideline to explore a side passage. A gap reel can also be used in an emergency situation in which a diver becomes lost or disoriented. After tying off his line, he can search for the permanent guideline and be able to return to his initial tie-off point. This enables him to search in different directions without swimming around in circles and getting lost worse than he already was.

There are many activities and occupations that are more dangerous than cave-diving: skydiving, bridge construction, high steel, and combat service to name a few.

The most dangerous job in the world is the Presidency of the United States. Of forty-four Presidents, four (or nearly 10%) have been assassinated in office; two (or nearly 5%) were injured by assassination attempts; nine (or 20%) escaped injury during assassination attempts.

Granted that cave-diving is not as safe as Ping-Pong, but cave-diving discipline entails a strong measure of control by incorporating well-defined backup procedures to overcome nearly every eventuality. A cave-diver must always be on the alert, must never let down his guard, must never become complacent, and must be ready to act assertively at a moment's notice.

Roughing It

I am not going to deliver a cave-by-cave account of all my Yucatan dives. Every dive displayed its own kind of excitement. A brief overview of unusual events will adequately evoke the fun and excitement of cave-diving in general, while stressing some of the systems and cenotes in particular.

A cenote might measure a foot or two across, while others might be the size of a football field. Divers can enter the smallest cenotes only by lowering their gear on ropes, then by descending a rope and donning their gear in the water. Large cenotes may have steps or ladders from the dressing area to the water.

Most cenotes are located on private land. Landowners charge a usage or entrance fee. Some large cenotes are used as swimming holes. Those that are the most commercial, and that cater primarily to swimmers and picnickers, have parking areas, bathhouses, restrooms, and food concessions. Small cenotes that are of value only to cave-divers may not have equivalent amenities. Entrance fees range from $5 to $10 per person, sometimes more for a diver.

Because the ground consists of solid rock with only a few inches of soil on top, pit toilets cannot be dug. A toilet must be placed above a catchment.

Most of the Yucatan Peninsula is covered by impenetrable jungle. A single main road runs north/south along the eastern shore. West of this road are few incursions. The rocky roads that exist extend only a few miles into the interior. These roads – or in many cases, trails – were hacked out of the jungle by the landowners. Therefore these roads are private, not public, although the landowners generally do not prevent people from driving on them.

Grading is usually impossible because the soil that has accumulated on the bedrock is only a few inches or a couple of feet deep. Vehicles that are equipped with four-wheel-drive or have high ground clearance are recommended. Some trails are so narrow that donkeys are used to transport dive gear. A special harness can carry two sets of doubles: one on each side of the animal's back.

Some cenotes have only recently been discovered. I wondered at first why you couldn't fly a plane over the jungle, and spot every watery opening from the air. I quickly learned the reason for new discoveries. As I noted above, some cenotes are so small that you could walk right past them and not notice them. These tiny open-

The road less traveled.

The cenote Uchben Hakata cannot be seen from the air. The water begins some thirty feet inside the entrance to what appears to be a dry cave or overhang.

ings cannot be seen from the air because of overhanging trees and encroaching vegetation.

Other cenotes are not open to the sky like swimming pools, but are concealed by an overhang, much like a dry cave whose vertical entrance is carved into a cliff face. Uchben Hakata is like this. It is one of many entrances to the system known as Uchben Nach Iloob (or Uxben Nah Iloob; the spelling varies).

Sergio Granucci and his Labnaha Expeditions discovered this cenote by following a long tributary tunnel until it surfaced in a room that was connected to a dry section by means of a short passageway. He doffed his dive gear and exited the cave to find himself in the middle of the jungle. He had planned ahead by carrying a GPS receiver in a waterproof housing. He found an opening among the trees where the unit could receive a satellite signal. He marked the location as a waypoint. Then he retreated through the water to his original point of entry.

Later, he cleared a road to a central location and established a permanent campsite from which to access the system. He hacked a mile-long path through the jungle from the campsite to the newfound entrance. These preliminaries enabled him to guide divers through a system that lay far off the beaten track. This was the "wildest" cave that I encountered in Yucatan. Only a few divers have explored it so far.

Marcie and I paid Sergio $200 for the privilege of having him lead the way through this almost untouched system. He used much of the money to hire "Sherpas" to carry our tanks and gear bags. These so-called Sherpas are actually indigenous Mayans, not Nepalese porters from the Himalayas. They are short and stocky in stature, and are incredibly strong. Each carried a set of double tanks by resting them on his shoulder, or by wearing the backplate and employing a tump line. After the dive, they carried our tanks and gear bags back to the campsite. This was an all-day excursion.

The trail was rough and rugged. The heat was almost unbearable. Marcie and I doused ourselves with insect repellent that is familiarly known as "deet." Don't buy the spray brands because they are diluted with aerosols and inactive ingredients. Buy 100% deet in liq-

Two of our stalwart Mayan "Sherpas" on the jungle trail, on their return from the cenote after dropping off our tanks.

Looking out from inside the cenote Uchben Hakata. I am standing in water which deepens behind me and leads to the submerged passageway. The dressing table is on the right. The jungle and some trees are visible through the opening.

uid form, pour some onto your palms, and wipe your palms over all exposed skin. If your skin is sensitive to the active chemical – N,N-diethyl-meta-toluamide – use a 75% solution to reduce irritation. To decrease the amount of exposed skin, wear a long-sleeved shirt, long pants, and a hat. If the bugs are really bad, wear fine mesh over your hat so that it covers your face and neck.

Marcie and I wore leather hiking boots; Sergio wore rubber sandals. I nearly bumped into Sergio when he came to a sudden stop. He pointed to a coral snake that lay only inches from his unprotected toes. He stepped around the venomous shake. I was carrying my camera gear because I didn't trust it to the Sherpas. I put down my underwater rig (waterproof housing and strobe); a loose digital camera swung on a strap around my neck. I snapped three quick shots before the deadly snake vanished into the undergrowth.

I was overheated and sweating profusely by the time we reached the cenote. A rock wall rose some twenty feet above the cave floor. Trees grew on top of this wall, as well as on the ground immediately in front of the wall. From the air one might see a discontinuity in elevation, but one could never spot the vertical opening.

The Sherpas had preceded us with our tanks, dive gear, and drinking water. Everything was awaiting our arrival. I gulped down some water in the cool interior of the dry portion of the cave. Sergio had erected a wooden bench to be used as a dressing station just inside the entrance. The dry portion of the cave was the size of a cottage. Water lapped a rocky shore about thirty feet inside.

We donned wetsuits and tanks. I waded into the shallows where I sat on a bed of soft sand to pull on my fins. When all three of us were ready to go, Sergio submerged and frog-kicked a score of feet to where the water was 10 feet deep. There we did an all-around bubble check. Then he went another score of feet, and showed us some animal skulls that were partially embedded in the sediment. They might have been prehistoric, but I couldn't be certain.

The tunnel measured fifteen to twenty feet in diameter. It undulated slightly like a kiddie roller coaster. The maximum depth was 30 feet. Visibility extended as far as all three lights could reach. Because the cave was not deep enough to encounter salt water, there was no halocline. The permanent guideline that Sergio had laid was always in clear sight.

Uchben Hakata was not as highly decorated as other Yucatan caves. Yet it had a charm of its own. Because the ceiling was so close to the surface, tree roots hung down like Rapunzel's hair. Sergio paused by one bundle of roots that grew from the ceiling all the way to the floor. Hiding in the mass of scraggly fiber were tiny albino blindfish that measured an inch or so in length. Evolution is a long and slow process that requires the passage of uncounted generations. That albino blindfish evolved from sighted surface fish said a great deal about the age and stability of this flooded underground environment.

Occasionally the tunnel widened to create a great

chamber. In one such chamber, stalactites thrust down into the water like so many spears. Sergio clipped a gap reel to the guideline. We followed his ascent to one side of the cave, and emerged in an air-filled hollow whose ceiling rose only an arm's length out of reach. This ceiling was almost a solid phalanx of stalactites.

We floated on the surface, removed our regulators, and raved about the splendor of so many stalactites. We puttered around the room as we talked, careful to swim between groups of stalactites so we didn't break any of them. I heard a cheeping or chirping sound that befuddled me until I spotted a small brown flying object that I soon identified as a bat.

We found clusters of bats hanging upside down in overhead holes the size of soup cans. Our dive lights awakened them. They opened their mouths and made grotesque faces at us, as if they were embodiments of living gargoyles. These airborne rodents could not have swum into the chamber. There must have been a dry passage for them to enter and leave. Try as we might, we never found a fissure with sunlight shining through it. We could only surmise that, like mice, bats had the

One of many huge root balls that hung in the tunnel. Albino blindfish hid among the roots. Note the stalactites in the background. Bats flitted in the air-filled chamber overhead.

ability to squeeze and squirm through hairline cracks in the limestone.

There were probably half a dozen bats flying back and forth. Marcie squealed every time one passed in front of her face. She screamed out loud when I pinched her hood, then slugged me for startling her.

These were the highlights of an 85-minute dive in 77° water, with no decompression.

After we dried off and donned jungle outfits, Sergio took us to some nearby dry caves. One that was house-sized had bunches of tree roots hanging from the roof like overgrown grapevines. Individual roots then stretched across like the starched tentacles of some alien squid or octopus.

Another cave had the rubble of foundations where manmade partitions once separated the room into cubicles or living quarters. In an offshoot of the latter cave there was a discarded clay container about the size of a beach ball; there was a large hole in the bottom. The rock partitions and thin clay vessel attested to ancient Mayan occupancy.

Outside, a troop of wild moneys swung from tree to tree by means of long arms and prehensile tails. The hike back to the campsite was anticlimactic.

Flowstone Wonders

The greatest attraction of Yucatan caves is not their tortuous length – although some systems have that too – but their limestone beauty. Every cave is decorated with flowstone in endless variety. Dissolved minerals have stained some formations in countless shades of brown: from dark tan to light auburn to burnt sienna.

Stalactites may be round in cross section, shaped like a sword, curled like ribbon, or bumpy like a teenager whose face is covered with acne. Instead of being pointed they may be blunt, like an upside down golf tee. Entire blocks of stalactites may be broken off and lying at bizarre angles on the floor.

Stalagmites, which form from the drippings of stalactites, might be misshapen into amorphous blobs with short carrot tops. Columns may be fat and fluted like those that adorn a Victorian mansion, or long and skinny like soda straws. Some small deposits on the walls may be crystalline, with twisted stems and folded leaves like pure white flowers.

My all-time favorite system is X'Tabay. I admit confusion about the name of the cenote. At the dressing station, a laminated map of the cave denoted the cenote as Chiken Ha; this is the name that I entered in my dive log. In *The Cenotes of the Riviera Maya*, the cenote is called X'Tabay (the same as the system).

The book lists a cenote called Chicken Ha (note the second "c" in Chicken), but as part of the Ponderosa system. Ponderosa was named after Tony and Nancy DeRosa, who, along with Steve Gerrard, were the first divers to explore the system (in 1990). The name of this system is sometimes spelled PonDeRosa.

According to the map in the book, the cenotes X'Tabay and Chicken Ha are close to each other. This implies that systems X'Tabay and Ponderosa might be one and the same. Time and continued exploration will tell.

One possible reason for the disparity in names is the publication date of the book: year 2000. Since then, the

X'Tabay

naming convention has been standardized, and some cenotes have been renamed.

Be that as it may, the cenote that I logged as Chiken Ha is separated from the main guideline by a distance of several hundred feet. The tunnel dips down as deep as 44 feet. The limestone rock in the saltwater zone is severely eroded by the high level of acidity. The surface of the walls has the appearance of crusty lichen, or defoliated petals; it crumbles to dust at the slightest touch.

The tunnel emerges from the halocline and enters a huge room that is appropriately called the Wizard's Den. The "den" is roughly circular and measures nearly one hundred feet across. The depth at the bottom of the den is 40 feet, while the depth at the top is only 5 feet.

This mammoth room looks the way a sea urchin would look if it were turned inside out. The ceiling is festooned with stalactites that have the appearance of Waziri spears that are aimed en masse at Tarzan of the Apes. These "spears" range in length from two feet to eight. The sharp points could easily impale an unwary diver who does not pay attention to the overhead.

Flowstone draperies adorn the walls. Offshoots and cul-de-sacs are filled with formations in miniature. In the long ago past, great blocks fell from the ceiling when

Wizard's Den

Swiss cheese beneath the halocline.

their weight grew so heavy that the force of gravity exceeded the cohesion factor. These tumbled blocks landed in odd attitudes: some on their side, others partially upside down. A view of the floor is as distorted as the view in a funhouse mirror.

Much to Marcie's chagrin, I wanted to return to the Wizard's Den time and time again. It is a photographer's paradise that lies only a thousand feet from the entrance. In deference to her preference to penetrate beyond the photogenic wonders, after shooting all my film, we followed the exit tunnel for several thousand feet until we surfaced in cenote Xochacalico, which was located at some isolated spot in the jungle.

This cenote is shaped like an upturned bowl; the sides slope inward toward the top, making it impossible to climb up and out through the overhead opening. Some enterprising diver had secured a thick manila rope to one side. This made it possible to doff tanks in an emergency, and scramble up a notch and out through a crevice into the jungle above. The return underwater required far less effort.

After I switched from a film camera to digital, I was no longer limited to thirty-six exposures. The following year I dragged Marcie back to the Wizard's Den for another photo shoot, even though she would rather have explored other systems.

Chac Mool is the perfect system for an introductory dive. Local dive guides use either of two cenotes as a starting point for divers who are not cave certified. A

Marcie leads the way in Nohoch Nah Chich. Note the guideline in the lower left corner. Air that is exhaled by open-circuit divers collects in "pools" or "puddles" overhead. Note the reflection of Marcie's rebreather in the air pools above her.

long cavern loop never leaves the light zone, yet exposes novices to a panoply of limestone formations of every type: stalactites, stalagmites, columns, curtains, ribbons, blobs, and exfoliated petals. One can see divers more than a hundred feet away as they pass through sunbeams that penetrate water that is as clear as mountain air.

Dos Ojos has more than a dozen cenotes, enabling divers to surface at a number of places in order to rave about the flowstone formations that they passed en route. The system is so highly decorated that it has often been used by film crews as an example to capture the beauty and wonder of the Riviera Maya. According to the published statistics, more than 35 miles of passageways have been explored in this system – and the end is not yet in sight.

Fun and Games

Cave diving must be taken seriously because there is no direct access to the surface. This doesn't mean that you can't have fun, as long as you don't relax your attention to detail.

I like to play games under water. My favorite is hide-and-seek. This is difficult to accomplish because exhaust bubbles give away my location. Recall what I did to Steve Berman in Ginnie Springs. I managed to spook a couple of other divers when they thought they were all alone.

The visibility was only six to eight feet on the *Empress of Ireland* when I spotted a beam of light through the murk. I switched off my light and ducked under an overhang to take advantage of the opportunity that the poor vis presented. My exhaled air was dispersed by the hull plate above me. John Moyer passed directly overhead. I leaped out from beneath him and clamped my hands around his left thigh. His entire body quivered like a shaken bowl of Jell-O.

I was swimming along a pitch black corridor at 220 feet inside the Promenade Deck of the *Andrea Doria*, when a glow of light attracted my attention. At this time in the wreck's evolution of collapse, deck plates were falling away one by one. The glow was diffusing through a rectangular opening in the "ceiling" of the Promenade Deck, which was the "floor" of the Boat Deck. Because the hull lies on its side, the opening was on the vertical surface to my right.

I placed the front of my light against my chest – I *never* switch off my light inside a wreck or a cave, because it might not switch back on again. I peered into the opening. On the Boat Deck, a diver was swimming at the same depth and in the same direction as I was. I pulled back so he couldn't see me. As he passed the opening, I reached into the Boat Deck and grabbed him around the thigh. John Yurga's reaction was identical to John Moyer's. His body shook and vibrated as he jerked his leg away from a phantom shark. When he glared back at me, I pulled my light off my chest so he could see my face. I waved.

In both instances, we joked afterward about soiled undergarments.

Hiding from Marcie was more difficult. She had purchased a rebreather and had completed her training course shortly before the trip. Part of checking the functionality of her rebreather was doing a pre-breathing exercise in 20 feet of water. We entered the cenote together. The main guideline commenced not far from the light zone – just far enough that a cavern diver was unlikely to find it. We had both been in this system before; we both knew how to find the guideline, for there was only a single tunnel that went nowhere else.

As the more experienced Yucatan cave diver, Marcie usually took it upon herself to lay the line from the cenote to the main guideline. Because she had to do the pre-breathing exercise, I had started taking the lead to the main guideline. In this instance I deviated from protocol.

I swam partway along the tunnel to where it was comparatively dark. Outside sunbeams cast a faint illumination – enough to enable me to see without a dive light, so I did not switch it on. I inflated my buoyancy compensator, rose to the ceiling, spread out my arms and legs, and flattened myself against the overhead rock like a legendary vampire bat that was lurking for prey. I

These are the kinds of signs that warn divers to proceed no farther unless they have the proper training and certification. The top sign is in Ponderosa. The bottom sign is in Taj Mahal. For those who are illiterate or foreign language impaired, the pictographic images should be universally understood: the personification of Death with his sharp weeding scythe, and the skull and crossbones found on bottles of poison.

waited. My black wetsuit blended with the limestone in the relative darkness.

Marcie completed her pre-breathing exercise. She swam along the tunnel in a horizontal attitude, frog-kicking slowly so as not to stir any silt that lay on the bottom of the passageway. Stealth diver that I was, I breathed slowly and quietly when I saw her approaching. She was studying her rebreather gauges when she passed beneath me. She did not look up.

Gently I released air from my buoyancy compensator. As I fell from the ceiling, I rotated my body so as to orient myself toward the interior of the cave. I tagged along behind her. When Marcie reached the warning sign to which the main guideline was tied, she looked around for my light. Everywhere was darkness.

At that moment I swooped down behind her and pinched her butt. She leaped up and spun around like a spring-mounted Jack-in-the-box; or perhaps, in this case, like a Jill-in-the-box. Immediately she knew that I was up to my old tricks. She gave me the "bad" sign by passing one extended index finger over the other. She was annoyed at being startled. I laughed aloud through my regulator. After we both settled down, we got serious and stayed that way for the remainder of the dive. But she had some stern words for me after we surfaced.

Stealth Divers

Nohoch Nah Chich is thought to be the longest underwater cave system in the world. It has dozens of cenotes and more than 40 miles of surveyed passageways. It is also one of the most decorated systems on the peninsula, if not on the planet.

The cenote that intrigued me the most in this system is called Casa. This cenote looks more like a river than a typical cenote, because it winds through the jungle for a quarter of a mile, with a cave entrance at either end.

The cenote access is a sandy lot next to a beach road that parallels the seashore. Spread across the lot are chunks of fossilized coral that measure anywhere from marble size to basketball size. I collected some small (and lightweight) specimens to take home.

The cenote is a favorite swimming hole for locals and tourists alike. The fresh water is warm and clear. The river measures some fifty feet in width. The current is not strong. Marcie and I swam upstream through schools of tiny fish that like to hide among the mangrove roots. At the upstream end of the surface river, we descended to a depth of 26 feet, tied off a guideline, and proceeded against the current into the narrow cave.

The permanent guideline started less than one hundred feet inside. The ceiling was less than ten feet above the floor. The fine silt was thick, and it was stirred somewhat by the fast flow of water, so that visibility was only about thirty feet. The walls were light gray in color. Formations were few and small in comparison to the those found in the fairyland that existed several miles upstream.

The drabness of the cave was pronounced. We penetrated less than a thousand feet when we decided to turn the dive. Back out in the open, we drifted slowly on the surface until we reached the downstream terminus. We ducked under swimmers and entered the cave. Visibility here was about fifty feet. There was no guideline so we deployed our own, and unreeled line as we proceeded through the tunnel with the current.

The floor was littered with seashells. Instead of tiny fish that we spotted upstream, fish that measured one to two feet in length swam around us. After proceeding about five hundred feet, we saw the dim glow of light ahead of us. The accelerating current propelled us through schools of saltwater fish.

We burst into bright sunshine that illuminated a colorful coral reef. We surfaced, and found ourselves in the ocean about a hundred feet from the beach. We climbed onto a coral ledge where we could sit, chat, and take in the sights.

Outdoor diners at a nearby restaurant pointed fingers at us, no doubt wondering about our unannounced landfall. We must have looked like a pair of World War Two frogmen who had emerged from the deep to lay explosive charges on an enemy-held strand; or perhaps a pair of Navy Seals on a search and destroy mission. We laughed about the obvious ruckus that we were causing ashore.

After five minutes or so, we rolled into the water and, in the eyes of the diners, disappeared forever. Swimming back against the current was a challenge. We had to skirt the fastest part of the flow by clawing along the rocky sidewalls of the tunnel. After fighting our way back to freshwater and the light zone, we spent some time collecting seashells and fossil coral.

A new group of swimmers was taking advantage of the waterhole when we climbed out of the cenote. They were American tourists who showed interest in our cave-diving exploits as we doffed our tanks. They quickly told us about the frogmen who had appeared out of nowhere in front of the restaurant, and later vanished into the deep, never to return.

Marcie and I laughed as we told them about the tunnel that passed under the road and the restaurant, and that *we* were the frogman and frogwoman who had astonished them at lunchtime.

Mexican Hat Dance

My first impression of Mexico – other than the extreme heat – was that the country was operating under military authority. From several pages back, you may recall my observations about the abundance of soldiers and constabularies that patrolled the highways and cities. The job of these various peacekeeping and law enforcement agencies was not to keep the general public in line by employing intimidation and armed confrontation, as in a dictatorship, but to protect the public and visiting tourists from outlaws.

Mexico is *not* a police state. It is a federation whose chief officials are elected by the citizenry. But the country is plagued by political corruption, economic devastation, drug trafficking, gun running, and other assorted troubles and criminal activities. In some areas, violent crime is practically a national pastime – but more so in border towns and major metropolitan areas than in the boondocks such as the Yucatan Peninsula.

The crackdown on drug cartels has resulted in much armed conflict. Bloodshed resulting from shoot-outs is commonplace. According to the official estimate, some 30,000 alleged criminals have been killed in the past five years. Not all these deaths are attributable to the army and local police. In addition to the war *on* drug cartels is the war *between* drug cartels; this internecine strife takes a terrible toll on competitors.

While local police are generally armed with handguns, the transportation of drugs by well-armed gunmen has made it necessary for soldiers to carry automatic weapons, in order to achieve fire superiority in a firefight. I saw these tightened security measures in action. In places the highway looked like a militarized zone: fortified outposts were strategically placed every few miles, and guard towers commanded an elevated view of approaching traffic.

The army established unscheduled roadblocks. Drug traffickers never knew when they might be stopped by a squad of uniformed and heavily armed soldiers.

Marcie and I were returning from a dive when we encountered such a roadblock. A squad of soldiers surrounded each vehicle in turn, conducted an examination, and released the vehicle with only a couple of minutes delay. I noticed that the examining officer always checked the top of the driver's side sun visor. We were told afterward that drug traffickers often kept a gun at that handy spot. When the car in front of us departed, the officer waved us forward.

The officer spoke in Spanish that Marcie had difficulty understanding because he used some words that she didn't know. He asked us to vacate the vehicle. Marcie was driving, so she stepped out on the left and engaged in conversation with the squad leader. I stepped out on the right. I took three or four steps so that the soldiers had a clear view of the vehicle. Marcie was still wearing her wetsuit, but I had changed into shoes, shorts, and T-shirt.

It was obvious that we were American tourists. The back of our vehicle was filled with tanks and dive gear. I understood nothing of what Marcie and the officer were saying. I glanced around at the troops.

I used to be an infantryman in Uncle Sam's army, so I paid particular attention to the soldiers. Half a dozen young men wore full kit in the blistering heat: long-sleeved olive drab fatigues, head gear, and combat boots, plus web gear and an automatic rifle. Four of them stood casually around the vehicle at a distance of twenty feet or so, while two others kept their eyes on the other vehicles in the lineup. They cradled their rifles waist high with the muzzles not pointing at anyone. Each soldier held his fingers around the trigger guard.

As I swept my gaze from one soldier to the other, I began to notice that their casualness was ingeniously deceptive. The first rule of engaging the enemy was to ensure that none of your comrades stood in your line of fire. The guards did not encircle the vehicle precisely at the four points of the compass, or at the corners of a square or rectangle. Instead, each one stood a few degrees off the perpendicular, and they stood at slightly different distances from the vehicle.

When I drew an imaginary line between any soldier and me, or between any soldier and Marcie, I saw that an extension of that line passed between the two soldiers on the opposite side of the vehicle. This ragtag grouping, or out of order stance, was too peculiar to be coincidental. I also noticed that their eyes did not stay focused on any one person, place, or thing, but roved constantly, although they did not move their heads.

I suspected that their apparent nonchalance was intentional; that they were cleverly giving the appearance of boredom and detachment in order to lull a potential enemy into a state of false security. I decided to test my theory.

I reached down and pretended to swat an insect on my bare leg. In the process of doing so, I stepped back, stood up, and sidestepped, thus moving like a knight on a chessboard. I looked around with indifference. None of the soldiers appeared to descry my subtle change in location, but they all took half a step or two that altered our relative positions, so that once again the line of sight left their comrades out of harm's way.

I repeated my maneuver with another nonexistent insect. Once again they realigned themselves with choreographed precision, better than a well-rehearsed chorus line.

I was duly impressed. These soldiers were trained professionals and experts in their field. I thought of testing them one more time, but I didn't. If they were as smart and as observant as I supposed them to be, they might interpret my seemingly innocuous movements as something sinister, and take appropriate action.

The officer had his final say. He signaled that we could pass. Marcie and I got into the vehicle and proceeded on our way. Back at the condo, I told everyone how I had danced with Mexican soldiers – and was soundly rebuked for my mischievous behavior.

Nonetheless, my experience at the roadblock made me feel secure. After all, the Mexican army was there to ensure our safety, and I thought that they were doing an excellent job.

Puerto Aventuras

I don't want to sound like a travel agency that is promoting its favorite resort because of the kickbacks they receive from making referrals, but I would be remiss if I didn't write a few words about accommodations in Yucatan.

Most visiting divers tend to stay in Akumal because the location is central to the systems that comprise the Riviera Maya. Akumal has lodging, dive shops, and guides. I can't say anything good or bad about Akumal because, although Marcie had stayed there when Steve Berman used to organize trips, she preferred the accommodations in Puerto Aventuras, so that is the only place I have ever stayed.

Puerto Aventuras is a modern tourist resort that is still under construction. It is a huge condominium com-

This is a roof-top view of only one condo section in Puerto Aventuras. The community center - which has a porpoise pond surrounded by restaurants, gift shops, jewelry stores, and so on - lies within easy walking distance.

plex that is complete with marina, golf course, swimming pools, white sandy beaches, gift shops, restaurants galore, a gas station, and two full-service dive shops. One dive shop caters to cave divers; the other runs daily charters to offshore reefs.

The island of Cozumel can be seen from the mainland; ferryboats shuttle people daily between the two. Saltwater game fishing is also available.

If you take lodging in one of the luxury condos in Puerto Aventuras, the only reason to ever leave the place is to dive in caves and visit Mayan ruins. Everything needed for a comfortable vacation can be found without leaving the self-contained community. Most condos have bedding for six friendly people, so the cost of lodging can be divided six ways. The condos are air-conditioned, come with a full-sized kitchen, and most have Internet access.

Puerto Aventuras is a gated community. The guards at the gate are not armed. They won't let you enter unless you are lodging there or have business there. Identification checks may be cursory, but they keep out the riffraff as well as the drug dealers and gun runners. Private police patrol the grounds and the streets to ensure the safety of lodgers and visitors.

Part of the charm of Puerto Aventuras is the central porpoise pool that measures some hundred yards across. For a small fee people can swim with trained resident porpoises. Surrounding the pool are restaurants that serve international cuisine, clothing stores, jewelry stores, gift shops, a visitor center, and so on. Fossil coral is so common that it is mixed with cement and is used to decorate the sidewalks.

Some restaurants play music or have a band to encourage dancing. Beer, wine, and spirits are on most menus. I had a Philly cheese steak which, while not as good as one from Pat's Steaks in South Philly, was not a bad imitation. For those who prefer to cook their own meals, a grocery store sells fresh meat and vegetables, as well as an assortment of canned victuals.

Montezuma's revenge is for real. Local water contains bacteria that contain toxins to which most travelers are not immune. Avoid drinking tap water or water that is served in a glass. Drink bottled water only. Do not pour bottled water or canned soft drinks over ice that is furnished by restaurants, because the ice may have been frozen from tap water. One bout of diarrhea will convince you of the sincerity of my cautions.

Fossil coral is so prevalent that it is mixed with cement to make concrete for sidewalks. Feel free to take some souvenirs home with you.

Puerto Aventuras has its own submerged cave system known as Valet. Across the road are two cenotes of the system Las Grutas De Maurilio. System Chac Mool is only a mile away. All the other well-known systems are southward.

The Mayan Way

I speak primarily for myself when I say that you shouldn't overlook Mayan artifacts on a dive trip to Yucatan. I have been interested in archaeology since I was a teenager. As an adult I visited ancient Amerindian cliff dwellings such as those found at Mesa Verde National Park (Colorado), Bandolier National Monument (New Mexico), Canyon De Chelly National Monument (Arizona), Gila Cliff Dwellings (New Mexico), and the extensive and monumental multistory stone structures at Chaco Culture National Historical Park (New Mexico).

I have also photographed hundreds of examples of Indian graffiti (pictographs and petroglyphs) in the Four Corners region: Utah, Colorado, New Mexico, and Arizona. This long and abiding interest in prehistoric man inspired me to visit the Mexican remnants of Mayan culture that were open to the public.

You hardly have to go out of your way to see the reconstructed ruins at Tulum, because you drive past the entry road en route to some of the caves. You can easily visit Tulum during surface interval between dives, or on the way "home" after a day of diving. Tulum is about 30 some miles south of Puerto Aventuras.

If you want to make an all-day excursion, I highly recommend the three-hour drive from Puerto Aventuras to the magnificent ruins at Chichen Itza. This is perhaps the best-known archaeological site in all of Yucatan, if not in all of Mexico. There you can see the classic Mayan ziggurats (step pyramids) in all their glory. Depicted are fine examples of Mayan art and sculpture. Some of the ruins have not been reconstructed, so you can see the way the structures existed when they were first discovered.

On the way back from Chichen Itza, take time to stop for a quick tour of Coba. The centerpiece is the tallest Mayan structure in Yucatan: a set of stone steps that climb to a hilltop on which a small building is perched. From this great height you can see for many miles in every direction. Coba also has the Mayan version of a volleyball court that is built out of cut stone. (No playing in the ruins is allowed.)

What is there to see and do in Yucatan? Everything.

Chichen Itza

The Rise of the Fourth Reich

Another Addition to NOAA's Ark

It will come as no surprise to my long-time readers that the enmity between NOAA and me shows no sign of abating. As long as NOAA continues its policies of arrogant dictatorship and territorial expansion, I will continue to act as watchdog for the American people. And as long as I continue to call attention to NOAA's subversive and anti-American activities, NOAA's administrators will continue to abhor me, my journalistic investigations, and my public declarations.

Round and round we go, in escalating conflict.

Here is another round in which we engaged in verbal fisticuffs, this time about NOAA's clandestine but ongoing expansion shenanigans. The saga begins meekly, but . . .

NOAA announced its discovery of the *YP-389*. I covered this World War Two gunboat in both *Shipwrecks of North Carolina: North* and *The Fuhrer's U-boats in American Waters*.

In June 1942, during a running gun battle that lasted for an hour, the *YP-389* was shelled and sunk by the *U-701*. Six sailors were killed in action, and many of the remainder were wounded by shrapnel. The survivors floated on the Atlantic swells throughout the night, until a Coast Guard vessel rescued them in the morning.

The wreck site was discovered in 1973 by a Duke University expedition that was searching off the Diamond Shoals for the Civil War ironclad *Monitor*. The side-scan sonar survey located more than a dozen targets during the course of a weeklong search. Examination of the side-scan images established that one of the sites was the *Monitor*. The other sites were relegated to the scrap heap because they were not relevant to the mission's goal.

NOAA obtained the coordinates of the other sites from Duke University. In 2009, NOAA dedicated three weeks of expensive shipboard operating time to survey these deep-water sites by means of a camera mounted on a remotely operated vehicle (ROV). One of the wrecks was subsequently identified as the *YP-389*.

The entire wreck was videotaped, and a photomosaic was created from frame captures. The photomosaic provided an overhead view from bow to stern, and clearly showed a gun that was mounted on the deck. Along with wreck-site dimensions that were scaled off a multi-beam sonar image, the gun lent credence to the supposition that the wreck could be the *YP-389*. This kind of identification is not indisputable, but I have no reason to doubt the wreck's identify. Nothing else remotely like it is known to have been lost in the area.

According to NOAA, the wreck lies at a depth of 300 feet. The precise location of the site is being kept from the public that paid millions of dollars for the survey.

One might wonder why NOAA spent taxpayer's money to conduct shipwreck surveys that did not serve any useful purpose for American citizens. The reason was NOAA's secret mission to expand its National Marine Sanctuary Program in order to increase its control over public property and resources.

Congress created the NMSP for the express purpose of preserving areas of biological and geological interest. On its own authority, NOAA has established a territorial imperative that goes far beyond the pale of its Congressional mandate.

NOAA, that archenemy of the American public and destroyer of democracy, has implemented an initiative to expand its dictatorial jurisdiction over shipwrecks. Because Congress placed a temporary hold on the creation of new marine sanctuaries, NOAA has focused its attention on a movement to extend the boundaries of the present sanctuaries, in order to exert domination over more shipwrecks.

Modern Day Pirate

Previously I revealed to the public that NOAA was lying when it stated that it had no plans to expand the *Monitor* National Marine Sanctuary – that in fact it had already devised a new name for the anticipated expansion: the Graveyard of the Atlantic National Marine Sanctuary.

After my news was made public, NOAA grudgingly admitted in subsequent public hearings that it did in fact have a plan to expand the *Monitor* NMS. However, it refused to divulge the particulars of the plan.

I then revealed more devastating information. I obtained a secret NOAA document that dated from 2005. In this document, NOAA clearly outlined its goals and established a timeline for its expansion program. Within the next few years, NOAA has plans to annex more than *1,200* shipwrecks.

You read that correctly but I will spell it out in order to avoid any suspicion of a typographical error: NOAA has plans to annex *one thousand two hundred* shipwrecks.

Notice that this document was created six years ago. This means that NOAA and its minions have been knowingly and consistently lying to the public ever since it adopted its new territorial imperative.

As noted above, NOAA's Congressional mandate says nothing about controlling shipwrecks or monopolizing access to wreck sites. NOAA has taken this tack on its own; has, in fact, violated its Congressional mandate.

The sole reason for creating the Marine Protection, Research, and Sanctuaries Act was, and I quote from the Act, "to protect valuable, unique, or endangered marine life, geological features, and oceanographic features." Nothing – I repeat, nothing – was ever mentioned about policing shipwrecks.

By definition of the MPRSA, the *Monitor* NMS and Thunder Bay NMS are illegal.

To add another absurdity, Thunder Bay is not even a marine environment; it is a freshwater bay in Lake

Huron. The definition of "marine" is "of or relating to the sea." By no stretch of the imagination can Thunder Bay relate to the sea. In fact, the sole reason that NOAA created the Thunder Bay NMS was to control the shipwrecks that are located within its boundaries. The same is true of the *Monitor* NMS (which at least is located in the ocean).

In the old days, pirates were hanged for robbing ships – for taking even a single ship. Yet NOAA is getting away with wholesale piracy, and with complete impunity.

Tomorrow the World

When will Congress wake up to the fact that the National Marine Sanctuary Program has been exceeding its authority ever since its inception nearly forty years ago; that although the MPRSA was mandated by Congress to "preserve, restore, or enhance areas for their conservational, recreational, ecological, research or esthetic values in coastal water," the program has never done anything to benefit the American people, and especially the "recreational" members of the public; that NOAA is hijacking shipwrecks under the guise of "preservation" for its own personal pleasure and use; and that NOAA is getting more out of control with each passing day?

One could hope that enlightenment might come as new blood is gradually infused into the National Marine Sanctuary Program, when new people are hired to replace those whose views are outdated and dictatorial. Instead, new employees are either infected by the diseased minds of their superiors in the hierarchy, or they are indoctrinated not just to maintain the status quo, but to further enforce aggrandizement of the Program.

If you want to read the sad truth about NOAA's past nefarious activities, read my book *Ironclad Legacy: Battles of the USS Monitor*. You can also read about NOAA's heinous handling of the Stellwagen Bank NMS in the chapter that is titled "The Stellwagen Bank Robbery," in my book *Shipwreck Heresies*.

Both accounts will make you cringe. Now it gets

worse . . .

An *eightfold* expansion is already underway in the Thunder Bay sanctuary. Next on NOAA's nefarious agenda are two other expansions: doubling the size of the already huge Stellwagen Bank sanctuary, and a *thousandfold* increase in size of the *Monitor* sanctuary. That's right – a *thousandfold* increase, at least. And that is only one step in NOAA's domination of the underwater world.

NOAA wants to expand the one-mile-diameter *Monitor* sanctuary to cover all the shipwrecks on the Diamond Shoals and along the Outer Banks. This new imperative will encompass scores of merchant vessels and a number of U-boats, all of which could be placed off-limits or be severely restricted in access. This expansion has nothing to do with historic preservation, but with control.

This planned expansion was the justification for the shipwreck survey in which the *YP-389* was re-examined. The publicity that NOAA garnered from promoting its identification of this World War Two gunboat has given additional impetus to its expansion program, and has resulted in a change of its naming convention. Now NOAA is referring to the proposed enlargement of the *Monitor* sanctuary as the Battle of the Atlantic National Marine Sanctuary.

This newly designated Sanctuary will be *thousands* of times larger than the core Sanctuary on which it is formed, perhaps to encompass the entire Eastern Sea Frontier. During World War Two, the ESF was an operational area that extended from Maine to Florida to a distance of approximately 200 miles from shore.

If NOAA gets its way, it will eventually control every shipwreck off the American eastern seaboard.

In light of NOAA's current enforcement policies, and the more restrictive policies that it is proposing, wreck-diving could then become a thing of the past.

This chapter is not just a well-deserved and vitriolic diatribe against NOAA. It is a wakeup call for all of you who are appalled by the government's excessive abuse of authority. Unless you want NOAA to keep getting away with cheating the public out of its birthright, lodge complaints with your State and federal representatives.

Don't waste your time by attending NOAA scoping meetings or public hearings. NOAA representatives will only lie to you and misrepresent NOAA's intentions and future plans, in order to convince you that it has your best interests at heart, and that it will not alter the status quo without your full consent.

Nor will it do any good to air your views about how Sanctuaries should be managed. NOAA representatives will suffer through your dialogue, then kiss you off as soon as the meeting is over. NOAA doesn't give a wit about your opinions or suggestions. The scoping meetings and public hearings are merely window dressing, designed to lull you into believing that NOAA cares about your viewpoints. NOAA will do whatever it wants to do and can get away with.

I repeat: complain to your State and federal representatives. A congressional leader interceded in my *Monitor* case, and forced NOAA to rescind its ban against issuing permits to dive on the wreck. But Congress hasn't been keeping a tight leash on NOAA. A new generation of NOAA minions is continuing to take away freedoms that are supposedly guaranteed by the Constitution of the United States.

There is only one logical manner in which to handle this situation. The National Marine Sanctuary Program must be abolished.

Thomas Jefferson once said, "The price of freedom is eternal vigilance."

That statement is just as true today as it was two hundred years ago. Perhaps more so.

Homage to Occam's Razor

"Who does not know that the first law of historical writing is the truth?"

– Cicero, 106 BC – 43 BC

The Fickle Finger of Fate

William Seach of Occam (or Ockham) was a twelfth-century philosopher and theologian who is best remembered today for his principle of methodology, known as Occam's razor (alias the law of parsimony). According to this principle, a theory that fits the facts by relying on the fewest assumptions and postulates is preferable to one that can be made to fit only by being overly complex and convoluted.

In lay terms: all things being equal, the simplest explanation is usually the best.

A corollary to Occam's razor is that *all* the facts must be brought into account.

An article that appeared in *Wreck Diving Magazine* not only failed to recognize Occam's razor, but ignored the existence of facts that contradicted the a priori theory of the authors. The article was entitled "The Fate of *U-869* Reexamined," and was bylined John Yurga, Richie Kohler, and John Chatterton. (Hereafter this article will be referred to as the Fate article.) It appears to have been written in response to (or in retaliation for) the 70-page continuation of my exposé of *Shadow Divers*, which I published in *Shipwreck Heresies* as "Shadow Divers Exposed in Retrospect."

Ordinarily I am glad to have people read my books and follow my exploits. In this case, however, it was brought to my attention that Chatterton (if not Kohler and Yurga) bought *Shipwreck Heresies* primarily to disavow the facts that I presented. Chatterton used some of those facts to denigrate me on an Internet chat room by claiming that, although we were on numerous dive trips together throughout the years, he and I barely knew each other; that we were only casual acquaintances. He can have it that way if he wants it.

I find it ironic, though, that I received an email from Facebook stating that Chatterton's wife Carla listed me as one of her "friends." This attempted friendship fell by the wayside because I was not a Facebook member. I could not access the Facebook website much less be someone's "friend."

The Fate article contained so many errors of fact, sins of omission, and leaps of faith that I hardly know where to start parsing it, or how to proceed with a rebuttal in an organized fashion. To describe the worth of the Fate article, two metaphors come immediately to mind: "A diarrhea of words and a constipation of ideas," and "A flood of words that contained hardly a drop of truth." Both are appropriate, so take your pick and shovel out the manure.

The premise of the article was to prove that a circular run of its own torpedo was responsible for the demise of the U-boat. Only those facts that supported this theory were brought to light. Any facts that repudiated the theory were ignored. Thus a reader who was presented with only this partial evidence might be led to believe that the circular run torpedo theory was tenable.

Additionally, the Fate article went to great lengths to avoid mentioning names and giving credit to researchers who obtained those facts that conflicted with the authors' pet theory – banishing them to literary oblivion, as it were, along with the efforts of their research. The Fate article further bemoaned the fact that after careful consideration of *all* available evidence, both the Naval Historical Center and the U.S. Coast Guard Historian's Office rejected the authors' circular run hypothesis, and gave credit to the *Howard D. Crow* and *Koiner* for the U-boat's destruction. The Fate article claimed that this reevaluation was "simplistic and self-serving." (P2p18)

(The Fate article was published in three parts: Part

1 in Issue 17, Part 2 in Issue 18, and Part 3 in Issue 19, all in 2009. The shorthand reference at the end of the preceding paragraph should be interpreted as Part 2, page 18.)

The Fate article then made the most stupid comment imaginable: "Other than the presence of the wreck itself, there was no physical evidence to indicate a submarine being sunk by the USS *Howard D. Crow* and the USS *Koiner* on February 11, 1945." (P2p18) This was the kind of illogic that permeated the article in pleading its case. On the contrary, the presence of the *U-869* precisely where two warships conducted a combined hedgehog and depth-charge attack on an escaping U-boat that one of them was following on sonar, is the most compelling evidence of all. Yet the authors dismissed this evidence without stating why.

The Fate article then contradicted its own ludicrous sophistry by noting that the loss of the *U-166* was reevaluated in 2001 for the very same reason: the discovery of a wrecked U-boat precisely where the *PC-566*, "whose crew always believed that they had sunk a U-boat," conducted an attack. (P1p17) The Fate article seemed to want it both ways: whichever way suited its purpose.

Clever Deception

The way the Fate article was worded, readers who had no previous knowledge of events surrounding the fate of the *U-869* were led to believe that the authors knew about the hedgehog and depth-charge attack all along, but discarded it after an exhaustive examination of the attack in comparison with other possibilities. Nothing could be further from the truth.

On March 1, 1998, the same three authors of the Fate article submitted the "Final Report on the Location and Identification of the World War II German Submarine *U-869*." In this so-called "Final Report," the authors claimed "that we meticulously searched the US Navy Eastern Sea Frontier Diaries and the Allied Anti-Submarine Warfare records. We examined the records searching for U-boat sightings, missing ships or aircraft, debris sighting, etc. We searched the record for the entire war and later focused more intensely upon late 1944 and early 1945. Having done so, we could find no entries whatsoever that we could specifically link to the wreck site." The *Howard D. Crow* attack was not mentioned. Perhaps the authors needed to look up the word "meticulously" in the dictionary.

Shadow Divers (published in 2004) was bylined Robert Kurson, but was based almost entirely upon information that was provided by Chatterton and Kohler. *Shadow Divers* claimed (pages 181, 185, and 187) that altogether Chatterton spent seven days in Washington, DC, conducting U-boat research. After supposedly pouring through thousands of documents, he failed to find a single anti-submarine warfare incident within 60 miles of the *U-869* during the entire war. (*Shadow Divers*, p187.) In fact, there were scores of incidents. Once again the *Howard D. Crow* attack was not mentioned.

Independent researcher Barb Lander made a list of ASW reports in the vicinity of the wreck for an eight-month period during the last year of the war. She found 28 incidents within a radius of 37 miles of the site. She went so far as to highlight the *Howard D. Crow* and *Koiner* report, which plotted at 4.5 miles from the wreck. She gave copies of her list to Chatterton and Yurga. They did not bother to look up the report. (For more in this regard, see *Shadow Divers Exposed*, pages 9 and 75-78.) As a result of this disregard, *Shadow Divers* made no mention of the *Howard D. Crow* or *Koiner*.

After the publication of *Shadow Divers*, Harold Moyers conducted his own research. He found the *Howard D. Crow* and *Koiner* reports after only ten minutes of leafing through the after war assessments. He passed this information on to the Naval Historical Center and the U.S. Coast Guard Historian's Office. He told me about it, and I gave him credit for the discovery in *Shadow Divers Exposed* (p84).

It appears that the authors of the Fate article were unaware of the report until Moyers made it public. Yet they neglected to credit their prior ignorance. Instead, they wrote Moyers out of the article and made it seem as if the attack was either already known to them or that it was common knowledge.

Ironically, the Fate article itself confirmed the fact that the authors did not conduct their research about the *Howard D. Crow* and *Koiner* incident until after Moyers publicized it. The National Archives maintains a policy of not releasing photocopies of documents that were stamped Confidential, Secret, or Top Secret, unless those documents bore a declassification sticker. (See *The Shipwreck Research Handbook* for a history and description of this policy.) A new sticker is generated each and every time a researcher asks permission to photocopy such a document, and the sticker bears the date on which the document was photocopied.

The Fate article reprinted a page from the Enemy Action and Distress Diary which bore the appropriate declassification sticker. (P2p13, in the upper right corner of the full picture of the page). The sticker was dated November 8, 2005, thus establishing the date on which the authors did their research – after they already know from Moyers what to look for and where to look for it.

Another Clever Deception

The Fate article stated, "We received information from Robert Coppock at the Ministry of Defense [sic] in London, that another Deschimag boat, the *U-869*, could possibly have been lost off the east coast of the United States, instead of off the coast of Africa, where historians had originally placed it." (P1p18; repeated non-verbatim P3p33) (Note: Allied *assessors* placed the *U-869* off Africa, not historians.)

What the article neglected to state was where Coppock received *his* information. This same deception was practiced in *Shadow Divers*. For reasons that I am unable to fathom, the authors (of the book and the article) refused to credit Mark McKellar with being the first to discover the Ultra decrypts that mentioned the *U-869* by name (or by number). He uncovered this crucial information in 1993 – two years after Chatterton and Kohler claimed to have discovered the wreck, and four years before they claimed to have identified it.

Not only did McKellar inform Coppock, he also personally informed Chatterton. Coppock later relayed McKellar's information to Chatterton, so that Chatterton received the information from two sources, both of which originated from McKellar.

The Navy intelligence department that was known as the Tenth Fleet was well aware that the *U-869* was proceeding across the Atlantic Ocean to the eastern seaboard, even if German U-boat headquarters was not. The Tenth Fleet tracked the U-boat from radio transmissions, and went so far as to dispatch a hunter-killer group to intercept it along its predicted route.

It appears that the *Howard D. Crow* and *Koiner* waylaid the *U-869* before the hunter-killer group could reach an intercept position.

In *Shadow Divers Exposed*, I gave McKellar full credit for his valuable contribution (pages 61-64, 71-72, 134, 196-197, and 223).

Yet Another Clever Deception

In a sidebar in each of the three Parts of the Fate article, the authors took credit for discovering the *U-869*: " . . . they worked on identifying the mystery submarine that they located . . . " (P1p21, P2p19, P3p39)

It was clearly stated in *Shadow Divers* that Kohler did not participate in the so-called discovery dive. He did not dive on the U-boat until the third trip of the year. Yet despite his own admission, he now laid claim to being one of the discoverers.

In any case, as I wrote in *Shipwreck Heresies* (p252-254), Chuck Wine and Bart Malone made the first descent to the *U-869*. They made their dive in 1988 – three full years before Chatterton, Kohler, and Yurga knew anything about the existence of the U-boat. The Fate article ignored this prior discovery in favor of the dives that the authors made three years later.

Deception or Scapegoat?

The Fate article gave credit for the circular run torpedo theory to Coppock. Yet in *Shadow Divers* (pages 232-233), Coppock was not mentioned in this regard, and full credit was taken by Chatterton and Kohler for inventing and developing the theory. *Shadow Divers* was replete with other instances in which Chatterton and Kohler took credit for the accomplishments of others, but nowhere did the book take credit away from them and assign it to someone else. This change in tune in the Fate article was ironic to say the least. But I can speculate as to why Chatterton and Kohler now wanted to distance themselves by one remove from this unwarranted theory.

Coppock did not pull the theory out of thin air. There are instances on record of a torpedo leaving its tube and circling back on the submarine that launched it. The Fate authors appended a dozen recorded instances relating to American subs (only two of which were actually struck by the torpedo) but did not append any recorded instances relating to German U-boats. Instead, they furnished a German warning to all U-boats that read, "On crash-diving after firing an acoustic torpedo from the bow tube, the boat must submerge to a depth of 30 meters – not in 60 seconds but as quickly as possible." (P3p35) They noted that four U-boats were "most likely lost to circular run torpedoes." (P3p35) Not only is "most likely" an exaggeration of "suspected" (the word that the article used on the previous page), but either distinction is not the same as "recorded." The reason these losses were not "recorded" is because there were no survivors, and because the Allied assessors could find no attack reports that coincided with the dates and places of loss.

Of the four U-boats that were noted in the Fate article (*U-47*, *U-305*, *U-377*, and *U-972*), at least one (*U-377*) has so far been reassessed as having been lost due to enemy action. (See Axel Niestle, ubootwaffe.net) The reason for the loss of the others was pure speculation.

NOTE: The crash-dive submergence depth for avoidance of acoustical torpedoes was 60 meters, not 30 meters, as the Fate article stated. There are numerous sources in this regard, including *Memoirs* by Admiral Karl Doenitz and uboat.net.

NOTE: None of the Fate article's actual recorded instances of circular run torpedoes referred to T-5 acoustical torpedoes.

Most telling of all, however, was that every recorded instance of a circular run torpedo occurred on the surface. There was no recorded instance – or even a suggestion – of a torpedo not only circling back on the submarine that launched it, but chasing the submarine down to the bottom of the sea.

Coppock suggested the theory based upon information that Chatterton and Kohler provided – information that was deficient in two main regards. They misinformed him about the extent of damage to the hull, and they did not inform at all him about the attack that was made by the *Howard D. Crow* and *Koiner*. As I noted above, the written record makes it appear that the Fate authors had no previous knowledge of the hedgehog and depth-charge attack until Moyers made it public, which was after *Shadow Divers* was published.

The written record also makes it appear that the Fate authors were unaware of the importance of the damage to the hull atop the after torpedo room. *Shadow Divers* mentioned this hedgehog hole only in passing: one sentence on page 163, and one sentence on page 209. The book offered no explanation for the existence of this massive hole, and ignored it completely in the imaginary sinking scenario that was described on pages 324-326.

Now that the *Howard D. Crow's* hedgehog attack has become public knowledge, the Fate article openly acknowledged the existence of the hole, although the article totally misinterpreted the origin and significance of the hole. In order to corkscrew this hole into the Fate article's theory, the article assumed that the hedgehog hole was instead a depth-charge hole. This assumption appears to be based upon a belief that the hole was as large 65 years ago as it is today.

Not only does the Fate article ignore the processes of natural collapse and deterioration, but it fails to account for the hedgehog detonation.

I submit that if Coppock had known about the hedgehog and depth-charge attacks, and the hole that a hedgehog blasted through the top of the pressure hull, he would not have suggested the circular run torpedo theory. He would have reached a simpler and more logical conclusion.

I also submit that, having publicly taken credit for the theory and having staked their reputations on it in *Shadow Divers*, Chatterton and Kohler have found themselves stuck with it, so they continue to advocate it – but they now put the onus on Coppock for originating it, as a way to save grace because the theory has fallen into disfavor in light of superior evidence.

Thus the rationale for a three-part article whose primary focus was to discredit the *Howard D. Crow* and *Koiner* attacks.

The Errors of Their Ways

Errors abound in the Fate article, due to either ignorance, carelessness, or intentional obfuscation. The article stated that the *Reuben James* and the *Buckley* "attacked a sound contact in the North Atlantic, east of Cape Cod, in over 7,000 feet of water." (P1p15). The crush depth of German U-boats was less than 1,000 feet. Although there were several instances in which U-boats exceeded their designed crush depth by a fractional amount, it was impossible for any U-boat to survive at a depth of 7,000 feet. Even modern nuclear submarines have a crush depth that is less than 5,000 feet.

According to the Fate article, "Hedgehogs had magnetic triggers that detonated when they contacted a ferrous object." (P1p18). This is not true. Hedgehogs did *not* have magnetic triggers. Hedgehogs had contact triggers that detonated on contact with a solid object, such as rock or the steel hull of a U-boat. A hedgehog that landed in mud or soft sand did not detonate, because the surface was not hard enough to depress the trigger.

If a hedgehog was launched at a U-boat in an area of soft sand, such as that found in the underwater desert off the New Jersey coast, a detonation implied a hit on the U-boat. If the authors of the Fate article indeed found a reference to hedgehogs with magnetic triggers, they failed to identify the source.

The Fate article claimed that the *U-869* lay 5.2 miles from the final attack position that was noted by the *Howard D. Crow*. (P3p18) In fact, the distance was 4.5 miles. Furthermore, the Fate article neglected to mention that the difference between positions lay right along the *Howard D. Crow's* original course, without deviation to port or starboard. The attack position was obtained by dead reckoning: that is, by estimating course and speed, and by extrapolating the distance traveled during the time from the last known or observed position. Thus the difference is only one of changing engine revolutions, as the *Howard D. Crow* first started chasing and then matched speed with the escaping U-boat.

By withholding information, *Shadow Divers* led its uninformed readers to believe that the discovery of the *U-869* at a place where it was not supposed to be, was a unique and unprecedented occurrence for which Chatterton and Kohler should be given great credit. The Fate article contradicted this thesis by noting that more than 100 U-boats have been re-identified or relocated since the post-war assessors assigned places and dates of loss. Yet, after admitting the truth of the matter, the authors then condemned the Naval Historical Center and the U.S. Coast Guard Historian's Office for reassessing the fate of the *U-869* in accordance with Moyers' newly discovered information.

The Fate article stated that the *Howard D. Crow* and *Koiner* "would never have left what they believed to be an enemy submarine on the bottom, without proof that it had been completely destroyed." (P2p19). This sentence demonstrated either a complete lack of understanding of escort duty, or a brash attempt to dupe unknowledgeable readers into believing that proof of sinking a U-boat was a paramount duty for a convoy escort.

The purpose of an escort was to protect its convoy from enemy attack, not to sink U-boats. A convoy could be protected simply by keeping a U-boat submerged by means of harassing fire until the convoy steamed out of range. This was exactly what the *Howard D. Crow* and *Koiner* did.

Night was the time when most U-boat attacks occurred. The skippers of the escorts would have been derelict in their duty had they remained on site until they were absolutely positive that the U-boat had been destroyed, while another U-boat torpedoed vessels in the convoy that the escorts were supposed to be protecting.

Doenitz orchestrated wolf pack tactics against convoys. In this tactic, a U-boat that intercepted a convoy did not attack it, but transmitted the convoy's location to its brother wolves. Not until all the wolves converged on the convoy did any of the U-boats attack – each from a different direction. Once the presence of one U-boat was ascertained, the convoy commander feared that other U-boats might be lurking nearby. This accounted for the recall of the *Howard D. Crow* and *Koiner*.

The Fate article stated that after the attack, the *Koiner's* whaleboat spent only fourteen minutes examining the water over the wreck (P2p13), and did not see any sign of debris. The article neglected to mention that the hedgehogs were launched about fifteen minutes before sunset. The first depth-charge attack took place after sunset. It was well after nightfall by the time the *Koiner* reached the scene. It was completely dark by the time the whaleboat was launched. That accounts for the reason that debris was not sighted.

The Fate article neglected to mention that Stanton Ring, the chief of the whaleboat, recovered a sample of diesel oil by soaking it up in a rag. He showed this oil-soaked rag to tank tender Ralph Kern. The Fate article disregarded this important testimony.

Selective Evidence Comparison

The Fate article drew attention to the mounds of debris that were picked up after the *U-853* was sunk. The Fate article neglected to mention that nearly everything that was recovered from the site was recovered in bright sunshine the following day.

The Fate article drew considerable attention to the fact that twelve hours after the *U-521* was sunk, the *Chickadee* reported a huge oil slick that emanated from the wreck site. (P1p15). Perhaps if the *Howard D. Crow* and *Koiner* had remained over the *U-869* until the following morning, they would have reported such a slick. But by that time they were not in the area to make such an observation. The article compared an observation that was made half a day after destruction, with an observation that was made only minutes after destruction, when debris and an oil slick had not yet had time to become noticeable on the surface and in the dark.

Worse, the Fate article neglected to state the duration of an oil slick *beyond* twelve hours. In the case of the *U-701*, for example, the oil slick was visible for at least three days after the U-boat's destruction. (See *Shipwrecks of North Carolina: North*, pages 194-201, and *The Fuhrer's U-boats in American Waters*, pages 284-292). For an oil slick to have completely dissipated by February 11, the *U-869* would have to have been sunk many days prior to the arrival of the *Howard D. Crow*.

Worst, the authors neglected to mention that of the more than 600 U-boats that were lost during the war, a large number disappeared without a trace: there was no oil slick, no floating debris, nothing to indicate that a U-boat had been sunk with all hands. This accounts for the reason that so many initial assessments were inaccurate.

The Fate article either neglected to mention or its authors did not realize that when the *U-548* sank in 7,000 feet of water, and "produced an oil slick that was two miles by one mile," (P1p15) the hull would have imploded after exceeding its crush depth – thus the reason for the dispersion of so much oil. The *U-869* sank in only

230 feet of water – far shallower than its designed crush depth – and therefore would not have released much oil.

The Fate article used the *U-853* as its only example of how anti-submarine warfare was conducted, and how much paperwork was submitted afterward, supposedly because ASW analysts wanted to determine "specifically what techniques, tactics, and weapons were actually sinking submarines." (P2p14). The destruction of the *U-853* occurred only one day before Victory in Europe, when the Navy no longer anticipated a need to study techniques, tactics, and weapons.

Navy personnel knew that peace negotiations were underway and that the war against Nazi Germany was about to end. This was the last opportunity for skippers to claim credit for sinking a U-boat, so everyone wanted to get into the act and ensure that his name was entered on the rolls.

In the event, it took more than two *hundred* depth charges to crack the hull of the *U-853*, and to release oil and floating debris from the hull – compared to *one* hedgehog and *one* depth charge that are known to have struck the *U-869*. When commercial salvage operations were conducted on the *U-853* in 1953, divers had to blast a hole in the hull in order to gain access to the interior: there were no original damage holes that were large enough to permit entry. (See *Shipwrecks of Rhode Island and Connecticut*, p155.)

Furthermore, the attacking warships were not employed in escort duty at the time of the attack. They were free to hang around the area for as long as they wanted. They could afford to expend all their depth charges because they would not be needed after the end of the U-boat war (which terminated the following day).

Fudging the Facts

The authors wrote that Harold Muth, the gunnery officer on the *Howard D. Crow*, contacted Kurson "as well as several other divers and historians." (P2p15) First of all, Kurson was neither a diver nor an historian; he was a paid biographer.

Second, the sentence misleadingly put the cart before the horse. In reality, Moyers tracked down Muth and several other crewmembers after he learned about the *Howard D. Crow* and *Koiner* incident. Moyers was the one who initiated contact, and who obtained the information that the authors of the Fate article took credit for obtaining.

Third, the Fate article stated, "Muth came to believe that the *Howard D. Crow* and *Koiner* were indeed responsible for the sinking of the *U-869*. A case was presented to the USCG Historian's Center [sic], and the USN Historical Center." These sentences were worded in such a way that the article deviously implied that Muth presented the case, whereas it was Moyers who presented the case, by submitting his written report along with supporting documentation (including written and verbal information that he obtained from surviving crewmembers). Once again the Fate article cheated Moyers out of credit that was due to him.

Not only that, but Muth did not "come to believe" anything – he had *always* known (or suspected with conviction) that the *Howard D. Crow* was responsible for sinking a U-boat. He told me that when I was writing *Shadow Divers Exposed*, and I included his convictions in the body of the text (pages 35-36). The Fate article twisted the sequence of events and gave the impression that Muth did not initially believe in the *Howard D. Crow's* successful destruction of a U-boat, but adopted the belief after the Naval Historical Center and the U.S. Coast Guard Historian's Office validated it.

The Fate article singled out Muth as a malcontent, dismissed his account out of hand, and neglected to inform their readers of Muth's assertion that the U-boat was underway at the time the *Howard D. Crow* conducted the hedgehog and depth-charge attacks. A moving U-boat contradicted the circular run torpedo theory.

Worse still, the Fate article readers were not informed that Muth's account had been corroborated by three other surviving crewmembers of the *Howard D. Crow*, all four of whom Harold Moyers interviewed:

George King (anti-submarine warfare officer), Howard Denson (sonar operator), and Ted Siviec (hedgehog launcher). (See *Shadow Divers Exposed*, pages 32-33)

Even those who might find fault with the testimony of subordinate personnel must accept that an account that was given by the attacking vessel's ASW officer was not so easy to dismiss.

Lewis Davis, commanding officer of the *Howard D. Crow* during the Korean War, corroborated the convictions of the former crewmembers in a letter that he wrote to me after publication of *Shadow Divers Exposed*. Based on his knowledge of the sonar equipment and on the observations of witnesses, he confirmed that the U-boat had to have been in motion during the hedgehog attack, and did not stop moving until afterward. The U-boat was stationary by the time the *Koiner* arrived on the scene and delivered the coup de grace. I reproduced Davis's correspondence in *Shipwreck Heresies* (pages 232-235). The Fate article conveniently ignored Davis's conclusions, and did not let their readers know of its existence.

The Fate article informed its readers about the report that was filed by Charles Judson, commanding officer of the *Koiner*. Judson reported that the target was not moving when the *Koiner* arrived. The Fate article did not suggest the possibility that the target was not moving because it was already flooded as a result of the hedgehog and depth-charge attacks made by the *Howard D. Crow*.

The Fate article overemphasized Judson's report in which no debris was sighted and "only a 'smear' of oil" (P2p15) had risen to the surface after the *Koiner's* whaleboat was in the water for only fourteen minutes, and downplayed Muth's assertion that bubbles of air rose to the surface and that the sea was covered with oil.

Ironically, while the Fate article placed complete faith in the *Koiner's* succinct action report, the article completely debunked the same kind of action reports that placed the *U-869* off Gibraltar. This designing attitude of acceptance and denial served the avowed purpose of the article at the expense of objectivity.

A Suffusion of Fantasy

The Fate article would have its readers believe that the *U-869* arrived at its ultimate destination some time prior to the day on which the *Howard D. Crow* attacked a moving target at the same location, that the *U-869* launched a torpedo at a target that did not report an attack, and that the torpedo circled around and detonated against the U-boat's hull with such violence that "This boat is virtually blown in two, amidships." (P2p17)

There are a number of fallacies in this argument. The Tenth Fleet was tracking the *U-869* via Ultra decrypts, knew its rate of progress, and predicted that it would reach its operational area some 70 miles off New York Harbor in the beginning of February. (*Shadow Divers Exposed*, pages 29-30) Based on this known rate of progress, Harold Moyers calculated the time it would take for the U-boat to travel the distance to its ultimate destination after its last transmission was intercepted and its location was triangulated. His extrapolation placed the *U-869* precisely where the wreck is located on the day of the *Howard D. Crow's* attack. (See *Shadow Divers Exposed*, p42)

The Fate article did not present any evidence to establish how the *U-869* could have reached its ultimate destination any sooner than February 11. The Fate article ignored the known travel speed and simply assumed that it must have traveled faster than its predicted speed. Additionally, a significant amount of time must have passed since the U-boat's destruction, in order for the putative oil slick to have completely vanished before the arrival of the *Howard D. Crow*.

The Fate article did not present any evidence to establish that the *U-869* ever launched a torpedo. It merely made that assumption. In fact, no torpedo doors are open on the wreck. If the *U-869* had launched a torpedo and was sunk seconds later, at least one torpedo door would be open.

The Fate article authors claimed that they spoke with "experts" who determined "that the center of the explosive force was inside, not outside the pressure hull," (P2p18) and that "if the pressure hull is blown out, then the cause has to be from an internal explosion." (P3p36) These putative experts were not named. (In both *Shadow Divers Exposed* and *Shipwreck Heresies*, I provided the names of my sources and quoted them verbatim, so there could be no doubt as to who they were or what they said, and so that follow-up researchers, historians, and journalists could confirm what I wrote.)

Readers of the Fate article were expected to believe that the *U-869* fired a T-5 acoustical torpedo that "possessed a 'shape' to the warhead explosive, as well as sophisticated fusing. Taken in total, it was designed to cause the maximum damage to a target, by 'cutting' into the hull. This was incredibly advanced technology for 1945." (P3p36)

In fact, the technology was so advanced that it did not exist! While it is true that there were two configurations of the shape of the nose of the T-5 acoustical torpedo – one flat and one rounded – the different shapes were designed to accommodate different numbers of hydrophones: the flat nose accommodated four hydrophones; the rounded nose accommodated two hydrophones. (See *Naval Weapons of World War II*, by John Campbell and N. J. M. Campbell, p264; and *Hellions of the Deep: the Development of American Torpedoes in World War II*, by Robert Gannon, p155; for additional information about T-5 acoustical torpedoes, see Gannon, Chapter 8, "A Torpedo that Listens," pages 99-101.)

The nose shapes had nothing to do with explosives or fusing, as the Fate article alluded. For that matter, what did the Fate article mean by "fusing." "Fusing" is the present participle of the verb "to fuse." "To fuse" is defined as "to melt, or to liquefy or reduce to a plastic state by heating," or "to blend, or to mix together as if by melting." These definitions are meaningless with respect to torpedoes.

The tip of a torpedo was fitted with a detonator to

trigger the explosive charge that was contained in the main body of the housing, not with a mechanism or chemical to melt or blend metal.

Furthermore, the Fate article failed to mention that U-boats were constructed with a double hull: an outer hull and an inner hull. Every U-boat enthusiast should know this.

In order for this fabricated "cutting into the hull" theory to work, the torpedo would have had to cut through the U-boat's outer hull without detonating, then penetrate the inner hull, and then explode inside the compartment, so as to create what the Fate article called a "reverse differential pressure wave." (P3p35) The Fate article based this entire premise on the oral allegation of an unnamed individual they just happened to bump into. (P3p36) The Fate article furnished no primary documentation or published corroboration.

Furthermore, the Fate article did not present any documentation to show that the *U-869* was armed with T-5 acoustical torpedoes. This was just another convenient assumption.

Acoustical torpedoes were designed to home in on the loudest sound within range. For this reason they struck their targets at the propeller or engine room: the noisiest areas of a vessel. U-boats could not operate their diesel engines while proceeding under water, because there was not enough oxygen inside the pressure hull to support combustion of the fuel. A submerged U-boat used a huge collection of large storage batteries to furnish power for electric motors, which in turn rotated the propellers. This system of propulsion was called "silent running" because it produced hardly any noise other than cavitation that was created by the propellers.

For the *U-869* to have torpedoed itself, it must be assumed not only that the guidance controls malfunctioned, but that the torpedo dived under the surface, then missed the noisiest part of the U-boat (its propellers) and struck the nearly inaudible control room.

The Fate article conveniently neglected to stipulate where in the water column this catastrophic event occurred.

If the *U-869* was "virtually blown in two, amidships" at the time of its demise, as the Fate article claimed (and which the proposed theory required), then the U-boat must have been resting on the bottom at the time it was destroyed. Had the U-boat been blown virtually in two on the surface, then the hull would have broken apart and the wreck would lie in two pieces. Had the hull remained in one piece despite this catastrophic damage, the conning tower and associated debris would not have come to rest next to the control room. The conning tower would have landed on the seabed astern as the U-boat's momentum propelled it forward, and other debris would have left a trail between the displaced conning tower and the place where the hull eventually came to rest.

If it is posited that the torpedo struck the U-boat *after* it settled on the bottom, then it must be assumed that the torpedo's hydrostatic pressure device (which set the torpedo's running depth) malfunctioned simultaneously with the guidance controls. The guidance system and the depth control were separate mechanisms; the malfunction of one did not affect the other.

In summation, in order for the Fate article scenario to work, it must be assumed that the errant torpedo missed its intended target, circled around and homed in on its launching platform, followed the U-boat down to the seabed (at 230 feet) on a three-dimensional curving vector, struck the outer hull at a place of comparative silence (and without detonating), then proceeded to cut through the inner hull before the detonator triggered the explosive charge, and then projected the explosive force through a small hole into the control room, instead of expanding outward and upward. Those are a lot of assumptions.

The Fate article called attention to inward bending of the *U-853*'s pressure hull "caused by depth charges or hedgehogs from the outside." (P2p16 caption) In fact, the so-called depth-charge or hedgehog damage that was shown in the pictures (P2p16) was caused by natural collapse many decades after the U-boat's destruction.

When I first dived on the *U-853*, in 1972, there was no damage whatsoever in the area that was depicted in the photographs. Both the pressure hull and the outer skin were intact. At that time, there was only one hole that was large enough for me to penetrate, and that was in the motor room in the port stern. This hole was blasted not by a depth charge, but by salvage divers in 1953, because they found no means of entry other than tight-fitting hatches.

Not until the 1980's did a barely penetrable hole appear in the area that was pictured. (P2p16) I published this information in *The Lusitania Controversies* (Book One, pages 230-231), which Chatterton purchased from me immediately after its publication in 1998, and in *Shipwrecks of Rhode Island and Connecticut* (p158, published in 2004).

The Fate article presented the "inward bending" of this hole as proof of what depth-charge damage should look like. As every wreck-diving expert should know, the hulls of *all* shipwrecks bend inward after a sufficient passage of time. Caving in is an ordinary mechanism of shipwreck collapse. The portrayal of this hole as original damage that was made in 1945, either displayed criminal ignorance of the processes of natural collapse, or brandished a vagrant attempt to bamboozle uninformed readers.

The Fate article noted "stress cracks" in the area surrounding the control room of the *U-869*. (P2p17). A great deal of imagination is required to see any stress cracks because every bit of exposed surface is thickly encrusted with marine fouling organisms. Even if cracks were visible, it would not be proof that they originated from concussion. Cracks appear in weak points of all steel plates as a shipwreck collapses due to the force of gravity.

No saltwater shipwreck appears today the same way it appeared 66 years ago. This includes the *U-869*. As I noted in *Shipwrecks of North Carolina: South* (p187, published in 1992) and in *Shipwreck Heresies* (pages 216-217), the conning tower was still standing on the U.S.

submarine *Tarpon* when I first dived on it in 1983. When I dived on the wreck in 1986, I found the conning tower lying on its side next to the control room – in the identical way the conning tower of the *U-869* now lies on its side next to its control room. I am fairly certain that the *Tarpon's* conning tower was not blasted off by a torpedo during the intervening years.

In order to fit its concocted theory, the Fate article assumed that the appearance of the *U-869* today is the same as it was when it sank. But hedgehogs and depth charges did not gouge gigantic holes in a hull; they merely broke welds, cracked steel plates, or damaged through-hull fittings, which caused the submarine to flood. The *U-853*, for example, had no major breaches in its hull, despite the fact that more than two *hundred* depth charges were dropped on it.

What the Fate article referred to as a major breach in the hull of the *U-869* (P2p17) was probably little more than a crack or a disjointed fitting in 1945. Since then the conning tower fell off as a result of natural deterioration, or was dragged off by the dredge of a fishing trawler, and the control room overhead subsequently caved in.

The Fate article claimed that the *U-869's* hatches were blown off by the torpedo explosion. (P2p17) Yet neither of the two American subs that sank as a result of circular run torpedoes had their hatches blown off. The Fate article noted these submarine losses (P3p39), and stated that there were survivors from both, but neglected to mention that the survivors of the *Tang* escaped from the submarine many hours after it crashed to the bottom, at a depth of 180 feet. The *Tang's* hatches were not blown off by any so-called "reverse differential pressure wave." (P3p35) The hatches were opened by the men inside when they made good their escape.

The Fate article neglected to mention the loss of the *U-250* and the miraculous survival of several of its occupants during a follow-up depth-charge attack. After the U-boat flooded, the skipper and several of his crewmen crowded neck deep in water under a hatch. A subsequent depth-charge explosion yanked the hatch cover off its hinges. The men were sucked out of the U-boat and blown to the surface with the escaping air bubble.

In order to appreciate how this can happen, the reader needs to understand the mechanism of an underwater explosion. An explosion is defined as a rapid expansion of gas. Gas is compressible but liquid is not. When an explosion occurs under water, the gas expands outward in all directions, pushing the water away and creating a temporary vacuum in the center. Once the bubble of expanding gas is stopped by the surrounding water, the water pressure collapses the bubble. Like a swinging pendulum, the collapsing gas passes through the center of the vacuum and continues out the other side. This alternating expansion and collapse recurs several times – the number of times being dependant upon the size of the initial blast – until the released energy is stabilized. (This mechanism is fully explained in the U.S. Navy training film, *Close is Near Enough*. The film also explains how subsequent bubbles are drawn toward the comparative hollow of a vessel's hull, thus causing more and more damage.)

Submarine hatches are not designed to keep pressure in, but to keep it out. The inner locking mechanism does not need to be very strong because the hatch is kept closed by external water pressure. When a depth charge explodes close over top of a U-boat, the suction force of the vacuum exceeds the breaking strength of the hatch's locking mechanism. The hatch is either swung back or sheered off its hinges, the air escapes from the pressure hull, and the submarine floods.

Divers then find the hatch covers gone or lying near the hatches.

Harold Moyers, Steve Gatto, and Jon Hulburt are members of the Society of Naval Architects and Marine Engineers (SNAME). They presented this scenario to SNAME explosives expert James Ruggieri. He agreed that this scenario was not just plausible, but likely.

Moyers explained: "The U-boat hatch diameter is 600 millimeters. That would be 23.62 inches for an area of 438 square inches. If the hatches were in 215 feet of water and the sub was flooded, then 48,387 pounds of pressure would be exerted on both sides of the hatch. If a depth charge went off outside the flooded sub then an overpressure would occur outside the hull. The explosion bubble would expand until the pressure of the expanding gas in the explosion equalized with the surrounding water pressure. The bubble would then collapse as the detonation consumed itself. Water would quickly re-exert itself into the void. But for an instant prior to that happening there would be a vacuum above the hull (and possibly a hatch). With near zero pressure above the hatch, and 48,387 pounds below the hatch, the hatch would pop off. They were held in place by three quick dogs (actuated by a hand-wheel), and one manual locking dog. Arthur Baudzus of *U-859* described the dogs to me as 'flimsy.' His submarine was torpedoed by the HMS *Trenchant* and no hatches were 'ripped from their mounts.' Baudzus and 19 other survivors made it to the surface and survived."

Point and Counterpoint

It is hypocritical to say the least that the Fate article asserted categorically that any hypothesis should take "*all* of the facts into account." (P3p39; italics in the Fate article). The Fate article cautioned its readers to "trust the evidence, and take nothing for granted. The evidence has no hidden agenda." (P1p21)

Despite these assertions, the Fate article concealed from its readers numerous all-important facts and most of the evidence, to wit: that there existed a great deal of evidence in addition to the reports that they quoted, that the target that the *Howard D. Crow* detected on sonar was in motion, that the *Howard D. Crow* chased this target as it attempted to escape under water, that the target continued to move in an evasive fashion after the hedgehog attack, and that the target did not stop moving until after the *Howard D. Crow* dropped depth charges it.

The Fate article neglected to inform its readers of the testimony of four surviving crewmembers of the *Howard*

D. Crow (Howard Denson, George King, Harold Muth, and Ted Siviec), all of whom agreed that the U-boat was in motion during the chase and the attack, until a barrage of depth charges brought it to a halt.

As an alternative to this simple and straightforward scenario, the Fate article proposed the following twisted string of events:

If the *U-869* reached its ultimate destination earlier than its known travel speed projected, *if* it was equipped with a T-5 acoustical torpedo, *if* the *U-869* fired a T-5 acoustical torpedo at a target that cannot be accounted for, *if* the torpedo's acoustical tracking system failed, *if* the torpedo's guidance system then ceased to operate, *if* the torpedo started to circle, *if* the torpedo's independent depth control mechanism malfunctioned, *if* the torpedo followed not only a horizontal circular pattern but a descending trajectory like a swooping bird, *if* the torpedo was tipped with a fusing or melting device that could cut through hull plate, *if* the torpedo cut through the outer hull without detonating, *if* the torpedo cut through the inner hull, *if* the explosive charge penetrated into the control room before detonating, *then* the *U-869* can be said to have been sunk by a circular run of its own torpedo.

The only *ifs* that are not implausible in this scenario are those that are impossible.

The Fate article further postulated that the *Howard D. Crow* dropped its hedgehogs and depth charges on the already sunken U-boat, that the hole above the after torpedo room was not a hedgehog hole but a depth-charge hole, that the hole adjacent to the control room was not a depth-charge hole but a torpedo hole. In doing so, the Fate article ignored the hedgehog attack, and offered no explanation for the hedgehog detonation.

This problematical and long-winded scenario is an insult to the intelligence of the Fate article's readers, and demonstrates a clear lack of respect for historical accuracy.

An incredible number of assumptions and postulates must be made in order to support a theory that can better be explained by relying upon the known actions of the *Howard D. Crow* and the observations of crewmembers who witnessed the event.

William of Occam must be turning over in his grave at this outrageous violation of the methodological principle.

Addendum

I intended to submit my rebuttal to *Wreck Diving Magazine* in the hope of educating the readers who had been misled by the negligence of the Fate article. After all, that magazine's readers were the very ones the authors targeted to deceive.

Joe Porter, the magazine's publisher, declined to respond to my query letter. Instead, he had his wife Heidi write to me and reject my article. It appeared that Porter, like the authors of the Fate article, did not want the magazine's readers to have all the facts, either. This clearly demonstrated no respect for either the truth or the magazine's subscribers.

In 2011, Dan Wright submitted an article proposal to Porter. Dan intended to dive on and photograph the *Monitor* and the *Andrea Doria*. He wanted to tie the two wrecks together by giving some background about their historical significance to the wreck-diving community. Porter liked the idea; he gave Dan the go-ahead to write the article, and promised to publish it after Dan obtained underwater photographs to accompany the text.

Dan wanted to use me as the thread to connect the wrecks. After all, he reasoned, my landmark court case against NOAA was solely responsible for enabling him and every other recreational diver to dive on the Civil War ironclad. My association with the *Doria* was abundantly well established. I had written the book about the *Monitor*, and I had written two books and numerous articles about the *Doria*. My name was inseparable from both shipwrecks.

Furthermore, the *Doria* trip on which Dan and I were together was the one on which I made my landmark 200th dive to the Grand Dame of the Sea. A photographic record of this event would add a fascinating fillip to the article.

When Dan approached me with the idea of photographing me on the *Doria*, and interviewing me about my experiences on the *Monitor* and the *Doria*, I agreed – but only if he first obtained approval from Porter.

Unfortunately for Dan and for the readers of the magazine, Porter nixed the idea in no uncertain terms. He told Dan, "Under no circumstances will Gentile's likeness or mention of his name appear in my magazine." This was in keeping with Porter's previous stance in which, in one issue of the magazine he listed a number of books about shipwrecks, and specifically excluded all 36 shipwreck titles of mine.

Porter supported the lies that were told in *Shadow Divers* and the Fate article. He repudiated the truth that I told in *Shadow Divers Exposed* and "Homage to Occam's Razor."

Such is the attitude of unreason.

These purveyors of falsehoods and partial truths persist in the belief that if they reiterate a lie often enough, the lie will eventually achieve the eminence of verity and historical authenticity; that by shouting lies loud enough they can convert their cowardly prevarications to gospel. Urban legends may die hard, but they always do die, and they leave egg on the faces of those who perverted the facts or made them up.

I joked with Dan about taking my picture and captioning it with someone else's name, then afterward revealing the "mistake;" and about slipping my name into the article just to force Porter to expunge it. Ultimately we decided against making Porter and his magazine the butt of another joke. The joke would be on Porter when his readers learned the truth elsewhere, and learned that Porter intentionally backed the falsehoods of his magazine's backers.

Now you know why you read the facts here first instead of in *Wreck Diving Magazine*.

Photographic Memories

"Arma virumque cano" (Of arms and the man I sing)
  The Aeneid, by Vergil

I have a photographic memory. Which is not the same as an eidetic memory. That's a horse of a different color, as the Wizard of Oz once stated.

According to the dictionary, the definition of "eidetic" is "able to recall or reproduce things previously seen, with startling accuracy, clarity, and vividness." A person who has an eidetic memory can remember a scene in detail, can repeat dialogue with precision, and can recite long passages that he has read in books.

To dispel a common notion, no one can flip casually through the pages of a book and then write down every word that his eyes skimmed over. This is how many people regard photographic memory: as the kind that snaps a picture of everything he sees, and then retains that picture so that the person with such a memory can regurgitate the words on printed pages as if he is reading them from a mental image. Notwithstanding the above, some people have displayed a remarkable talent for recollection, making it appear that that is what they are doing.

Prime Minister Winston Churchill once recited eighteen *hundred* lines of poetry without batting an eye, missing a beat, or referring to notes. By contrast, in high school I studied for hours in order to recite fourteen lines of Shakespeare in front of the classroom: "But soft, what light through yonder window breaks? It is the east, and Juliet is the sun. . . . " That's as much as I can remember today.

Biochemist and prolific author Isaac Asimov could read a dozen reference works about a particular subject, collect and collate all the information in his mind, then sit down at his typewriter and type ninety words a minute to produce a ten-thousand-word article in a couple of hours, or a full-length book in as many weeks, without ever looking back at his sources.

I could go on with other examples but you get the point. Some people have phenomenal memories along with instant recall. Other people have photographic memories but their minds have no film.

In twelfth grade, I read all three hundred pages of Vergil's *Aeneid* in Latin. Today I remember only the first three words of the first Cantos, quoted above. (For those who don't remember – or never knew – *The Aeneid* was the Roman version of Homer's Greek epic poems, *The Iliad* and *The Odyssey*: sagas of the Trojan War and the long return journey of Odysseus, or Aeneas.)

By exclaiming that I have a photographic memory, I mean that when I see a photograph that I took years ago, the image evokes instant memories of events that occurred concurrently with the scene on film. The merest glance serves to spark reminiscences that may have long since been buried in the well of my subconscious.

Because this is a book of reflections, I decided to peruse my vast photographic library – I have taken hundreds of thousands of pictures throughout my life, starting when I was but a youngster – in order to see what reminiscences my mind's eye would summon. It should be fun for both of us.

Myakka River dreamer.

Gators Galore

Alligators are not endangered in southeastern United States. On the contrary, in waters in which *Alligator mississippiensis* predominates, the only endangered species is *Scubadivor unsapiens*.

The largest concentration of American alligators I have ever encountered was on the Myakka River, in Florida. When I canoed the fourteen-mile stretch of wild and untamed river between put-in and take-out, my paddling partner was Cheryl Novak; Ted Green led the trip in his kayak. The twisting river had more doglegs than a pet shop. Around every bend we saw monster alligators sunning themselves on the sandy banks.

Oddly enough, despite their size, ferocity, and reputation, alligators are rather skittish. As soon as they spotted us, they leaped into the water with a tremendous splash, sometimes close enough that we were doused by the spray. What made Cheryl more nervous than anything was when they dived under the canoe and the top rows of their armor plates grated along the soft keel of our 17-foot Oldtown Tripper; it made a sound like a guitar pick dragging across the corrugations of an antique washboard.

I've seen alligators while canoeing on other Florida rivers, as well as on backwater swamp creeks in North Carolina. But the next largest concentration I observed was on a diving trip.

The Cooper River meanders through the State of South Carolina until it flows into the Atlantic Ocean in the vicinity of Charleston. The convoluted river has more squiggles than an epileptic rattlesnake. Toward the end of its peregrinations it cuts through an alluvial plane whose sediment was laid down millions of years ago, when the planet's water level differed from that of modern times.

During ice ages, when much of the world's water was bound in the form of ice, the Charleston area was high and dry, and was inhabited by prehistoric mammals. During interglacial epochs, the area lay deep under water where ancient sharks swam.

Sleeping with both eyes open - and wary.

Nowadays the flow of water gradually erodes the banks so that deposited material is continually exposed and falls into the riverbed, where it is swept along by strong current and shifting tides: a never-ending and constantly replenishing source of fossilized bones, horns, and teeth. On any given day a diver might spot the bone of a primitive camel, the horn of an extinct ungulate, the vertebra of a primeval shark, the tympanic bone of an ancient whale, a stingray plate, a turtle shell, a mastodon or woolly mammoth tooth, a coprolite (fossilized fecal matter), an arrowhead, a spear tip, or a Colonial china shard. My friend Pete Manchee once found the fang of a saber-toothed tiger.

Most people search for fossil shark teeth, in particular those of *Carcharodon megalodon*: "meg teeth" in the local vernacular. That is the chief draw to diving in the Cooper River and its tributaries, and in nearby rivers that shared the same alluvial flood plane.

On one trip the pontoon boat was easing into an anchorage when a ten-foot gator swam serenely past the hull against the current. Aghast, one diver said in a shaky voice, "Are we going into the water with them hanging around?" His question was rhetorical. If he wanted to collect shark teeth, the only way to do so was by diving for them.

I commented dryly, "We're not competing for the same resource. We're after rock and they're after food."

He was not mollified but went diving anyway, albeit with great trepidation. No one had any encounters of the third kind.

On another trip in a johnboat, four of us returned from a slack-water dive then moved to another spot. By the time we arrived the tide had turned. It is almost impossible to dive in the Cooper River when the speed of the current is augmented by the outgoing tide. Nonetheless, Pete Manchee and I decided to go for it. Jim Hinton was along for the ride; he had no problem with chasing after us if we got swept downstream.

Andy Ogburn and Mike Phipps chortled as floating debris sped past the anchored boat at twice warp speed.

They catcalled Pete and me the "old geezers" because we belonged to an elder generation. They stayed on the boat with Jim while the "geezers" went diving.

It was tough going on the bottom. They say that the trick is to stab your knife into the riverbed and hang on with one hand while you fan the gravel with the other. But here the bottom consisted of marl with a hardness of nine on the Mohs scale. My knife would not penetrate more than a fraction of an inch.

I made myself heavy by letting all the air out of my drysuit and buoyancy compensator. I grabbed a boulder and jammed it into my weight belt. I dug in with my fingertips and knees. And *still* I was shoved downstream. I vectored to the bank and clawed my way upstream, then ferried across the river to the opposite side where I repeated the process.

Eventually I returned to the left bank a short distance astern of the boat. I used brush and submerged branches to pull myself upstream to the port side. There I doffed my tanks and weight belt, helped to get them aboard over the gunwale, then climbed up the side like a Navy seal. Pete did the same.

Now the laugh was on Mike and Andy, or, as I referred to them, the "young whippersnappers." Pete and I each had a collection of teeth and assorted oddments.

I said, "Just remember that the geezers went diving while the whippersnappers stayed on the boat."

It was all in fun, just as it should be.

Slinking into the water after unwary divers.

When I wasn't shooting alligators (with my camera), I spent my time collecting shark teeth and other fossils. A sampling of teeth of different shark species is pictured above. Shown below are (clockwise from upper left) unidentified bone, turtle shell, whale rib (the big thing in the middle), turtle scute (a plate that covered the caudal base), whale bone, and a giant ground sloth claw (or so I was told).

Thousand Islands Undressing

The St. Lawrence River is the major artery that connects the Great Lakes with the Atlantic Ocean. Monster vessels ply this narrow waterway virtually nonstop. In many places these steel-hulled giants pass within the proverbial stone's throw from shore. Okay, maybe you couldn't hit the hull by throwing a stone, but you could definitely hit it with a potato launcher.

The deep-throated thrumming of diesel engines sounds so loud under water that you might think that you are about to be run over by a passing deep-draft vessel. Once when I was diving on (and inside) the *Lillie Parsons*, the water vibrated with such intensity that instead of ascending straight to the surface, I swam to the bow and followed the wreck's anchor chain across the rocks to Sparrow Island, where the anchor was displayed on land as a topside tourist attraction. Then I swam around the small island to the slip where the boat was docked.

In actuality, most of the wrecks in the Thousand Islands aren't in the shipping lanes. But this doesn't mean that they are out of the way of small boat traffic. So be careful wherever you dive.

One story that I heard through the grapevine I was later able to verify by hearing the details straight from the horse's mouth. The horse's mouth, by the way, is different from the horse of a different color that I mentioned in the first section of this chapter. In this case, the horse's mouth asked me not to mention his name because he had already received enough grief from the diving community, which castigated him as a horse's . . . well, enough about equines and their anatomy.

Diver Dan (not his real name) was exploring the wreck of the *Roy A. Jodrey* when the incident occurred. The starboard bow of the wreck is pressed against the underwater cliff face that drops off the south side of Wellesley Island. A convenient cove is located next to the wreck site; the cove is just large enough for a dive boat to enter. Instead of dropping anchor, crewmembers scamper ashore with lines that they tie to nearby trees.

Above: Inside the *Lillie Parsons* looking out through the fractured stern. I was able to penetrate all the way to the bow of this upside-down wooden schooner by passing over the cargo of coal. I guess that makes me a coal passer. She sank in 1877.

Below: The anchor of the *Lillie Parsons*. You can see the chain leading down into the water. Maximum depth was 70 feet.

Above: The *See Way Vision* is sequestered in the cove near the *Roy A. Jodrey*. The mainland of New York State is in view across the Narrows at a distance slightly more than the length of a football field.

Below: Ted Green is swimming out of a forward window on the pilothouse of the *Roy A. Jodrey*. Note how zebra mussels cover much of the surface. Although Ted can be a pane you can't see through him.

With the bow nudged into the end of the cove, the stern hangs over 6 feet of crystal clear water. Divers can lower sling bottles onto the rocky bottom, then retrieve them after they jump off the swim platform, and either carry them throughout the dive or stage them at a convenient depth. The wreck is reached by one of two means: in either case you must angle about forty-five degrees to the left and pass over a bare hump of rock to a depth of about 30 feet, then (1) drop over the edge and glide down to the wheelhouse whose top reaches up to 150 feet, or (2) continue on the angled route to about 60 feet, where thoughtful divers have secured a rope that goes directly to the crane abaft the pilothouse.

The layout of the *Roy A. Jodrey* is typical of Great Lakes vessel design: the pilothouse is perched nearly atop the bow. The decks of the pilothouse are great fun to explore. The glass is gone from most of the windows on the navigating bridge, so it is easy to swim into and out of the large compartment. Ladders lead down to successively lower decks. You can go down four decks and exit through a huge hole on the starboard side where the outer bulkhead was scraped away by the rock face as the wreck slid down to the bottom.

You can swim over the port rail at a depth of 200 feet, then drop down to the riverbed at 240 feet. Don't do this if the current is moving fast, or you will find yourself dragging along the mussel-encrusted hull and perhaps unable to regain the main deck.

The wreck measures 640 feet in length. Abaft the crane there are only cargo holds until you reach the superstructure at the stern. This was Diver Dan's goal. Swimming nearly 600 feet at a depth of 200 feet, while wearing double tanks and two swing bottles, is an onerous task. He made it all the way, but then found that he did not have enough breathing gas to accomplish the return against the current.

Because the hull angles away from the shore, attempting to swim directly to land is problematical at best. By approximating the angle and using the Pythagorean Theorem, I estimate that the distance is

Above: From the *See Way Vision* in the cove near the *Roy A. Jodrey*, you can see how close Great Lakes freighters pass the dive site. Note the inflatable in the lower right corner, and the hard-hull boat above it; these boats brought additional divers to the wreck.

Below: The Coast Guard station and dock are visible at the right of the picture. The *Roy A. Jodrey* access cove is located to the left of the metal tower, at the far left in a notch between trees.

about 300 feet – and that through open water or by swimming along the bottom. The additional time that he must spend at depth would have added exponentially to his already extensive decompression penalty.

Diver Dan took the only option that seemed practical to him (and which seems logical to me): he deployed a marker buoy and sent a decompression line to the surface.

The shipping channel between Wellesley Island and the mainland of New York State is so narrow at this point that President Washington could have thrown a silver dollar across it, as he is supposed to have done across the Potomac River. (I disbelieve this historical legend, although it is just possible that he might have *skipped* a silver dollar across the river.) In any case, the stern of the wreck was so far from shore that Diver Dan's marker float hit the surface in the way of large vessel traffic; and, coincidentally, directly in front of the Coast Guard station.

An alert coastguardsmen (or coastguardswoman) spotted the marker and realized it for what it was. A diver decompressing in the middle of the channel called for immediate attention. To prevent Diver Dan from being run over, the Coast Guard broadcast a warning for all vessel traffic to cease operating in the Narrows. This meant that upbound vessels had to stay in place while maintaining steerageway against the current, while downbound vessels had to reverse their propellers in order to hold their hulls against the tide: a tricky maneuver at best, as vessels don't steer well going backward.

The Coast Guard dispatched a cutter to watch over Diver Dan for more than an hour, until he completed his decompression. After they plucked him out of the water, they soundly rebuked him for his inconsiderate action.

I was well aware of this story when I made my first dive on the *Roy A. Jodrey*. I made no attempt to repeat Diver Dan's mistake. I confined all my explorative activities to the pilothouse and to the structures around the crane. My dive buddy was Ted Green. We did our deep stops by clinging to the cliff face for vertical orientation.

After we rose over the hump into the shallows, instead of staying put the way most divers do, we decided to overcome the boredom of long decompression by swimming back and forth along the shore. Very quickly we discovered old bottles that had been tossed into the river before the time when trash disposal in water became a hotly debated environmental issue.

We passed the time by ranging far and wide. I stumbled over an intact deer skeleton. I spotted walleye and great northern pike. I flushed smaller fish out of the grass and algae. I recovered some nineteenth-century bottles to add to my collection. It was the most fun I'd ever had during decompression – or any fun, for that matter, during decompression. Ted agreed.

Apparently, however, we ranged too far and too wide. Unbeknownst to us, we had gone past the Coast Guard station and docking area during our underwater peregrinations. This was considered a no-no. Divers were prohibited from that vicinity for fear that they might run afoul of passing boat propellers if they surfaced where and when they shouldn't.

This made perfect sense to me when I learned of it later, but at the time I had no idea that a Coast Guard station lay right around the corner from our entry point. Nor did the Coast Guard post warning signs under water for unwary or unknowing divers.

The Coast Guard sent an officer through the woods and over the rocks to the secluded cove, in order to reprimand our skipper about his divers' transgressions. The skipper (Brent Brown, *See Way Vision*) passed along the reprimand to us. Duly chastised, we promised not to repeat our indiscretions.

The most delightful and cost effective way to explore the Thousand Islands is by houseboat. Steve Lewis organized such a week-long excursion which allowed the group to dive on a number of shipwrecks along a twenty-five-mile stretch of the St. Lawrence River, from Brockville, Ontario to Wellesley Island, New York. The boat was our lodging as well as our dive platform. There is no better way to make new friends and to enjoy the

Above: After a dive on the *Roy A. Jodrey*, most divers decompress the way this pair is doing: reposing on rock ledges at the appropriate depths. I found this method too boring, so I went exploring along the shore.

Below: This yellow perch was kind enough to hang around while I focused my camera. The pike and walleye were more skittish; they never came within range of my wide-angle lens. Scrounging through the weeds and algae was a lot more rewarding than clinging to rock like a limpet.

Above: The *Pippen II* is the boat on the left. Note the large expanse of windows and the all-around railing on the weather deck. Plastic chairs adorned the deck so that passengers could relax in the sun, but they were so flimsy that the legs snapped off when anyone tried to sit in one. The square end of the boat is the bow. Captain Lewis is walking on the dock.

Below: The spacious interior of the *Pippen II*. Note the tanks on the after deck beyond the corridor. One cabin is aft of the galley, the other up a ladder in the corridor into the low deckhouse that is shown above.

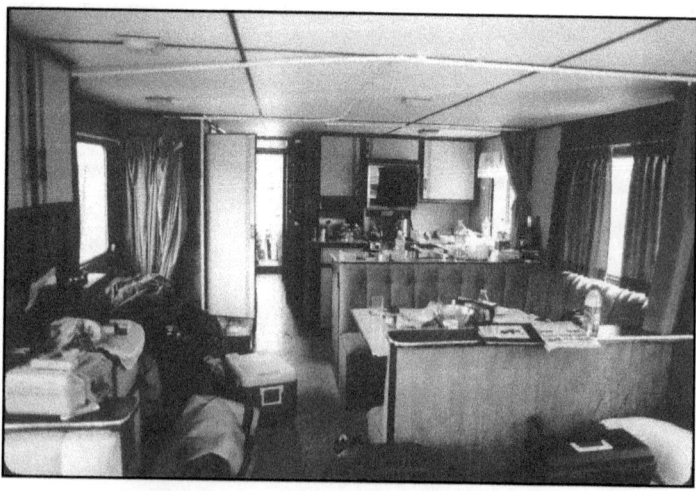

camaraderie of constant company than to live together for a week in a mobile motel.

The name of the houseboat was *Pippen II*. The interior floor plan was laid out in a great room concept that included a full-sized galley, a mess room, and a common area with chairs and a pair of sofa beds. A short passageway led to two small staterooms and a shower. The boat was quite literally a small home away from home.

There was endless hot water courtesy of a tankless coil water heater. I was fascinated by this ingenious device. I had never heard of one that didn't have a tank which was filled with water whose high temperature was constantly maintained. The tankless water heater was a fraction of the size of standard house units because, obviously, it did not have a storage tank. Instead, the unit consisted of a tight copper coil full of water that was heated by propane gas. When not in use, the propane valve was closed and the water temperature equaled ambient. When the unit was switched on, the propane valve opened, an automatic igniter lighted the gas, and the flame heated the water in the coil in a matter of minutes. In the shower, the user was sprayed with hot water from the end of the coil while cold water was introduced into the beginning of the coil. By the time the new water circulated through the coil to the end, it was heated. All eight of us could take showers (in sequence, not together) without ever running out of hot water! This marvel of modern technology saves energy. It needs a good promotional scheme in order to see more widespread use.

I was first of the group to arrive at the dock. I leaned into my van to pull out my tanks – and my back slipped out of place. I was unable to lift a tank for the rest of the week. I had to depend on my fellow divers – most of whom I had never met before – to carry my tanks for me. They willingly obliged.

No license was required to rent or operate the boat. After Steve arrived, an employee of the rental company spent five minutes in showing him and me how to start the engine and work the controls; he did not take us on a trial run. The most difficult part to master was dou-

Above: Although there may not be a full thousand islands in the area, it certainly looks that way. Some islands are privately owned, and are only large enough to fit a house. The castle is a tourist attraction. The customs station is the building to the left. Divers are expected to pass through customs every time they plan to dive on a wreck that lies across the border.

Below: The *Keystorm* lists way over on its starboard side. I am looking straight up through the wheelhouse. The anchor chain at right rises to a mooring buoy on the surface.

ble-clutching the gears in order to switch from forward to reverse and back again. This "crash" course in boat handling was aptly named.

The greatest weakness of the houseboat was its poor maneuvering characteristics. Instead of turning on a dime and giving ten cents change, a king's ransom was needed in order to effect a change in course. Sometimes it took the full width of the river to turn around. Docking in a narrow marina was like turning around an eighteen-wheeler in a one-lane driveway. To depart, Steve had to go backward while turning the wheel in one direction, forward in the other direction, then backward, then forward, then backward, then forward, then so on and so on until the bow was pointed the opposite way.

The highlight of the trip may have been the time when Steve was parallel docking and the gear shift lever hung up. He spun the wheel frantically and tried to shift into reverse – to no avail. The wooden hull struck the dock with a resounding crash that tore boards off the bow and sprung planks in the deck. We recovered the loose boards from the water, saved them, and turned them in with the boat at the end of the week. The owner said nothing about it. Apparently such damage was considered par for the course.

Even though the accident wasn't his fault, I called Steve by the name of Crash Corrigan for the remainder of the trip. He accepted the moniker with good grace, even in front of his students.

His primary purpose for organizing the trip was to give the in-water segment of a mixed-gas diving course. Five of the passengers were his pupils. Tim Harmon and I were tag-alongs who either dived as buddies or who went our own way while Steve led his class through their paces. We started by diving on shallow wrecks such as the *America* and *Kings Horn*, dived on several wrecks at intermediate depth, and ended up on the *Roy A. Jodrey*.

The only accident occurred one evening on the boat. Some people brought prepared meals that were kept in the freezer, while others (such as I) chipped in to buy drinks and food to cook onboard. Candlelight dinners

Above: The diver provides scale for the massive propeller on the *Henry C. Daryaw*. The wreck lies upside down at a depth of 90 feet. One can swim under and into the hull to explore the compartments and passageways.

Below: The *Keystorm's* propeller is as large as the one on the *Henry C. Daryaw*. Note the encrustation of zebra mussels. Biologists are still arguing over whether zebra mussels are black with white stripes or white with black stripes. Zebra mussels don't care one way or the other.

were cozy times to discuss the day's events. I struck a match to light the candles when a sparkling bit of phosphorus broke off the head and flew across the table into the eye of one of the students (whose name I cannot recall – I should have taken his picture).

He screamed, dug his finger into his eye to flick out the offending particle, then poured water over his eyeball. He was okay; the tiny black scar on the white of his eye did not affect his vision. But what a bizarre event!

The water temperature during this second week of June was a comfortable 58 degrees. Ambient light visibility was in the forty-foot range. Tim and I made a night dive on the *Kings Horn*. Steve and I dived as buddies on the *Henry Daryaw*. All the students passed the course and received certifications for mixed-gas diving. I can honestly say that a good time was had by all.

An addendum to this particular trip I found personally fulfilling. Joyce Hayward and I decided that, as long as we were in Canada, we would add a couple of days to the trip by diving off Kingston, Ontario. We made an interesting dive on the *J.H. Munson* before the weather turned sour and we made a mad retreat to the dock aboard a nameless boat that was either so poorly ballasted or so poorly balanced that it rolled out of control whenever someone moved from one side to the other. Even the tanks and gear boxes had to be stowed with precision or the boat listed badly. We were told to remain seated at a prescribed location on the bench lest the boat capsize in mounting seas.

Notwithstanding the above, the owner of the local dive shop was one Dan MacKay. When Joyce and I checked in, Dan was wearing Canadian army fatigues because he was in the reserves, had just returned from maneuvers, and had not yet had time to change before going on duty at the counter. We got to talking about military service. When he told me the location of his army base – in Algonquin Provincial Park – my ears perked up.

Now I need to go back fifteen years. In October 1986, Jack Schieber and I went on a week-long wilderness ca-

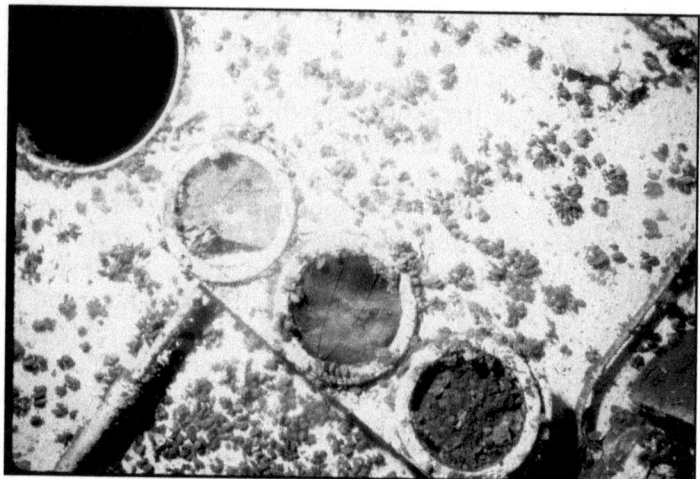

Above: Three gauges next to a porthole on a bulkhead of the *Roy. A. Jodrey*. The inner passageways and compartments of the wheelhouse structure are exciting to explore.

Below: Divers have collected china and glassware from various hidden places inside the *J.H. Munson*, and placed the items together for all to see. The temperature on this dive in Lake Ontario was a brisk 41 degrees: a cold shock after the previous day's dive in the comparatively warm water in the St. Lawrence River.

noe trip down the Petawawa River. (I related the entire saga in *Wilderness Canoeing*; I will distill only the pertinent and salient features here.) We finished the trip in what we had been told was a Boy Scout camp. Turned out that it was actually army camp that the government let the Boy Scouts use during the summer when the army had no need for it.

Jack and I landed on a beach next to a building where soldiers thronged like ants whose nest had been disturbed. They ignored us. Olive drab jeeps and trucks drove back and forth on the soft sandy road. We entered the building, asked if there was a public phone we could use, and were directed to a corner by a sergeant. I called the driver who had dropped us off at the put-in, and who was supposed to pick us up in my van at the take-out, to let him know that we had arrived. He did not answer his phone.

We explained our quandary to another sergeant. He suggested that I hitch a ride with the civilian garbage truck that was due to arrive shortly on its daily rounds. I did; Jack stayed with the canoe and our camping gear. The army camp was so isolated that it took an hour to drive through the forest on winding dirt roads to reach the front gate that was located next to a paved highway. The captain who was on guard duty acknowledged the driver and his helper, then asked about me. I told him my story and presented identification.

The captain wanted to know how I got on the base. I told him that we paddled down the river and landed on the left bank by the large single-story building.

"How did you get past the sentries?"

I asked, "What sentries?"

The captain then said, "By rights, I have to arrest you for trespassing on military property." He explained that base security was currently operating under full alert status because that very night – and it was already dark – an "invasion" force was planning a parachute drop into "enemy" held territory.

I quickly deduced the situation. Despite the highest level of security, two civilian canoeists slipped unwittingly onto the base because *someone had neglected to post sentries along the river*. Once we were inside the security checkpoints, our presence was ignored – everyone assumed that we had a right to be there. Heads were going to roll over this military snafu – I just didn't want it to be mine that was put in the guillotine.

Under the circumstances, the captain didn't have the authority to release me; that could come only from someone with a higher rank. He said, "I'll have to call the colonel."

As he escorted me to the guard shack, he explained that the colonel was asleep because he was leading the parachute drop. The captain would have to wake him up. Inwardly I groaned. I envisioned spending the rest of the year in the stockade while the red tape was unraveled.

To make a longer story short, the colonel authorized my release. I didn't have to hitchhike because the garbage haulers drove me to town (some twenty miles away, but *on* their way). I retrieved my van and returned to the base.

In the meantime, the captain checked out my story by driving to the take-out where Jack was bundled up in the dark awaiting my return.

A lieutenant took the captain's place at the guard shack. In the absence of the captain, he wouldn't let me pass without obtaining permission from a higher authority. He picked up the phone and roused the same colonel out of bed. This time I might have groaned out loud. Despite two awakenings before his nighttime parachute drop, the colonel did not order me to be shot at sunrise. The lieutenant warned me to drive directly to the take-out, not to take any other roads, and to return as quickly as possible. I followed orders.

Fast-forward to 2001. The incredible coincidence that developed was that Dan McKay was on active duty in 1986, and he participated in that very parachute drop. He was a member of the Canadian Special Forces. He parachuted into territory that was defended by the British SAS (Special Air Service). It was from him that I obtained the other side of the story that I wrote in *Wilderness Canoeing*.

Last day on the Petawawa. Did I mention that we had a blizzard on the first day? After the snowstorm, the temperature remained only slightly above freezing. That's Jack in the canoe; he is dressed appropriately for the weather.

Into the Wilderness

I was born and lived my first year a few blocks from the famous intersection of 10th and Wolf, in Philadelphia, Pennsylvania. Then the family moved from South Philly to the Great Northeast: a suburban section of the city. I continued to live there throughout my life - first with my parents, then in my own house - until I realized that, because I traveled so extensively, I didn't really live in Philly any more. My house was just where I kept my stuff.

Eventually, because I had accumulated so much stuff, I outgrew my modest home and rented warehouse. I started to search for bigger premises from which to run my growing publishing business. I moved to a secluded mountain retreat in the Poconos, about eighty miles north of Philly. The new house provided two floors for lodging and an 1,100-square-foot basement that was ample space in which to store my book stock.

Because the acre-and-a-half property borders State Game Land, the house offers photographic opportunities that I never anticipated. A babbling brook in the back is a watering hole for local wildlife. Animals perceive the large back yard as a meadow in which to roam or forage for food.

When I look over my computer in my second-floor study, I see deer and turkeys every day. I often see mice, voles, squirrels, chipmunks, rabbits, raccoons, skunks, groundhogs, opossums, porcupines, bears, and bobcats; to say nothing of passing crows and hawks and all the birds that are attracted to the feeders on the deck.

The place from which I type these words is a nature photographer's paradise. I keep my cameras on a table next to my computer, always ready to snap a few frames of activity in the clearing behind the house.

The hiking and biking possibilities are endless. From the side door of my two-car garage I can bushwhack half a mile through the woods to the top of a bluff that overlooks the Lehigh River from a height of a thousand feet. My only regret is that I didn't move here years ago.

The following is a bonus section. Enjoy!

Christina Young took me flying in her vintage Super Cub, allowing me to take aerial photos of my house and the surrounding forest. Unseen is the thousand-foot dirt road that leads to the driveway that is hidden by the treetops. One winter I snowshoed to the top of the ridge so I could look down into the Lehigh Gorge. I have paddled my canoe and kayak through this picturesque gorge numerous times, enjoying the solitude and beauty as much as the challenge of the whitewater. Notice the many rapids in the Lehigh River.

Staring at me from a distance of forty feet is a twelve-point buck - a broadside view that any hunter would give his eyeteeth to see. (Being vegetarians, deer don't have canine teeth.) That's a six-point buck to the left; a four-pointer is off-camera farther left. No big deal for me - I see this all the time. I observe more does and speckled fawns than bucks. Witness the two fawns who are suckling from their mother. I do all my shooting with a Canon instead of a Remington, so my yard is a safe haven for the denizens of the forest.

Photographic Memories

From the large to the small. The chipmunk above is slinking across the deck in search of birdseed. They don't eat the seeds on the spot, but stuff them into cheek pouches until the furry flesh bulges like inflated balloons; they scamper back to their burrows and eat the seeds later. Squirrels come from all around to feast on sunflower seeds. They are crafty fellows. There is no squirrel-proof birdfeeder that they can't steal from. I must have the fattest squirrels in the world.

The only species of humming bird that inhabits the east coast is the Ruby Throated. Plastic flower petals attract them to the feeder, which is filled with water in which sugar is dissolved, sugar being their prime source of nourishment. When they get too fat, I substitute aspartame for sugar (only kidding - I wouldn't want them to contract cancer). If you don't like humming birds, the feeder pictured above comes in a bug zapper model (again, only kidding). After leafing through my hawk identification book, my best guess is that the one pictured below is a Rough-Legged Hawk. But I could be wrong. So many of them look so much alike, and I am not an expert. I shot this picture through my study window.

Sometimes while I am working, I hear gobbling outside. I glance up from my computer screen and see a flock of turkeys in the yard. I don't mow the back over the leech field so the grass will go to seed; I also spread corn in the yard. The picture of the tom was taken in mating season. My record count is 49. The picture below shows 47, but two more turkeys were scratching through the snow off-camera to the left. I felt foolish in the grocery store buying an oven-stuffer for Christmas dinner, when I could have filled my larder with one shotgun shell. But I don't hunt. I would rather let the butcher do my killing for me.

Mice are nearly impossible to photograph in the wild. The method I used to take these pictures is too long to fit in a caption; see the following pages for the explanation. After studying an identification guide, my best guess is that these are either deer mice or white-footed mice, but I wouldn't swear to it. They could be voles instead of mice; voles are often called meadow mice. The differences are minute: long or short tail, blunt or pointed snout, variations in fur coloration, and so on. No matter what they are, I think they are cute - but not cute enough that I want them in my house, chewing through food wrappers and leaving tiny turds that look like black grains of rice. My mouse stories are amusing in retrospect, but they were not amusing at the time of occurrence. Read on . . .

Of Mice and Men and Women

I never had mice in my Philly house. My initial experience with them arose from an infestation at Cheryl Novak's house in the Dismal Swamp of North Carolina. They made nests in the closets, marauded the pantry, ate food in the kitchen cabinets and drawers, and left droppings just about everywhere: behind the furniture, under the sofa, on closet shelves, and so on.

Cheryl wasn't fond of the mess they made or the food they destroyed. Actually, she hated mice. She used steel wool to plug the spaces around the pipes under the kitchen sink, but still the mice got into the cabinets and drawers. In the evening, when the house was quiet, we could hear them scratching. When I pulled open the drawer from which the scratching sound emanated, a mouse leaped out like a jack-in-the-box. I grabbed for it but missed; it scampered away and vanished. Other times they dashed across the living room floor as if they were jet propelled.

Like any other woman, Cheryl wanted to get rid of the mice by killing them. I disliked killing animals so much that when I was a kid, I walked around or carefully stepped over anthills in sidewalk cracks. I couldn't abide pain or suffering either. As an adult, I stopped on the road and carried sunning turtles into the weeds. I scooped up spiders on a sheet of cardboard and carried them outside for disposal. Okay, I know I'm weird, but that's the way I am.

I formulated a bold plan. I baited the mice's favorite drawer with the remnants of the candy bar whose wrapper they had already chewed off. I told Cheryl to tell me when she next heard scratching in the drawer. I would tiptoe across the kitchen floor, whip open the drawer, and quickly scoop out the munching mouse.

So there is no misunderstanding: Cheryl was fully informed of my humanitarian intentions to catch the mice and release them out-of-doors.

The very next night she called me from the kitchen and told me that she heard scratching in the baited drawer. I did exactly as I had planned: I tiptoed across

I bait my traps with peanut butter. Any brand will work; smooth or chunky doesn't matter. It is important to check traps often so the mice don't suffer or die from dehydration. If the mouse seems weak, I pour water into the trap before I release it. I cannot account for the "wet look" of the mouse at the bottom of this page and the bottom of page 236. These mice seem to have groomed themselves with moisture. Identification of any mouse is complicated by the fact that biologists recognize subspecies and varieties that can be distinguished only under microscopic examination in a well-equipped laboratory for which my garage or basement does not qualify.

the linoleum floor, listened for a moment to the scratching, yanked open the drawer, and slammed my hand into it blindly.

Sometimes Cheryl has lapses of memory; or she does things without thinking of the possible consequences. During the twenty-four hours that lapsed between the time at which I baited the drawer and told her about my plan - which she agreed to let me try - she went out and bought a mousetrap and placed it in the very same drawer under the candy. She never thought to tell me what she did - not even when she called my attention to the scratching.

As a result, my hand went right into the mousetrap.

Before you picture my fingers being amputated by a spring-driven guillotine, banish the thought. It was worse. In keeping with my idiosyncrasy about not killing mice, Cheryl bought a mousetrap that was actually a trap, and not a euphemism for a slaying device.

This kind of trap consisted of a rectangular plastic dish that was slightly larger than a 3-by-5-inch index card. The dish was filled with a grayish sticky concoction that had the consistency of soft silicone glue. In principle, a mouse's feet would get stuck in the glue when it stepped onto the plate to nibble the bait.

And it worked! Two mice were stuck in the trap.

My hand was also stuck in the trap, with the mice caught between my fingers. I had never heard of this kind of trap, so I had no idea what I had gotten into. I yanked my hand out of the drawer. In their fright, the mice were biting my fingers to pieces.

I ran out of the house with the captured mice stuck to my hand literally like glue. On the lawn, in the dark, I pulled the glue dish off my hand. My fingers were torn and bleeding. After I got over my shock, I examined the trap and figured out how it operated. I pulled the mice off the glue pad and dropped them onto the leaves and pine straw.

They didn't run away because their tiny feet were coated with glue. They lay on their sides and scrambled in place. Their useless motions might have been comical if I wasn't so concerned about their survival.

I picked them up and pulled off the leaves that were stuck to their feet. This also pulled off some of the glue. I did this several times to each mouse, until they came completely unglued. Then they ran away.

Cheryl apologized for forgetting to warn me about the trap. I was not placated. She made up for the error of her ways by cleansing my wounds with hydrogen peroxide and then coating them with an antibiotic. The bites did not get infected.

Glue traps can be cruel. If you hear the mouse trying to escape immediately after it is caught, pulling it off the glue pad is easy. But after a while, the struggling mouse gets glued by the tail, the chin, the underside - until it either dies a lingering death, or is impossible to remove without tearing it apart. We stopped using them.

At my Jim Thorpe house, I use a storebought plastic box that a mouse can enter by walking up one side of a seesaw. The mouse's weight tips the seesaw down when it passes the fulcrum to reach the bait. The rising seesaw closes a metal gate; then, when the mouse steps off the seesaw, it is weighted so that it tips up to the top of the removable lid. The mouse is trapped. See page 238.

The mice that are pictured on page 236 I photographed after I released them in the woods, but before they gathered their senses enough to run away. Cheryl says that I should mark the paroled mice with variously colored paints, as a way to determine if I am capturing the same mice over and over again.

Mice have so many natural predators that I don't need to add myself to their problems. In my area they suffer predation primarily from bobcats, coyotes, foxes, opossums, owls, hawks, and eagles.

Several mice that I released climbed a nearby tree after leaping out of the trap. Others were so meek or afraid of my presence that they wouldn't leave the trap, but hid under the seesaw. I had to remove the lid completely and turn the trap upside down to get rid of them.

What Cheryl views as a nuisance I view as a photo op. To each her or his own.

Photographic Memories

I calculate that I have spent some two years of my life in the woods on various hiking, backpacking, and wilderness canoe trips. In all that time I never saw an undomesticated feline of any species in the wild. It is therefore ironic that the first one I ever spotted was in my own back yard: the bobcat pictured above. As Dorothy said in *The Wizard of Oz*, "There's no place like home." Pictured below is the only marsupial that inhabits North America. The correct name of this animal is opossum, not possum, despite the common phrase "playing possum." It is also called Virginia opossum or American opossum.

Bearing the Brunt

From a photographer's point of view, it doesn't matter whether a black bear is shot in color or black and white, because, obviously, black bears are black.

Prior to moving to Jim Thorpe, my only black bear encounters took place in Glacier National Park in Montana, and in the Dismal Swamp in North Carolina.

Cheryl Novak had more trouble with bears than she had with mice: bears kept coming out of the swamp behind her house and stealing her trashcans. We sometimes spotted bears when we canoed along the desolate swamp creeks. They always ran away as soon as they detected our presence . . .

. . . except on one occasion. It happened like this:

The canoe was on the roof as we motored along the road to our planned put-in. I passed a big black dog walking along the treeline. When I realized that the dog was actually a bear, I jammed on the brakes and turned around. By that time the bear was crossing the road.

I stopped on the gravel shoulder and leaped out of my van with my camera in tow. I snapped off some quick shots of the bear's retreating butt - but it paused at the treeline on the other side of the road, turned its head, and peered over its shoulder at me. I kept shooting.

Slowly it turned; step by step it recrossed the road.

Now I was able to get pictures of its face instead of its nether end. I centered my telephoto lens on its muzzle, rotated the focusing ring, pressed the shutter release, pulled back the field of view, rotated the focusing ring, pressed the shutter release, pulled back the field of view, rotated the focusing ring, pressed the shutter release, pulled back the field of view - but the camera wouldn't focus.

At the same moment, it occurred to me that I was no longer pointing the lens horizontally or at a slightly downward angle but that I was pointing it straight down!

Suddenly it dawned on me. I moved the eyepiece away from my face - and found myself staring into a pair of eyes that were staring up at me. The bear was sniffing my kneecap!

When a photographer becomes so fixated on his subject that he loses all sense of his surroundings, it is known as "photographer's fixation."

I was so intent on obtaining full face images of the bear that I paid no attention to impending danger. I could have reached down and patted the bear on the head, but I knew that that would be a bad thing to do. I resisted the impulse.

When the bear's curiosity was satisfied, it stopped gazing up at me and proceeded along the path from which it had emerged when I first spotted it. Idly I wondered, "Why did the bear cross the road?" Or more to the point, "Why did the bear cross the road again?"

Who knows what strange thoughts lurk in the minds of bears? Not I.

This was my closest bear encounter until I moved to Jim Thorpe. I vividly recall the exhilaration I felt the first time I spotted a black bear stalking across the yard. I dashed for my camera and snapped a shot through the glass sliding door. Then I stepped onto the deck. The bear whirled its head in my direction when it heard the door slide open, stared for a moment, then ambled off through the woods in no particular hurry.

The bear above followed me back to the house. The one below sat and watched me as I replaced the birdfeeder on the hanger.

Little did I know that this was only the beginning of my encounters with Carbon County bears. After a while, bears lumbered through my yard on a weekly basis; then daily; and sometimes hourly. I've had as many as three bears rumbling in the yard at the same time.

It wasn't long before I calculated that I had seen more bears in my own back yard than I had seen elsewhere in the rest of my life. By now - if you can believe it - I've seen more bears on my own back *deck* than I've seen elsewhere in the rest of my life.

The reason for this last turnabout is that the bears like my birdfeeders; or, more precisely, they like the sunflower seeds that are *in* the birdfeeders.

Bears are great thieves. They are also persistent. I have chased away the same bear three times in as many hours. They keep coming back to see if I am still on alert.

What do I mean by "chase," you may ask? On more than one occasion I have literally kicked a bear off the deck and chased it a hundred yards into the woods, running as fast as I could, until it dropped the birdfeeder that was in its mouth.

What do I mean by "kick," you now ask. I mean that I heard the bear on the deck, slid open the door, then, as the bear ran down the steps, I booted it in the butt before it got out of reach. Then I ran down the steps behind it.

The first time this happened I simply reacted on instinct. The bear dropped the feeder in the yard but stopped at the edge of the forest and watched me scoop up the mangled frame. Then, when I turned back to the house, it followed me like a puppy.

When I stopped, it stopped. When I continued, it continued. When I turned and walked toward it, it turned and ran away - but stopped after twenty feet. That appears to be the distance of a bear's personal space.

Most of the time they are too fast for me; they escape before I can slide open the door and swing my foot. They outrun me in the woods, too, but I keep after them until

they let go of the feeder. Now I keep a pitchfork by the back door, so I don't have to chase after them unarmed.

My bear stories are legion. One followed me back to the house, then sat on its rump like a circus bear or a toddler, and watched me from a distance of ten feet.

A different one circled through the woods and attacked the deck from the other side. Instead of walking up the steps, it dug its claws into the support beams, scampered up the posts, and climbed over the railing.

One that I cornered on the deck clunked its head on the posts in its madcap flight to get away from me. It then leaped right over the doggie gate that barred the steps (and kept the dog from escaping when she was playing outside).

On the opposite page, the upper bear eyed me and the birdfeeders alternately, wondering if he could get away a snatch. The lower bear stole quietly onto the deck in the hope that I wouldn't catch it in the act; the glare resulted from shooting through the glass. The punching bears above were siblings who wrestled between bouts of eating grass. So many bears meandered through the yard that I nailed a "BEAR CROSSING" sign to a tree. I herded a bear to the sign in order to snap the picture below.

Another one tried a nighttime assault at 11:30 p.m., after I went to bed. When I heard clattering on the deck, I threw off the covers, raced through the house, switched on the outside lights, slid open the door, and chased the bear off the deck. Then I stood there in my birthday suit and shouted, "And don't come back!"

Not only do the bears mangle the feeders but they bend the iron rods from which the feeders are hung. In order to straighten the rods, I have to put them in my bench vice and apply strong leverage. They wind up with an S curve, but at least they are still usable.

Bears have incredible strength. Sometimes they tear the brackets right off the railing, either by ripping the boards apart or by bending the three-eighth-inch bolts that secure the brackets to the railing.

I now have more pictures of bears than of any other mammal.

Oh for a spray can of Bear-Off!

PARTING SHOT
Now I've seen everything, and so have you!

Books by the Author

The Popular Dive Guide Series
Shipwrecks of Massachusetts: North
Shipwrecks of Massachusetts: South
Shipwrecks of Rhode Island and Connecticut
Shipwrecks of New York
Shipwrecks of New Jersey (1988)
Shipwrecks of New Jersey: North
Shipwrecks of New Jersey: Central
Shipwrecks of New Jersey: South
Shipwrecks of Delaware and Maryland (1990 Edition)
Shipwrecks of Delaware and Maryland (2002 Edition)
Shipwrecks of Virginia
Shipwrecks of North Carolina: Diamond Shoals North
Shipwrecks of North Carolina: Hatteras Inlet South
Shipwrecks of South Carolina and Georgia

Shipwreck and Nautical History
Andrea Doria: Dive to an Era
Deep, Dark, and Dangerous: Adventures and Reflections on the Andrea Doria
Great Lakes Shipwrecks: a Photographic Odyssey
The Fuhrer's U-boats in American Waters
Ironclad Legacy: Battles of the USS Monitor
The Kaiser's U-boats in American Waters
The Lusitania Controversies: (Book One)
 Atrocity of War and a Wreck-Diving History
The Lusitania Controversies: (Book Two)
 Dangerous Descents into Shipwrecks and Law
The Nautical Cyclopedia
Shadow Divers Exposed: the Real Saga of the U-869
Shipwreck Heresies
The Shipwreck Research Handbook
Shipwreck Sagas
Stolen Heritage: Grand Theft of Hamilton and Scourge
Track of the Gray Wolf
Underwater Reflections
USS San Diego: the Last Armored Cruiser
Wreck Diving Adventures

Dive Training

Primary Wreck Diving Guide
Advanced Wreck Diving Guide
The Advanced Wreck Diving Handbook
Ultimate Wreck Diving Guide
The Technical Diving Handbook

Nonfiction

The Absurdity Principle
Wilderness Canoeing

Science Fiction

A Different Universe
A Different Dimension
A Different Continuum
Entropy (a novel of conceptual breakthrough)
A Journey to the Center of the Earth
The Mold
Return to Mars
Silent Autumn
Subaqueous
The Time Dragons Trilogy
    A Time for Dragons
    Dragons Past
    No Future for Dragons

Sci-Fi Action/Adventure Novels

Memory Lane   *Mind Set*
The Peking Papers

Supernatural Horror Novel

The Lurking: Curse of the Jersey Devil

Vietnam Novel: *Lonely Conflict*

Videotape or DVD

The Battle for the USS Monitor

Visit the GGP website for availability of titles:
http://www.ggentile.com

THE LUSITANIA CONTROVERSIES
THE TWO-VOLUME
HISTORY OF WRECK-DIVING

There is more to a book than its title. There is the subtitle. A subtitle is an explanatory device which describes the topic of a book more fully than its title. A case in point is The Lusitania Controversies. At first glance the title implies the sole subject of the Lusitania. But each of the two volumes possesses a subtitle which explains in greater detail the global premise of which the Lusitania is but a part.

Together, both volumes present the entire history of wreck-diving, from its meager beginnings in the 1950's to the advent of technical diving in the 1990's.

Book One is subtitled Atrocity of War and a Wreck-Diving History. One quarter of the volume is devoted to the construction, career, sinking, and aftermath of the Lusitania. Three quarters are devoted to the history of wreck-diving and to autobiographical experiences of the author, who became an essential element in wreck-diving and a pioneer in technical diving. Coverage extends to 1979, and includes a section on the author's first Doria trip, in 1974.

Book Two is subtitled Dangerous Descents into Shipwrecks and Law. This volume continues the history of wreck-diving from 1980; describes numerous dives on ever-deeper shipwrecks; a number of incredible penetrations into the vast interior of the Andrea Doria, including the recovery of two bodies; and details the beginning of mixed-gas diving to the point at which an expedition to the Lusitania became practical. The volume concludes with a detailed description of the 1994 Lusitania expedition (of which the author was a part) and subsequent legal activities.

The two volumes are larger than the sum of their parts. They comprise biographical content with incredible underwater adventures: some hair-raising, others deadly, all exciting: a fascinating excursion into the real world of wreck-diving and the evolution of the activity.

www.ingramcontent.com/pod-product-compliance
Lightning Source LLC
Chambersburg PA
CBHW051044160426
43193CB00010B/1059